Bottom to Top

Mount Everest
Without Bottled Oxygen

By James Brooman

Acknowledgements

Dedicated to all the people who made this adventure and this book possible, to the people who took me there and brought me back safely, to the people whose support has made all the difference.

IMG
Greg Vernovage, Eric Simonson, Dallas, Luke, Andy

Sherpa
Thunang, Phinjo, Dawa, Ang Jangbu, Funuru, Philen, Kama Rita

Climbers
Thom Pollard, Brooks, Ben, Ellen, Brad, the two Jims

Friends and Family
Alexis Tosti
David Brooman, Claudia Brooman, Tanya Brooman
Stephen Mortimer, Logan Mortimer, Astrid Mortimer
Rachael Harris, Zephyr Andrew, Jessica Hastings, Maggie & Connor, Lauren, Robert Lariviere, Henrik Scheel
Alex Evans, Carole Tomaszewics

1

The Void of Darkness

My universe was one of darkness, suffering and bitter cold. Nothing more.

Drained of intensity by the freezing temperature, the dim beam from my head torch barely illuminated the next few feet up the steep snow slope onto which I now clung. In my right hand, nestled deep in the palm of my thick and dexterity-robbing mitten, passed a thin red rope that was now my sole connection to the world. Above was a path towards an unknown fate, while below was my lifeline back down to earth. Periodically I would feel the rope tug as my Sherpa guide Thunang took his step upwards, but beyond that rhythmic reminder I was alone. Neither light nor sound could penetrate this dark void and all I could hear was the crunching of sharp metal crampon spikes as they clawed into the ice beneath my feet, muffled only by the swirling wind as it stung and scratched the few bare patches of bare skin not covered by balaclava or ragged beard.

Each step pushed us ever higher into the death zone. I could feel my heart hammering furiously, each best striving desperately to supply enough oxygen for my continued survival. I had chosen not to use bottled oxygen, and at these altitudes above 8,000m / 26,250ft the cells in my heart and neurons in my brain were dying in their millions. Teetering at the limit of consciousness there was so much that could go wrong. For every five people who have climbed without bottled oxygen to where I now stood, one will die.

For an age I ascended through the blackness, single slow footsteps up an infinite and unknown staircase. Time drifted through my mind and every ounce of concentration was focused solely on the next foot placement. There was precious little spare capacity for other thoughts, not even to dream of reaching the summit or ponder the dangers which surrounded me. All I understood was the urgency to continue and that only the next step forward mattered. It was OK if I couldn't reach the summit. Real failure was to quit before reaching my limit, for then I would forever wonder "what if", a pain worse than anything the mountain could inflict upon me. Trading this day of suffering for a lifetime of regret was the easiest exchange I would ever make.

And yet everyone has their breaking point. After hours of continuous exertion my resolve began to weaken and I stopped for the briefest of rests, hoping that this momentary respite might reset my focus. Looking away from the snow I stared into the nothingness around me, expecting to see pure black as I had with each prior glance. This time, however, something was different. It was almost imperceptible, but I could just about make out the dullest of reds glimmering through the shadows.

It was the coming of dawn.

Even in such minimal light I risked a switch to sunglasses from my fogged goggles, and with a new clarity I slowly witnessed the colors grow until a pastel blanket covered the pristine white snow and jagged gray rocks of the high Himalaya. Far below I could make out the yellow tent in Camp IV which I had left all those hours ago, and better yet, from this vantage point I could finally see above us to a place known as the Balcony. This was our first milestone on summit day. There was now a sense of progress, and for the first time since waking in my sleeping bag I felt something which wasn't pain, cold or relentless pressure. I felt hope. I had fought, struggled and had not been beaten, at least not yet. There was still a long way to go, but maybe, I thought, *just maybe*, I could rise to meet the challenge of this mountain.

Maybe I could win.

2
The Crash of Paper

Nine months prior I sat at my desk in a nondescript office and stared at an envelope in the outgoing mail tray. Inside that innocuous paper pouch was a completed application form and a check for sixty-five thousand dollars, money I had earned with blood, sweat and tears. Both were about to disappear in return for the chance to reach for a dream; a dream which could easily get me killed. The perverse irony of paying a small fortune for an opportunity to play the expedition equivalent of Russian roulette was not lost on me, and more than once I fought the urge to retrieve the envelope from its resting place in the tray, rising from my chair only to sit back down empty handed.

When the check cleared I would be a member of the International Mountain Guides expedition to climb Mount Everest the following year. It is a dangerous undertaking at the best of times, yet I had elected to now attempt the summit in a way that was fifty times more dangerous and difficult than the regular way. Only a fool or madman would choose to do this, and I was currently unsure which of those I would prove to be. I hoped it would be neither, but I've been wrong before.

The mail guy eventually arrived and bundled the contents of the tray into his gray US Postal Service sack before swinging it over a broad shoulder and pulling open the nearby exit with a deft heave. I watched him leave and as the lock clicked loudly shut behind him this adventure became real. It was in that moment I felt the exhilaration and terror of signing up for an expedition. The world now took on a more vivid hue. Everything would now be done with a heightened awareness, like the last look at a place you know you will never see again. From that moment your life is focused on that one defining event which, from now until the day you win or lose, will influence every facet of your existence. It impacts the food you eat, when you go to bed, when you get up and the risks you take. It alters where you spend your money and what you do with your weekends. Like a high stakes poker player waiting for the final card, little else seems to matter. It is a situation which I despise and which I love. Without it life is easy. Without it life is empty.

I was now committed and it was time to get serious about this challenge. If I didn't train hard I could easily be dead in just 9 month's time.

No joke, that.

3
Once Upon a Time

I've always felt my soul is connected to the mountains, not that my childhood gave any sense of it, surrounded as I was by the rolling green hills of England. Just an unremarkable boy growing up in an unremarkable place. No crashing ocean waves, no great forests, no vast desert or towering mountains could be seen from my bedroom window; not much of anything unless you count a swathe of unattractive brutalist-style architecture. In general, my home town was not known for its superlatives unless you include the preponderance of nutters binge drinking and fighting in the streets on a Friday night. Then it's world class. Although some of my childhood friends quite liked it and never left, a fan I was not. In those early years, when I had only my imagination for transport, I yearned to escape, and knowing only my sheltered microcosm of the world I believed that anywhere else would probably be an improvement. As I dreamed of reaching some ephemeral paradise there were two places which rose above all others in the mind of this small boy.

One was California. A fabled land of beaches, redwood forests and beautiful people; a land of smiles, surf boards and beachwear. During the early 90s, when American culture dominated, it was just so *cool*, so completely at odds with my boyhood surroundings. As I watched the winter drizzle fall from gray clouds onto cold mud and damp concrete it seemed to be located impossibly far away, a paradise at the ends of the earth, or perhaps some distance beyond even that. It was a place of unreachable dreams.

My other paradise was the Alps. Oh, the Alps! To fully understand me, and the hold mountains have over me, it is necessary to understand my mother.

This wonderful lady is from a small village in Italy, a rural high alpine community just a stone's throw from both the Swiss and Austrian borders. I always viewed her early years as something from a different world and in many ways it really was. Each story she told seemed to verge on a fairytale, replete with princesses, wood cutters and magic spells. As my late godmother was in real life the handmaiden to the princess who lived in the castle perched on a mountain a few miles down the valley, you can see where I got that impression. Of course, the reality of her upbringing in the mountains was often far from a fairytale; it was a harsh and unglamorous life, yet I still felt a sense of wonder about this faraway place.

Her early life seemed equally make-believe, at least compared with my dreary reality. My mother remembers a winter with so much snow that they could only leave the house by clambering out of an upstairs window. Where I grew up, the traffic grinds to a halt with an inch of snow, and more than six inches on the ground is a rarity. Despite the cold of those alpine winters there was no central heating in my mother's house; instead a large wood-burning stove in the small kitchen radiated heat as far as it could. As a young girl her winter mornings began with a dash from beneath a real eiderdown duvet, past icicles *inside* the bedroom window and across a cold stone floor to the kitchen for a bath. I say bath; it was a metal tub filled with water heated on the fire. As I said, glamorous it was not.

The school for that part of the valley was high on the slopes above the village. When there was snow she would ride in the back of a tractor-drawn cart up the hill each morning and ski back home in the afternoon. Many of my mother's cousins were mountain guides and one of my far-removed cousins was even a world champion skier. I remember being amazed when I visited his mountain chalet when I was a young boy, gawking at his beautiful glass trophies neatly arranged inside a large wooden display cabinet.

Later, my mother attended boarding school further down the valley at a convent. Despite being educated by nuns my mother is now not religious in the slightest, and from her stories about that period of her life it is easy to see why. Strict and scary nuns; reality for my mother, but for me that was just another classic fairytale situation!

The convent in those times offered the opportunity to spend a summer helping the nuns who work at the Vatican, and that was her chance to escape. She felt the same pull of adventure and escape as I later did, and such a distant journey to a great city, well, that was an unknown adventure a world away from the confines of her upbringing. This was the 1960s and the bustle of Rome must have felt a million miles from those isolated mountain paths. Two months of discovery and freedom beckoned, so she packed her bags and one day found herself on the train to the capital.

Things went well by all accounts. While her day to day tasks sounded fairly monotonous she soon discovered that once each week the nuns performed a set of duties within the walls of the city state itself, and my mother pestered them to be allowed to accompany them. She was often taken. With entry gained and with no specific tasks to do, she and a friend were left to roam the gardens behind the basilica of St Peter. "No tasks" soon transmogrified into "mild-mannered mischief" and the Swiss Guard were an easy and obvious target. Famous for their colorful Michelangelo-designed uniforms and sworn neutrality, guards are positioned as sentries at certain points around the Vatican gardens and have express orders not to move a muscle while at their posts. Disrupting this command was seen as a challenge by my mother and her friend, who persisted in their light-hearted torment of one lone and unlucky soul. Distracted by their mischief they failed to hear the soft footsteps of someone approaching from behind.

"You know, you really shouldn't do that," said a voice, and in shock they swiveled around sharply. Expecting to see another guard there stood instead a man dressed in white. It was Pope John XXIII.

Much commotion ensued as my mother simultaneously professed innocence and offered profuse apologies. For the poor guard this was certainly a sweet victory, and a wry smile passed across his lips; a smile which did not go unnoticed.

"Ha!" shouted the Pope with a triumphant air and pointed finger. "I made the guard move! I can do it! Although I suppose I am the Pope!"

He spoke to my mother about where she was from and why she was at the Vatican before making her recite three "Hail Marys" as punishment, to which she happily obliged. He soon said his goodbyes and continued on his way. For the remainder of her stay she would get a wave and a "Hello!" on the occasions the Pope passed by. This was the era before popemobile and bulletproof glass, remember.

"He was such a nice man!" my mother would remark when telling the story, and he certainly sounded like it. Making friends with the Pope, that's not a bad result for a summer internship. Certainly beats just doing the photocopying.

Growing up with these tales somehow instilled in me a sense that such exploration was permitted. I had no idea how to go about it, was terrified of the concept, rarely entertained thoughts about it, wasn't looking for it and generally considered anywhere outside my zone of experience to be impossibly dangerous. Yet at least at some level I knew it wasn't just something which could only ever happen to other people. If my parents had managed to have some adventures, I figured, then there was no reason I couldn't have some either.

4

Into the Unknown

That small English town upbringing, while benign enough, inevitably created a somewhat myopic view of the world. While many people went to a sunny part of Europe for their summer holidays, just as our family usually did, going long haul was a scarcely unheard of luxury amongst the people I knew. Only one or two kids at my entire school had been to the USA and were envied, and I didn't know anyone who had gone anywhere even more "exotic", for want of a better term.

When I was 15 years old, my dad splashed out and bought us a family vacation to the Caribbean, figuring that might be our last big holiday before myself and my twin sister grew too old for such things. He wanted to do something special, and special it most certainly was. I'd never been to the tropics before and landing in St Lucia was like landing on another planet. It was just so different! The island paradise I'd seen in movies was apparently real and for two weeks I piled high memories and experiences I will cherish forever. That includes the experience of being swept out into the Atlantic Ocean alone in a tiny sailboat and having to be rescued by the coastguard. I mainly remember it because it's just so very strange to lose sight of land as you drift inexorably towards an endless blue horizon, and because I saw flying fish on the speedboat ride back to shore. At my age and with experiences up to that point it was basically the best afternoon adventure ever, although I'm sure that my parents didn't see it quite the same way.

For all such wonder, though, those two magical weeks still felt somewhat like a one-off. The concept of seeing places outside an organized resort or an organized tour was still alien to me, and it was a feeling which persisted for a long time afterwards. I remember being in a geography class at school when the teacher played a video about Brazil, and Rio de Janeiro might as well have been on Mars, so far away it seemed from that dull classroom. I certainly didn't entertain any thoughts that I would ever visit somewhere like that for myself. I barely realized you were actually allowed to go there. Travel to South America? Impossible. Who could possibly go to such a place. The danger, the difficulty, the distance, the expense. Impossible!

And so that view remained for the next few years until it was time to pack my bags for university. I'd been accepted to study mechanical engineering at Imperial College in London, and I was looking forward to learning new things and meeting new people. It did not disappoint.

During freshers week, as the first week of university for new students is known in the UK, there was a big event where all of the sports clubs set up tables to advertise their existence and attract new recruits. Along with the standard fare of soccer, rugby and such like, there was a smorgasbord of more esoteric clubs offering the chance to do activities I had only ever heard about, and some things I hadn't. I still don't understand what lacrosse is. By the end of the afternoon I was signed up for the parachute club and the rock climbing club. I'd always enjoyed climbing up the tree in our back garden at home and I wondered what climbing on rock might be like. I'd never done it before and I didn't know that indoor climbing walls even existed until the club explained where they went each Wednesday afternoon. Joining that club in particular was one of the turning points in my life, perhaps indeed *the* turning point. Through it I met some truly special people; daring, athletic, adventurous and worldly types who had already traveled to the four corners of the earth and had - gasp - lived to tell the tale! These people represented a previously unknown universe of exploration beyond the artificial confines which had previously been installed in my mind, and I looked to them with a degree of reverence which even to this day I think would surprise them. To them I was just another friend, but to me they were gods. They were the people I wanted to be.

Nick was the guy that at the time I would probably have chosen to be if I could have been anyone. He was tall and muscular, one of those men with that half-bodybuilder, half-athlete physique that you see on the cover of fitness magazines or in the Olympics. With my thin, straggly limbs such a physique represented an unobtainable goal and was an achievement to be admired. He was also super smart, genuinely nice and generally awesome, the sort of person who got on fabulously well with others and was liked and respected by those who met him. All in all, I thought he was a legend.

He had also taken a gap year before starting university and his tales about the months he had spent in Australia were captivating. It was a brave new world. He'd also spent 8 weeks backpacking in Sub-Saharan Africa that summer. I'd been brought up in a place where taking 2 weeks to go to Spain was a luxury, so eight weeks in Africa was something that would never have crossed my mind. He epitomized the daring and adventurous maverick I wished I could be, but never knew how and was also too scared to attempt.

It was during my second year at Imperial College that Nick and a couple of other people in the rock climbing club had the idea of doing an expedition to the Himalaya. No ordinary trek, though. Oh no, where would be the youthful daring in that! Instead, they decided to trek the longest stretch of continuous ice outside the poles; one hundred and three miles of continuous high altitude glacier located in part of the Himalaya called the Karakoram. Which happens to be in Pakistan, and more specifically in Kashmir.

"You should come," Nick suggested to me one night as we were hanging out in his room inside the student house we shared in west London with some of our other friends.

Even the idea was terrifying. Pakistan? Kashmir? A few people who lived at the end of the street where I grew up were originally from Pakistan, and although they seemed to be lovely people, the country itself seemed worrisome. Never in a million years did I ever think I would go there. In my sheltered young mind I thought that anywhere you'd leave in order to move to my home town must be a bit grim. I knew very little about it except that Kashmir only ever seemed to make the evening news for the wrong reasons, and that it seemed to be full of men with long beards shooting AK47s. Traveling there initially seemed full of downside and not much upside, plus I'd also never stood on a glacier before, let alone trekked a hundred miles across one. In fact, I'd barely even gone hiking before.

"What, really?" I replied, not sure if he was serious. "Urr, maybe? It does seem pretty amazing, but ... I've never done anything like it. Can I even do it?"

"For sure! It's going to be incredible," Nick replied. "And don't say maybe. You always say maybe and that always means no; I know you."

"Uh, maybe…."

"Don't say maybe! Say yes!" he interrupted.

"Is it really going to be that great?" I asked, trying to invent excuses while my brain processed this very unusual offer.

"You are going to love it," Nick replied. "Say yes!"

"But it's expensive, right?" I countered. It was, especially for a student.

"You can make it work, I'm sure. That's what working over the summer is for, right!" he responded. Which was basically true, and I was running out of excuses.

"Actually, screw it, let's email Simon and Nigel right now," Nick continued. "Then you can't say no!" And with that he swiveled around on his desk chair and began to type.

The two men behind this idea were Simon and Nigel. Simon was a larger-than-life personality; strong, brave, adventurous, confident, fiercely intelligent and good looking, he was the sort of guy that guys want to be. He was also an outstanding athlete and expert kayaker, as well as being very funny. Just an amazing person and one of those special few individuals you meet in a lifetime.

Nigel was his foil. Equally strong, equally smart and equally impressive, Nigel was the reasoned voice of the duo, the logic to Simon's optimism, the man who would insist on dividing every estimate given by Simon by about 2.3 to get a more reasonable number. This number incidentally became known as the "Simon Factor" after his consistency with optimistic embellishment. Apart, Nigel and Simon were formidable; together they were unstoppable. They helped open my eyes to the wonders of life and I've never looked back.

I trusted Nick, Simon and Nigel implicitly and absolutely. After all, I figured that each week they held one end of a rope as I rock climbed while attached to the other, so I was already putting my life in their hands, at least to some extent. All three of them are natural leaders, leaders I would happily follow, and perhaps that is what turned this expedition from a Himalayan folly to a compelling idea. Perhaps it was my new-found desire for adventure, or perhaps subconsciously this would be a way to become more like Nick; to actually go with him on his travels. Perhaps it was a response to the faith they had in me. Whatever the reasons, they were enough.

"Ok, Ok," I reluctantly replied as Nick's typing continued, half-terrified at what I was agreeing to and half-grateful that Nick had seen through my excuses. "Let's do it."

I didn't know it, but those few keystrokes set my life on a very different path to the one I had previously imagined. Or perhaps subconsciously I understood at some level just how consequential this moment would be, because despite the intervening years I remember it like it was yesterday. It was a Tuesday. The room had the bedside light on but not the main one. Nick's double bed up against the back wall window was unmade, with a dark blue-green sleeping bag spread open on top of it. The stiff brown carpet was covered with clothes around the bed, with the only meaningful clear space concentrated around the desk and computer on the opposing side to the door. These were moments when time slows and everything is absorbed, because it's just so damn important.

"Email sent," Nick confirmed. "Congratulations on your first expedition!"

A few days later the ink was drying on our group's application to the trekking company in Pakistan and that was it. I was going now, come hell or high water. For the first time I felt the exhilaration and terror of taking a leap into the unknown.

Without it life is easy. Without it life is empty.

5

Unexpected Wonders

Five months later I walked along a narrow rocky trail surrounded by the immense mountains of the Karakoram. Before us, shining and shimmering in the blinding sunshine and cold air, lay a vast expanse of ice which filled the wide valley into which we now turned. At my sides walked Nick, Simon and Nigel, plus two other friends on our expedition, Faisal and Andy. Behind us walked our guide, Mehdi, an affable Balti man - for we were in the sub-region of Pakistan known as Baltistan - who was a pleasure to know. Behind *him* walked his assistant guide, quickly followed by our cook and his assistant cook. Behind *them* walked forty-four porters. And behind the porters walked a goat on a leash. Forty-four porters and a goat! This was proving to be a proper expedition, just like the ones I'd seen on TV.

For the next thirty days we blazed a path across ice, rock and snow in what was a transformative month in my life. I stared up at those dramatic peaks and down into the icy black depths of each crevasse. I shivered in the nighttime cold as we camped on the snow and sweated in the daytime sun. I jumped over streams, crunched over ice and climbed over rocky moraine, all the while looking in wonder at a landscape which I had barely even imagined. It wasn't just the incredible scale and mass of those mountains which staggered me, although that was part of the wonder. It was the stark and unforgiving beauty of this utterly remote place and the concomitant sense of intense solitude which really affected me. It sounds strange to say, but it was exactly that solitude which created the strong bond to where I was. It was as though everything had been made just so I alone could experience it. In that frozen world of black rock and bright ice I felt strangely comfortable.

As we trekked, I learned about the local people from Medhi, about their history and their culture. I learned about my friends and about the mountains. Most of all I learned about myself. A veil had shielded my eyes to the possibilities of the world, a veil which had focused me towards the well-trodden paths of modern life and trapped close to my chest the fears I had of what might happen if I strayed too far from what mainstream society considers "normal". As we walked during those thirty days that veil slowly dissolved, and like a butterfly emerging from its chrysalis I emerged from Pakistan a changed man. With new horizons now possible, I wondered what else I might do.

6

The Thinnest of Air

During the trek we had climbed on several occasions to around 6,000m / 19,700ft on the mountains adjacent to the glacier. It was here I got my first taste of high altitude alpinism. The challenge of the terrain. The pure air and unspoiled nature. The breathtaking vista revealed as a reward for your determination and effort. The camaraderie in success or failure. Inevitably, still staring up at even higher peaks from those lofty vantage points my mind wondered what it might feel like to stand at the very pinnacle of all this. I thought of the fabled 8,000m peaks.

There are just 14 mountains greater than 8,000m / 26,250ft, all lying in the Himalaya and Karakoram mountain ranges. They are the big boys, the highest of the high, the toughest of the tough. For many mountaineers they are the ultimate challenge.

In Pakistan I had the chance to see one of these monsters up close for myself. At 8,126m / 26,660ft Nanga Parbat rises as a single monolithic mass an improbable 18,000ft above the surrounding hills. I first saw it as we drove along the Karakoram Highway and even from a distance it appeared colossal. The second time I saw it was on a flight back to Islamabad after the expedition, when it took 10 minutes just to fly around it. To climb something so high and so imposing, well it seemed impossible for mortals, and doubly so for a mortal like me. These 8,000m peaks were undoubtedly and forever beyond my capabilities.

After seven weeks in Pakistan I was back in the UK and my life changed rapidly. I had joined the Erasmus exchange program which facilitates student swaps between universities across

Europe, and moved to Germany scarcely two weeks after returning. There, sidetracked by an intense study schedule and removed from my climbing peers my goals slowly changed. I'd been bitten by the traveling bug in Pakistan and the now beaches of Thailand and the rainforests of Borneo beckoned. In need of a rest and a distraction after so much work, some proper fun and genuine relaxation became my vacation goals as the pull of the high mountains diminished.

Diminished but not forgotten. This zombie of an idea was still alive until I made the "mistake" of reading "Into Thin Air" by Jon Krakauer. It's a book you may well have read, and if you haven't I think it's worth the time to do so. The narrative follows the author, who was climbing Mount Everest in 1996 when five people lost their lives in a single storm. It's quite a shocking story and very much reinforced my previous opinion that above 8,000m / 26,250ft you are putting your life on the line, quite literally. The quoted death rate for non-Sherpa on Mount Everest is somewhere around 2%, meaning for every 50 people who reach the summit, one climber will die making the attempt. However, quite a lot of climbers abandon their attempt early or don't reach the summit, so your actual chance of death during an attempt is probably closer to 1 in 100. At that time, frankly anything much above zero seemed scary. I valued the chance to make a difference in the world and dying on a distant mountain at a young age felt like I was leaving a lot on the table. I still had so many things to do!

As I finished the last page of Into Thin Air and put down the book, I knew Mount Everest would remain forever beyond my reach.

7

The Desperation of a Fool

Fast forward 15 years. In the time between I'd had my ups and downs, as most of us do in life. Using my well-honed knack for timing life badly I'd graduated with an MBA in 2010, right into the depths of the financial crisis. By May of my graduating year I'd been unsuccessful in finding a job I actually wanted to do. "Reach for the stars," they'd told me, but I was still on the ground grasping impotently skyward as the floodwaters of unemployment sloshed around my ankles. It was not an awesome time to say the least.

And then the phone rang.

It was a Vice President from one of the big US investment banks asking if I'd like to come for an interview in San Francisco. Someone on their team had just quit and apparently I happened to have the perfect resume for the job. Ironically it was a job many business school students graduating in my position would have half killed for, yet I was still hesitant. I'd sold my soul for this kind of job out of undergrad and it had been hard enough to buy it back the previous time. However, debt and unemployment during a recession has a way of motivating even the most recalcitrant, plus the job was in California. If I had to park myself somewhere to ride out the storm there were worse places to be, so I accepted the interview and flew to the West Coast a few days later.

I spent the entire day interviewing with the team. There were four or five other (better) qualified candidates also at their offices that day and it was a terribly stressful experience. A tiny chance of success and no idea what I would otherwise do next. At 4.30pm it was time for my final interview, this time with the global head of the entire group. This was the big one, the make or break.

"Thanks for coming," said the boss, welcoming me into his large office with a handshake. "Have a seat," he continued and motioned me towards the low chair in front of a large hardwood-veneered desk which had been polished to an excessively slippery shine. It had a solid front and therefore no space for my legs to go beneath it, forcing me to perch awkwardly on the chair. The whole thing seemed designed to transfer as much authority as possible towards the person whose office it was, and as I sat there, subjugated to this man who now dominated the entire room, I suspected this choice of desk had not been an accident.

The boss quickly found my resume from the pile on his desk and I braced for the expected onslaught of near-fatal and ultimately awkward questions, such as why I'd not applied to a single bank while at business school or why I'd never gone to a recruiting event at his bank. Usually, *missing* one of the multiple recruiting events was enough to get you blacklisted.

"Oh! I see you've ridden a bicycle from Alaska to Argentina," he remarked as he reached the Activities section of my resume. "That's great! My mother rode a bicycle all the way across the United States, from Boston to LA!"

I could not believe my luck. For the next 25 minutes of the scheduled 30 we talked exclusively about the adventures of his mother. I say "we". What I mean is that he offered a 25 minute monologue of her adventures and of life in general and I was not inclined to interrupt. All I did was nod and smile at all the right places, thinking only of Abraham Lincoln's immortal quote:

"It is better to stay silent and have people think you are a fool, than to open your mouth and confirm it."

I therefore stayed almost silent, with only a few utterances of "Oh, absolutely!", "Really?" and "Wow, that's great!", to prove I was still listening. Luckily bankers love to talk. At the end he wondered if I had any questions about the job so I asked about the team culture. Yeah, yeah, I know, but you always need at least one question and that question is pure gold to ask the boss of any team. They *always* think their culture is amazing even if it isn't. And so I survived until the end, at which point he shook my hand and I left the room. I knew he had gained exactly zero understanding of my abilities, motivations, personality or if I'd be any good in the role. But hey, if he thought I was made of the "right stuff" that might be all I needed.

It was. I got the job.

The first year working for the bank could be described as a "mixed bag". I worked exceptionally long hours doing mostly dull things while ruing the fact that a well-motivated chimpanzee could have done 90% of it, during which time I could have been sitting on a tropical beach drinking Pina Coladas. I felt perpetually exhausted and permanently aggrieved towards my captors for metaphysically chaining me to the office for no discernible benefit in either direction. They said time in the office didn't matter, but when I later I witnessed an extremely capable junior banker being criticized in his end of year review - and docked some significant bonus dollars - for essentially being too efficient and going home once his work was done, I knew I had read this unwritten rule correctly.

On the upside, I was working for a team which was actually very good so at least I learned a few things. The most senior bosses in it were also extremely reasonable, at least as far as bankers go. Given my previous moan that might seem a contradiction, but compared to some other teams I had it easy; the guys in our LA office were worked so hard that several of them had breakdowns. In our team's weekly meeting the boss would ask if there was a reason to come to the office at the weekend, and if there wasn't they suggested you didn't. Often though, some over ambitious middle manager would waste your Saturday, Sunday or both with powerpoint slides no-one would ever look at. At least the senior guys acknowledged that you might occasionally have a weekend off. By the rock-bottom standards of banking that was actually pretty good.

Also on the plus side, the 5% of my time which involved using some brain cells was actually interesting and I was being paid for my suffering, although not as much as you probably think. My secretarial assistant made more per hour than I did. Not overpaid and conscious of the tenuous permanence of my employment I subsisted mostly on oatmeal and free late-night take-aways at the office to save money. I'd occasionally spend my money on some guilty pleasures like a motorcycle track day or a new surfboard, but that was about it. Whereas my colleagues tended to buy fancy things or get bottle service in a nightclub in order to restore their sanity I would have an early morning surf session. Getting up in the dark after three hours of sleep just to get half drowned in the freezing ocean wasn't always pleasant, but at least my oppressors couldn't reach me out there. For an hour I was untouchable. For an hour I was free.

After a year the "mixed bag" became less mixed as they somehow managed to remove the good parts. The capable senior people either left or were maneuvered aside, whereupon the resulting leadership vacuum was filled by the inmates of this particular asylum. Around that time I remember reading a book titled "Psychopath" and noted that my boss ticked all the boxes to be one; clever, manipulative and unable to empathize with the pain he inflicted on others. A combination of crap management and sociopathic bosses with zero accountability turned my life from a bit rubbish to painful, and then to diabolical. You do not want a sociopath to hold an unaccountable dictatorship over your life, let me assure you.

I will spare you the many tales of woe which filled those last few years as that would be a book in itself; an unpleasant book no-one would want to read, I might add. Yet indulge me for a few minutes to regale you with just two short examples, simply to instill a tangible sense of just how utterly desperate I became to escape.

In my final year at the bank I spent perhaps forty percent of my working time, around 2,000 hours, on one particular project which ultimately earned the bank US$33,000 in revenue. That might sound like a lot of money, but for a small team expected to bring in over one hundred *million* dollars each year this was zero. Every boss spent more than that each month on travel expenses. I calculated that during this project I had printed enough sheets of paper to reach my office window from the ground outside, and I worked on the 22nd floor! The project probably cost us US$33,000 in paper and photocopying. With such a colossal waste of resources, people, trees, time and brain cells it was clear there would be implications for the banker in charge of this unmitigated disaster; the same psychopath I previously mentioned. There were. He was given a large bonus and promoted early.

Another project I worked on was run by the head of a different group. We'll call it group Alpha so this cretin doesn't sue me. I remember a client conference call to discuss part of the work stream. As the mid-level person on the team I had created the entire analysis we were discussing and thus knew more about it than anyone else, period. So when one of the clients asked a technical question only I knew the answer, and so unmuted the phone to answer it. Just a regular, uncontroversial question with a regular, uncontroversial 30 second answer. I was about 10 seconds in when the deputy leader of this project cut me off and finished my answer, getting it wrong as a bonus. Not cool, but I figured it was his prerogative to sound like a moron in front of his own client, so whatever.

After the conference call, though, he immediately phoned me directly and began screaming at me. Literally screaming. How DARE I speak on a conference call! Even though I was on the team, 32 years old and actually knew the answer. Because HE WAS HEAD OF ALPHA GROUP! DID I KNOW THAT! The fact his team consisted of exactly four shared employees was a minor detail for such an appalling human. I don't think I'd ever met a real bonafide narcissist before and it was something to behold.

The barrage of unwarranted abuse was unrelenting, but I was unable to respond and still keep my job. So I did the only thing I thought was reasonable. I put my desk phone on mute, put him on speaker so the entire open-plan office in San Francisco would be aware of his idiocy and went to the office kitchen to brew a pot of coffee. He was still talking when I got back with a fresh cup and he never even noticed I was gone. He eventually stopped talking, expecting a long, profuse and abject apology from me, but instead only received a long pause followed by a single "OK". Never has an awkward silence sounded sweeter.

Four years in that place were probably three too many. Yet leaving was a big deal. I was a Brit in the US on a work permit so leaving meant I'd effectively have to deport myself within 60 days of quitting my job. Believe me, it's no fun to be trapped in a painful job knowing you'll have to move *continents* if you resign. To justify the decision I needed to do something big, something epic, something which would seemingly make all the suffering worthwhile. Something which would restore my faith in myself.

To this day I couldn't tell you how, when or why I thought of Mount Everest. Maybe it was after some sleep-deprived, stress-induced brain spasm at 2am during some god-awful week when being allowed to freeze to death on a remote mountain felt like progress. Who knows. All I know is that one day the idea was there and that it wouldn't let me go.

8

Tigers and Sheep

I've never really had a plan for life. I've always wondered what it must be like to have a real purpose, that thing you've wanted to become since you were little. It must be wonderful, at least in the beginning. For the rest of us, we seem to wander around a bit lost, frankly. For me, I seem to have a large amount of wandering mixed in with short periods of focus, where an idea somehow takes root and a path lays itself out. Climbing Mount Everest was one of those ideas.

Why this idea and not others? Perhaps it's all about the reasons. With the right idea in the right place and the right time, there is something to hang onto. These ideas seem to pull you forward rather than you having to push. Yes, there were huge unknowns and risks to climbing Mount Everest, but there were also great benefits, my mind told me. The more the idea turned around in my head the greater those benefits outweighed the downsides.

Of course, the downsides are great, with an unpleasant death being foremost amongst them. We'll get into all the other nasty medical problems later on, so for now just know they are potentially traumatic and are not uncommon. And then there is the time, money and effort which this endeavor requires, and the impact all of this has on your friends and family. None of it is trivial.

So what does one gain from attempting this climb? I imagine most climbers have similar reasons, at least deep down. None of this "because it is there" fluff which people write on Instagram.

Personally, I wanted to experience the harshness of the death zone and see if I could actually survive; to feel the brutality of altitudes above 8,000m / 26,250ft rather than just watch YouTube videos of people shuffling around up there. Of course, to see if I could do something and not die is a selfish desire. If I was wrong or unlucky, my parents would be distraught and my niece and nephew would grow up barely remembering Uncle James. No doubt about it, at some level every single person who climbs Everest is putting themselves above the people who love them. But perhaps that is OK. I mean, there is a small risk of dying every time you cross the street, right?

Another reason for the climb is to prove yourself, both to yourself and to others. Subconsciously Mount Everest was to be my vindication after those tough years. Yet was climbing this mountain even "big"? In the end, you merely stand on a very small, very specific piece of ground somewhere on planet Earth. Y'know, cool. It is only "big" because of the outsized value us humans and society seems to put on it. There are far more difficult mountains to climb, more interesting mountains to climb and prettier mountains to climb. You climb Mount Everest purely because it's the highest, and when you succeed you join a small and unique club which everyone knows about. Strangers ask you about it at parties. You get invited to things because of it. Rightly or wrongly, the response of other people to this achievement is a powerful tool in the quest for self-worth.

You will succeed where others have failed. Few of us are motivated by a desire to prove ourselves to ourselves; mostly it's about proving yourself to others. Everest is like an Ironman triathlon in that way. Many people sign up to see if they can complete the distance or not, but everyone still records their time.

Performance is not just defined in terms of completing the course but also about how many people you beat when you do. In the results they literally tell you the exact number of people you passed on each segment of the triathlon so you know *precisely* how many people you beat. And there is nothing wrong with that. We enjoy the Olympics and the World Cup exactly because of that competitive spirit, but it's still a relative test, not an absolute one. On Everest you want to summit not only to see if you actually can, but also in part because you know others cannot.

The more I thought about climbing this mountain the more I thought about not climbing it. There became a "fear of missing out" which grew in my mind until I knew that not making the attempt would be as painful as trying it.

In life I've done a lot of things which have scared me half to death. I've BASE jumped from one of the world's highest waterfalls. I've ridden a motorcycle around the racetrack, elbow dragging on the ground. I've rock-climbed a thousand feet above the ocean and surfed 15ft waves. I swam without a wetsuit from Alcatraz back to San Francisco. I taught myself to breathe fire. These things terrified me, just as they might most people, and I got no joy from the fear itself. Tentatively climbing over bridge railings before BASE jumping into the void was a distinctly horrible moment for me. I am definitely not an adrenaline junkie despite what people seem to think, yet I was willing to push through my fear for the uniqueness of each experience and the flood of euphoria which comes afterwards.

It was not fear which drove me on but that fear of missing out. The regret if I forgo those euphoric moments, the kinds of moments which I will remember on my deathbed, far outweighs the in-the-moment fear of each pursuit. It is a perspective of life which has changed during the years, but I know the exact moment my mindset changed. It was on day 22 of our trek during that formative experience in Pakistan.

We'd just set up camp on the edge of the glacier and our leader Simon had gone exploring, eventually returning to proclaim he had discovered a stream of melted snow cascading over a huge boulder. Despite this stream being as cold as cold water can be, Simon decided this was a good opportunity for a shower. He now smelled incredible in comparison to beforehand, and we smelled the opposite. It's amazing how dirty you can get without noticing, at least until someone clean turns up and breaks the olfactory illusion. His radiance and our pungency now made this waterfall shower more or less obligatory.

The thought of stepping under that torrent was my worst nightmare. If you ever need to torture me there is no need to pull out any fingernails. A simple bucket of ice water is all you need. It will be far less messy and I will tell you anything you want to know. *Anything.* Whatever nerve endings relay signals of cold to the brain I have far too many of them, making even cold showers at home an unbearable experience. I've sometimes been unable to get in the ocean in California with bare ankles because the pain is so intense it literally makes me throw up. Cold water is not my friend, and I told Simon this in no uncertain terms. He listened politely to my protestations before giving me some sage advice, advice which I have remembered for all my days since.

"It is better to live one day as a tiger," he informed me, deliberately leaning in my direction, "than a thousand days as a sheep."

Yes, I know it's a total cliché, but it stopped my protestations dead. Sure, I could chicken out and not go under the waterfall, but that's what a sheep would do, and more than anything I wanted to be a tiger. Just like Simon. Soon our whole team was walking to the boulder and with encouragement from the others I stripped to my underwear and approached my doom.

It was a moment I remember with an eerie level of clarity, as though those seconds were to be my last. Years later I can tell you the exact shape of the boulder, the color of the rock, the look of the stones beneath the waterfall and the exact picture of the snowpack feeding the stream. With my senses heightened and my demise imminent I took a deep breath and stepped beneath the water.

Except it wasn't water which flowed over that boulder. It was pure liquid pain. I could feel it tear the life from my body, one spasming nerve cell at a time. I stood there screaming in exquisite agony, and I do mean screaming, for about 10 seconds before jumping away as though I'd been electrocuted. After a quick towel dry I sat there on a rock, shivering and hyperventilating as my senses slowly returned.

To me that cascade was the next level of diabolical hideousness. But you know what? I wouldn't change that experience for anything. I'd mustered my courage and faced my mini nightmare. The reward was the feeling I'd overcome something difficult for me and I had been given a vivid experience which I will remember for my entire life. That is a lot of reward for 10 seconds of suffering, no matter how bad that suffering might be.

I thought of this moment as I thought of Everest. To climb Mount Everest was to be a tiger. It was to face a fear and overcome it. To forgo an Everest expedition because I was scared would create a place of disappointment inside my soul that would be impossible to remove, and that is not the soul I wish to have. In the end it is a philosophy about living, and is neither right nor wrong. In any case, I think Laird Hamilton, the renowned big wave surfer, once captured this philosophy wonderfully, if not all that succinctly, after successfully riding the most dangerous and powerful wave ever attempted.

"I don't want to not live," he said, "because of my fear of what *might* happen."

Damn right.

9

All Hail the Believers!

I wanted to climb Mount Everest, that much I knew. The question was then *should* I climb Mount Everest? Could I actually be successful? I started with a bit of online research, but as with most things on the web it was difficult to discern facts amid the cacophony of morons. It was evident that I needed to speak with someone who had actually been there.

I pinged a few people who knew of such things and discovered that an alumni of my business school had climbed Mount Everest a number of years previously. He fortuitously happened to live in San Francisco and even more fortuitously worked just around the corner from my office. I sent him an email and we met up for a drink early one evening at the Irish pub down the street.

"So how old are you?" he asked as the conversation turned towards the climb.

"Early thirties," I told him.

"Right. So you could climb it. But let me explain why this might be a bad idea," was his response. "Look, there are loads of people up there who shouldn't be. It's a disaster on summit day, and many of these people are like you. They get to a certain age, want a challenge and now have some money. So they just buy their way towards the summit."

"OK, I appreciate that," I replied, "But I don't think I'm one of those people. Look at the other things I've done." I then tried to sell him on the "but I'm different" notion with some of the other things I'd done. It didn't make much impact.

"Yeah, but look, I'd had a whole lifetime of climbing," he told me after I'd finished. "I've climbed all these 14,000 footers, I had the experience to go and do it safely. If you don't have all that experience you're just like the others having a midlife crisis."

Harsh. He might have been right, though. I didn't have anywhere near as much climbing experience as he did and it was prime time for a mid-life crisis.

Many people at my age have had the same house, same kids, same mortgage, same job, same everything for a while. For some, such a stable and safe life is what they yearn for. These are the people who dream to one day retire to a house on the golf course where they can spend most of their time worrying about whether their new bath towels match the sink fittings. There is nothing wrong with that, but for me this is like waiting to die. Instead of stability I see the end of adventure and the end of my expansion as a human being. As middle age approaches there is a heightened yearning for uncertainty, for something to prove your best days are still ahead.

But what?

You could buy a Ferrari? Expensive and not as fun as you might think. You could buy a boat? Even more expensive. Or perhaps you could climb Mount Everest?

People see the challenge, the excitement and the recognition which comes with "conquering" the highest mountain on Earth. They've read those articles on the internet which say Everest is easy, that it is a walk to the top. It's the message they want to hear, and they believe. As we've seen in this current world, people have an infinite ability to believe utter nonsense when it suits them. In such scenarios people seem happy to trust the marketing brochure. I remember my mother talking to someone she worked with about my climb, and listened as that person declared "It's easy! My friend climbed to the summit in running shoes."

To this day I'm not sure how you climb fifty degree sheet ice without metal crampon spikes, let alone in jogging attire. Also tell this nonsense to the man whom I witnessed lose *both feet* to frostbite despite wearing the US$1,000, super high tech, triple-insulated mountaineering boots which *all* Everest climbers use. So yeah, sure, running shoes.

Such believers arrive at the mountain unprepared and untrained. Only then do they discover the harsh realities of climbing Mount Everest. Often they discover them the hard way. Some are lucky and only pay with failure and money. Others pay with frostbite and amputation. Some pay with their lives.

My alumni friend worried whether I was one of these believers. Perhaps he was right at some level. I did feel the slip of life after years of soul-destroying work. I felt as though I'd achieved nothing for so long and wanted some way of being relevant again. Perhaps this was just my own personal brand of crisis. In any case, at least I was trying to be a skeptic, although perhaps an optimist one.

When our drinks were done we parted ways and he wished me luck. Looking back on it I'm sure he saw me as another overconfident "banker bro" type who was going to buy his way up Mount Everest, endanger lives, fail to summit and somehow devalue his mountain and his achievement in the process. He warned me of the risks, a warning I did take on board. And yet I wasn't swayed from the idea; I figured that if I did this expedition right I could eventually prove him wrong.

10

In The Company of Condors

Virtually everyone who climbs Mount Everest uses a guide company in some capacity or another. The hassle of trying to arrange food deliveries and equipment to base camp for an extended period is immense so even the professionals usually partner with a local company to handle these kinds of logistics, as well as to facilitate climbing permits and so on. For less experienced climbers like myself it was normal to join a fully organized expedition, where you effectively just turn up and do what they say. With so much delegated responsibility it is thus critical to select the right guide company. Unfortunately, this is not always so easy.

Some companies will take climbers with little or no experience and give them minimal support, as my alumni friend alluded to. The consequences can be grave. I heard an anecdote from a respected Everest guide about a particular company some years ago whose record during one season was apparently four summits, four fatalities. That is not the kind of record you are looking for.

The good guide companies understand the outsized risks and potential consequences of taking potentially unsuitable people to one of the harshest and least forgiving environments on Earth. They understand they have a responsibility to keep their clients safe, at least as far as is reasonable, but also that this responsibility must work both ways to be successful. If you want to join one of these better expeditions you must first demonstrate your abilities, competence and non-craziness. Most companies prefer you to have climbed another 8,000m peak. A successful summit of Aconcagua, the highest peak in the Andes at 6,961m / 22,840ft, is pretty much the minimum threshold for high altitude proficiency, or at least as evidence that you probably aren't a complete liability.

Although not as high as the big peaks in the Himalayas, Aconcagua brings its own challenges. The expeditions tend to be short so your acclimatization time is minimal. Summit day on Aconcagua is very long and the mountain is renowned for high winds and intense cold. More than a hundred people have died climbing it and many more have been frostbitten. An expedition here is a short yet representative experience of high altitude mountaineering, and if you struggle with Aconcagua you're probably not ready for Everest.

I was currently still enslaved at the bank and it was the end of summer, meaning that there wouldn't be enough time for a climbing trip to the Himalaya climb that year. Summiting Aconcagua was therefore my first, last and only hope to meet the Everest entry criteria for the following season. The highest I'd previously reached was around 6,000m / 19,700ft and although I'd rarely had any problems with altitude this climb would test me at the next level. It was early September when I signed up for a December trip.

With three or so months to go I put my training into overdrive. Or rather, drive. It was a struggle. Most days involved an evening run or visit to the gym before returning to work until the late hours. Fortunately, I lived in San Francisco, where the ubiquitous hills facilitated some hiking-type training without too much planning. A few times a week I'd step out of my office building and trek up California St wearing a backpack containing

30 or 40lbs of finance textbooks and water bottles. Each lap only gained a few hundred feet, so to get more vertical climbing I began running up and down the stairs inside my 55 floor office building. It was going fine until I was one day stopped by building security, upon which all hell broke loose. Perhaps waving to the security cameras in the stairwell by the roof hadn't been the best idea.

Those three months went quickly and before I knew it I was on the plane to Argentina, excited to see what I was made of. My guide, Alejandro, picked me up from the airport and got me settled in the hotel in Mendoza, the largest town in the area. We spent a day organizing money and permits in the city before taking a van up into the Andes. Dropping us off in the early afternoon we were soon on the trail into the heart of the mountains. Condors soared high above as we meandered up the valley, and as the evening light began to shine we reached camp. Named Confluencia, this popular stop at 2,800m / 9,200ft was a good place to spend a few days to acclimatize as I'd been at near sea level until now. Surrounded by rugged terrain and vast peaks, high rickety bridges and wild rivers I felt at home once more.

11

Better Lucky Than Good

On day four we began the long walk to the main base camp for Aconcagua, named the Plaza de Mulas. The gain in altitude from Confluencia was significant and the difference in the environment was more than noticeable. Here, the brutal cold and seemingly perpetual wind makes for a harsher environment than its altitude of 4,000m / 13,000ft would suggest. Fortunately, it was still the early part of the season and the crowds were minimal, so a tranquil and pleasant camp atmosphere softened the discomfort. We were even invited to a barbeque by the camp staff, a genuine rarity by all accounts and a wonderful peek behind the curtain of camp life.

From the Plaza de Mulas, the first part of climbing Aconcagua along the main route is very mellow, at least on the scale of climbing big mountains. The main trail all the way up to around 5,900m / 19,300ft is all on gravel paths and it's not much more than a steep trek, provided there hasn't been any snow. Summit day, though, is a different beast entirely.

It was far below freezing when we left high camp in the predawn hours, slowly ascending along a thin line of dirt by head torch light towards the first resting area at around 6,200m / 20,300ft. Aside from Alejandro there were two other climbers on our little expedition, both from Canada, and so far we'd all done well during the prior week. I felt good and the pace of our little group was steady. As dawn broke we arrived at the rest area having gained several hundred vertical meters. Here we coincidentally met one other team which was also heading to the top that day, a chance encounter that quickly became a momentous stroke of luck.

We now discovered that neither of the Canadians were doing as well as expected. One had a headache and nausea, while the other had lost some of the feeling in his toes. These weren't encouraging signs and with the challenge set to increase from here they decided to turn back. That was probably the right call, but it put me in a tough spot. Together they were a majority and if they went down, so must the guide. If he went down then so must I, meaning that not only would my Aconcagua summit bid be over but also my chance for Everest. As you can imagine I wasn't too thrilled at the prospect of turning around.

"Hey, Alejandro, you understand the situation, right," I asked him. "Obviously if the others need to go down they should go down, and I'll come down if we can't find another way. But *is* there a way I can keep climbing?"

"I don't know James," he replied. "But look, there is another team here and I know the guide so let me have a talk." And with that he walked across the small plateau and began speaking with the other guide. Shortly he came back with the other man alongside him.

"James, this is Elan. He is an excellent guide. His team is in the same situation as us. So I will take down one group and Elan will continue up with those who are fit enough to continue. Do you want to go with his team?"

"Is that a question? Of course!" I replied. I turned to Elan and offered a heart felt handshake. "Great to meet you, and thank you for letting me come along! You have saved my expedition!"

As Alejandro and the others turned and started down, I turned and began to climb in the opposite direction. Our makeshift team soon reached the ridge that marked the start of a long, long traverse around the mountain and Elan turned to our ad-hoc group.

"We are lucky today!" he exclaimed, pointing to the sky. "This is where the wind normally hits us, but today it is calm. Oh yes, we are very lucky!"

Oh yes we were.

The group had some experienced climbers from France and Switzerland so the pace Elan set was brutal. Quite a shock from the leisurely climbing of the last week, but I gritted my teeth and just about managed to keep up while not looking like I was struggling too badly. After what seemed like an age on the long traverse we reached a large overhanging rock where we stopped to put on our big down jackets and take a drink. Clouds had now risen to engulf us and we began the final 400m / 1,300ft vertical push to the summit in a cold, thick mist. The terrain now was far steeper with a mix of boulders, scree, snow and ice. It was tricky, but I for one was happy to be scrambling over snow and doing something which approximated real actual climbing for once, rather than just high altitude walking.

Of the nine clients who set out that morning across the two teams, three of us reached the summit itself. With the mountain now completely shrouded in dense clouds I was denied a pretty view as my prize. That didn't matter. What *did* matter was that I'd made it and that I'd done so with no altitude sickness symptoms at all. Very encouraging. We stayed only a few minutes up there before descending to retrieve two clients who had oddly decided to halt their bids just short of the summit plateau. 13 hours after departing my tent I was back inside it, exhausted but happy. I had reached the summit of Aconcagua and, just as importantly, my Mount Everest expedition was still on.

12

The Journey of a Thousand Miles

Most expeditions to climb Mount Everest arrive in Nepal sometime around the end of March or early April, which gave me a couple of months to recover from Argentina and refocus on my training. With the right plan and enough effort I would be in peak shape, mentally honed and ready for the challenge. All I had to do was get right back to it.

So, naturally, for three weeks I did nothing. Not one workout. No running, no hiking, no gym sessions, nothing. I'd set up a spreadsheet to track my training and a missed day was given bright red shading as a visual admonishment. Now the swathe of yellows and greens from more successful weeks and months were terminated in an ugly block of abject failure. Had Aconcagua made me overconfident about my chances for success on Everest, or was I subconsciously sabotaging myself, pre-empting an excuse for failure if things didn't go well? That last outcome is a familiar pattern for me. Rather than train I procrastinate until I am forced to rely on luck. And luck is not a good strategy, except that unfortunately it often works! I'd suffer greatly and I'd underperform, but nine times out of ten I would make it to the finishing line, now armed with a story about how I did it without training. And if it went wrong the worst outcome was just a bit of embarrassment. On Everest, though, in the worst outcome I wouldn't have to worry about embarrassment. Or about anything, ever again.

It was only the quite real fear of dying that finally snapped me out of my malaise. Ironically I was only back in action for a few days before I had a minor accident, once again stopping my training. This is why luck isn't a strategy.

I'd gone to a friend's house party and had a couple drinks as one does. In that small San Francisco apartment they had assembled a pole-dancing pole for some inexplicable reason and I decided it would be a good idea to check whether I could do the "flag"; that position where you hold yourself out horizontally from the pole with just your arms. When I was 18 I couldn't quite do it, so why I thought my untrained, heavier and weaker self could now achieve this feat is a mystery. It turned out that I still couldn't do it. Not even close.

I jumped into a horizontal position and immediately crumpled back down, crushing my elbow into my side during the process. Now, it turns out that dislocating the cartilage that connects your ribs to your sternum is a strange feeling. It feels like your ribs aren't connected to the front of your body any more. Well, actually that's exactly what it is. Fortunately, I didn't seem to have damaged anything particularly life threatening so I didn't overly worry or even visit the doctor. When I did eventually mention it a few weeks later as I picked up some meds for the expedition she confirmed the treatment.

"Try to rest," was the advice. Medical technology at its most advanced. In hindsight I should have got a prescription for some better painkillers. Laying down in any position had been agony since the injury and deep breathing was even worse. Sleeping was nearly impossible, with every turn waking me up with a jolt. Training was also nearly impossible. Yet it was the mental stress which hurt more than the physical pain. I couldn't believe I'd come so far and got so close only to be derailed at the finishing line by this wanton act of self-inflicted stupidity. The urge to train through the pain was nearly irresistible, but I knew this pain was the bad kind, pain which informs you about damage actually being done. Still, you always second-guess yourself every moment. Could you be doing more? It is an anguish which every athlete will understand.

With two weeks to go before flying to Kathmandu the pain finally subsided. I was able to do a few gentle workouts, and at least traveling from San Francisco to the UK was a bit more tolerable. I spent a few days with my parents and saw some friends before saying my final goodbyes. It's a crushing feeling to know it may be for the last time. Giving my mother a hug on the back step of the house in the cold early morning, she in her dressing gown and me in my stiff hiking boots, is a moment I'll remember forever. Was it the last time I'd see my mum? I thought about it as my dad drove through the cold mist to Heathrow airport. It was a hard, hard thing to think about, and I wondered if I was making the right decision. I knew she would worry every single day and I felt terrible for putting her through all that stress and uncertainty.

Was I doing the right thing? Was I ready? Would I even come back?

I had no idea.

13
Shangri-La

Our plane circled high above Kathmandu, waiting to land as the first rays of light began to appear across the world. Below, the city and the foothills of the Himalaya were shrouded in lowland mist, but the high, snow covered peaks stood proud in the clear, cloudless sky. Each pass of the plane showed a jagged horizon against an ever-brighter sky until the endless mountains were silhouettes against a background of fiery orange. Amongst these tall mountains stood the true greats, the fabled summits of Shishapangma, Cho Oyu, Makalu, Lhotse and Kanchenjunga. These reached further and higher than all the others, and from their tops I could see smudged lines of black, drawn sideways from each of these peaks like the trails of dark comets. They were the shadows of spindrift, snow blasted from the highest slopes by the ferocious winds of the jet stream.

Yet even amongst this great vista one mountain rose noticeably higher than all the rest. It was the pinnacle of this mountain range, of all mountain ranges. It was as magnificent as it was vast, as terrifying as it was high. Even from this distance the sheer size of the mountain was imposing. With the longest of the spindrift trails the violence of the summit winds was unnerving. That any human being, let alone me, might exist in that place was beyond my comprehension. To summit this mountain seemed impossible.

Orange skies expanded to become a dazzling blaze of reds and yellows as we ended our holding pattern and began to descend, and as we passed into the mist my view of the distant mountains was slowly replaced with the emerging sight of a city far below. And what a shock it was. I knew Nepal was a developing country, but the name of Kathmandu had inspired thoughts of Shangri-La, that mythical hidden paradise of the Himalayas. Yet instead of paradise I stared at what I thought looked quite a lot like a war zone. Endless concrete buildings, assembled haphazardly next to each other, looked unfinished or in a state of disrepair. There seemed to be no suburbs, no green parks or woodland, just gray cubes interspersed across a dusty brown wasteland. Shattered in an instant, my preconceptions were now a blank slate. Perhaps the mist had obscured a more favorable vista beyond and I held out hope that the reality of Nepal I was about to experience might be restored. Yet at this moment, heading towards the unknown, my eager anticipation had turned into mild trepidation. I could sense the butterflies building in my stomach and had the start of a feeling that this whole expedition thing might not be quite as straightforward as I had hoped.

Before long we landed with a gentle thud and soon the mobile stairs were driven up to the plane for us to disembark. Stepping through the aircraft door was a step into another world. It was a little after 6am but already the warmth of the sub-continent flooded over my body. Each breath carried the unmistakable tang of south Asia, that heady mix of incense, tropical foliage, car fumes and the slightest hint of sewage, now mixed with the unmistakable scent of burnt jet fuel for added oomph. To some that might sound unpleasant, but to me it was the smell of travel in this part of the world; it was the smell of intrigue and adventure. A wide smile flashed across my face and I skipped down the steps with some much needed optimism.

As expected, immigration and baggage claim soon offered the usual dose of developing world confusion, but for now I was far too stimulated by the experience to be irked by the bureaucracy, transfixed as I was by the differences which make traveling so interesting. The traditional Nepalese hats worn by the men, the Buddhist and Hindu imagery, the unfamiliar symbols of Nepalese script. I just drank it all in.

With passport control and baggage claim successfully navigated I heaved my large yellow North Face duffel bags onto a cart and maneuvered towards the terminal exit. There, outside of the sliding doors I could see a gathered mass of humanity thronging with activity. Only now did it occur to me that I hadn't asked the guide company what was going to happen when I arrived, glibly assuming that someone would be there to meet me. But would someone? I realized I didn't actually know. And even if there was, how would they find me amongst so many people? I certainly didn't know how to find them. Steeling myself for an onslaught of pushy hawkers and this serious upcoming problem I rose up to my full height, took a deep breath and pushed my cart with fake confidence through the doors and into the maelstrom.

My concern lasted for about three seconds.

"Mr James! Mr James!" came a voice from behind the makeshift barrier about five deep in the crowd, and I turned to see a young man surging through the people towards me, smiling and excited.

"Hello Mr James, welcome to Kathmandu!" he repeated as he reached the barrier, leaning over to shake my hand vigorously before pointing to a place a few yards down where the barrier ended. A quick zig zag around the crowd and in no time he was with me.

"It is great to have you with us! Welcome!" he effused once more, and placed a traditional garland of fresh golden marigolds around my neck. What a truly wonderful welcome and a most unexpected gesture! The flowers were gloriously vibrant and released a heavenly smell; the petals felt so soft on my skin that I was scared to touch them. As I write this I feel as though I still wear it, so fabulous and memorable was this introduction. It was the best airport welcome ever.

This charming fellow was Mohan.

"We will go to the bus now and then to the Hotel Tibet. I am sure you would like to rest a little after your flight," Mohan continued. "Please, let me carry your bags."

"Oh, that's OK, I can carry one," I replied, but he took both of them anyway and deftly hoisted both my heavy duffel bags across his shoulders. Impressive.

"How did you find me in the crowd?" I asked him as we began our rapid snaking through the people and cars.

"We have the photo from your application!" he replied, "And your bags, or course!" I guess those bright yellow North Face duffels, a mainstay for mountaineers on these expeditions, had given me away. That, and being a tall white man dressed in a bright green T-shirt.

"Come, we shall be at the Hotel Tibet in no time," he continued and in no time we reached a small minivan, where inside a driver was waiting. With Mohan, myself and the bags on board, a lot of horn honking and some deft maneuvering extracted us from the clutches of the airport and we were on our way towards the heart of Kathmandu.

The minibus had seen better days, quite a few in fact, but it seemed every bit in keeping with where we were. Driving along dusty roads, past filthy canals and well kept, fragrant temples, I gazed out of the window to see a land already awash with the stirrings of humanity, even at that early hour. The sights and smells were in many ways familiar from my travels in India, yet somehow a little different. A different cultural veneer on common, long forgotten foundations, perhaps. I can scarcely convey the joy I felt as that minivan roared and banged along those roads. There was a sense of exploration and of the quest to come. It was all so intoxicating and with my spirits lifted my soul danced.

James was back in action.

14

Perfect Preparation Probably Prevents A Preposterous Purchase

We at last turned down a narrow side street and then into an even smaller alleyway before passing through a set of ornate gates and pulling up in front of the Hotel Tibet. Mohan escorted me into the hotel and helped me to check in. I was filling out the paperwork when I heard a voice greet me from behind. A familiar voice, this time with an American accent.

"Well there, is that James?"

A man strode the last few steps towards me, hand extended. He was slim and athletically built; nowhere near as scrawny as I was, despite being a good deal taller at maybe 1.95m / 6 foot 5. His medium length scruffy brown hair was hidden under a dark blue baseball cap with "IMG" embroidered on the front, and below were brown eyes and a wide smile. He exuded the optimistic calm of a man who is the master of his surroundings. Which he was. That was the first time I met Greg, our expedition leader.

Greg managed all of IMG's Himalayan climbs and oversaw the Everest expedition from the ground, first in Kathmandu to organize the arriving climbers and then from Everest Base Camp directly. IMG had one of the biggest commercial expeditions on Everest and in the discussions I'd had with them during my preparations I'd been impressed with their approach and experience. The founder of the company, Eric Simonson, had been an Everest pioneer way back in the early days on the mountain, long before there were any real commercial expeditions. Greg was also a highly accomplished climber with multiple summits of Everest, Cho Oyu and Lhotse to his name as well as many other high peaks around the world. He was also an Olympic gold medalist in volleyball! There was some real firepower in this team, both physically, mentally and experience-wise, there was no doubt about it.

I remember the first call I had with Greg and Eric, all those months before when I was deciding which guide company to whom I would entrust with my life on the mountain. The conversation was not what I had expected. Rather than a relentless sales pitch, they spent more time interviewing me rather than the other way around. And that inspired a lot of confidence. Picking the right team is the key factor in creating an effective expedition and the history of Everest is flooded with examples where things did not go to plan precisely due to problems in this department. Their interview process for me was both their and *my* first line of defense in minimizing the idiot factor on this expedition, and the more selective the better. It was an encouraging start, and I was just relieved they thought I was good enough to join their team.

"How was the trip here?" asked Greg.

"Yeah, pretty good," I replied. "That week in the UK definitely took a bit of the jet lag out of it, at least compared to you guys coming all the way from Seattle. Feels fantastic to be back in this part of the world again though!"

"I know what you mean! But it's all work for me from now so no jet lag is allowed!" I didn't doubt it.

"Hey so while you are here, this is the itinerary for the next couple of days," he continued. "The only thing we will try to do today is your gear check, so we can get that out of the way. The rest of the day is all yours, just get yourself settled, check out the city. All the clients and guides are arriving today and tomorrow so you'll meet them all at some point."

"Sounds great!" replied? It did.

"Then really only the briefing tomorrow is the next thing you can't miss. It's at 10am up on the roof terrace. Please don't be late," he warned me, "And then there is a dinner for all the team members who are here at 6pm, on the lower patio over there," he continued, pointing through the dining room to an ornate patio just visible through some French windows.

"Until then, if you need anything just let me or Mohan know." And with that we parted ways as I followed the eager porter who had whisked my bag up a wide staircase before I could tell him not to worry.

The Hotel Tibet was the go-to place to stay for IMG's Nepalese expeditions when in Kathmandu and I approved of their choice. The hotel aesthetic had a vibrant Buddhist / Tibetan theme in contrast to the Hindu and lowland influences more commonly seen in Kathmandu, and it felt more in keeping with my naïve expectation for the mountain valleys I would soon be visiting. My vision of the Himalaya included wise old monks and improbably located monasteries amongst the snows, and the Hotel Tibet helped to continue this spirit of imagination. The lady who owned it was herself from Tibet and as she glided like a spirit through the hallways there was a sense of authenticity to the place. Downstairs, the outside dining area was a nice patio while there was another, smaller patio on the roof. Anywhere I can sit on a roof and watch the sunset with a beer in hand is a good place in my book.

Despite the excitement during those first few hours in Nepal I could not escape the reality that I had just flown half way around the world. Jet lag was beginning to get the best of me, but several team members had arrived the previous day and there was a steady stream of new people knocking on the bedroom door to introduce themselves.

There was also that gear check to perform, something which all climbers on our expedition had to do before heading to the mountains. It basically involved emptying the contents of both duffels onto your bed and ticking off each item against the IMG checklist as one of the guides assessed your choices. It was a failsafe device; simple things like bringing enough water bottles were a huge hassle saver and forgetting even a single small yet critical item could make the difference between success and failure. You can't summit Everest if you forget your head torch. Although there was the possibility of trying to buy something in the village of Namche Bazaar in the Khumbu Valley, it involves a 14 hour walk from Base Camp and no guarantee you can find the item you desperately need. And then the walk back. It was infinitely better to bring everything with you at the start. Perfect Preparation Prevents Poor Performance as they say, and in this case also prevents an extremely long shopping trip.

The gear check felt like a high school field trip. Stuff strewn all around the room, packing and unpacking, all under the gaze of adult supervision! It was quite a long process from the sheer amount of stuff, the discussions about the suitability of each item and the steady stream of visitors who appeared in the doorway. First was my roommate that night. Andre was Brazilian, middle aged and athletically built with an upbeat, extroverted personality. I liked him, especially in smaller doses. Also introducing himself was Ben, a student who had somehow persuaded his university to fund his trip. I remember thinking that was more impressive and difficult than summiting the mountain. Similarly outgoing as Andre, I liked him as well.

And then there was Thom. Amongst our expedition was a group making a film about another of our climbers, a chap named Jim, who was aiming to become the oldest American to summit Everest. Thom was the director, cameraman, and general man-on-the-ground for the film. He'd been on many Himalayan expeditions over the years and had shot some well-known documentaries, including the 1999 expedition to Mount Everest which finally found the body of pioneer George Mallory, one of the most famous climbers in history. Thom had been high on Everest with Conrad Anker that day and had the unique experience of rifling through Mallory's pockets to discover what was in them. He is also the one and only person who has seen Mallory's face, revealing a secret which I will let him tell. To me he was an instant legend. He also happened to be a thoroughly wonderful person. Very easy to get along with, his upbeat demeanor and easygoing approach was just what the doctor ordered for this expedition. We became and remain good friends.

Later that afternoon a group of us wandered the short distance from the hotel along the busy main road to the district of Thamel, the beating heart of old Kathmandu. Now *this* was more like what I had expected. Narrow alleyways of wall-to-wall shops, all competing to sell you everything you could ever need on your visit to Nepal. Souvenirs to snacks to supplies. A crush of tourists and locals thronged through the streets, woven into a moving tapestry of motorbikes and small cars, all fighting furiously for every yard of progress. Above, power cables and telephone lines formed a spider's web around a myriad of signs and billboards. A complex mix of incense, hot food, hot garbage, dust and exhaust fumes once again pervaded the air. It wasn't necessarily good or bad, it was Thamel; a last remnant of a rapidly disappearing world.

Amongst the vast array of fake and knock-off equipment available for purchase there exists a few shops in Thamel which actually sell genuine gear. There is even an actual, true to life The North Face shop. These shops are a blessing for climbers and with their plentiful stock you could get everything from a Nalgene water bottle to a high altitude down suit. I had been diligent in my packing so I think I only bought one or two small and mostly superfluous items, but a couple of the guys made more use of the opportunity. One even bought a completely new backpack, which I considered a big bet this late in the game. What if it didn't fit him? Still, he bought the same brand and model I had settled on so I couldn't argue with the man's sense of quality and style!

15
Who's Who Or Who is Who?

The next morning I was up early, sipping instant coffee on the patio as the sun began to warm the world. After enjoying about 6 trips to the breakfast buffet I eventually shuffled my way to the roof terrace where Greg was to give our introductory briefing. To be honest I don't remember much of what was said. All I remember is filling out the piece of paper which enabled us to be included in the semi-official summiteer database, and that I got a "free" IMG baseball cap. Even in the Himalayas it seems that marketing is important. After the meeting I spent the afternoon wandering around and exploring the city as there wasn't much else to do before we left for the mountains the next day. I discovered a temple located on the top of a high rocky cliff above the streets, giving me a slight respite from the thick traffic fumes. Plus watching the monkeys jump around the ancient stone temple at the top made it additionally worthwhile. By early evening I had made my way back just in time for the big team dinner.

IMG took three groups to the mountain, each "phase" on a slightly offset schedule to efficiently use their resources on the mountain. There wasn't enough space at the higher camps for the whole expedition at once so staggering the climbers into teams made infinite sense. In the evening all the members of my "Hybrid" phase, the first of two "Classic" team phases and a couple of separate groups were drinking cocktails on the downstairs patio of the Hotel. It turned out to be an interesting, successful and quite eclectic group. Mostly consisting of Type A people; everyone was impressive in some way or another, with

CEOs, bankers, doctors, soldiers, surgeons and firemen among the mix of career paths.

Yet despite these impressive resumes we were still a haphazard group of individuals who had been thrown together by chance, common purpose and little else besides. It is the nature of commercial expeditions and the real price of simplified passage to these previously inaccessible heights. To some extent you must put your life and dreams in the hands of strangers, regardless of your ability or of theirs. If your team turns around on the mountain, so do you, whether you are a Climbing God or not. Although the reputable expeditions have mitigated that scenario to some degree by designating a personal Sherpa for each climber, your dependency on the others still remains.

That evening I felt surprisingly pensive as I met the rest of the climbers at the pre-dinner drinks. I did my best to present a happy and extroverted exterior, but like a business networking event there were deeper thoughts at play. It reminded me of a job interview where the potential employer takes you to lunch. It's all very civilized and everyone seems relaxed, yet you know that every move is being scrutinized at some level or another. Each of my fellow climbers seemed driven to succeed, in their lives and also on this expedition, and no one yet stood out as crazy. But who were these people? Would they help or hinder my chances and my safety? Would they turn this experience into a dream or a nightmare? While the initial signs were promising I knew this was a secret only time could tell.

I only remember meeting two people at the dinner that night; Brooks and Dan.

What to say about Dan? I liked him, but others would be more effusive in their praise. He was without doubt an exceptionally charismatic fellow, while being good looking and athletic into the bargain. A genuine alpha male with an air of supreme confidence, no doubt about it. This was a man who made a big impression either way and certainly stuck in your memory. Lots of people just loved this guy, but I guess I'd met enough of these folks to be swayed too much by the showmanship. Still, it was a big shock to read a year later that he had been killed by a falling rock when the infamous big earthquake hit Nepal in 2015. He was a guy you thought would live forever. Of course, at that dinner no-one would know how the chips of fate would fall. Very much a bright light dimmed far too soon.

The other guy I vividly remember from the dinner was Brooks. He is another rare breed. He was a banker and former boss of Goldman Sachs in South Asia. Brooks was one of the old school. Basically, before what is known as the big bang in the 80s the banks were seemingly selective with their tiny pool of high quality recruits, so rather than the greedy immoral misfits which have characterized many of their hires since, those early folks tended to be genuinely impressive people on many dimensions. Brooks was one of those people, and despite my mixed emotions about bankers in general he was one of the exceptions. He is someone I came to like and respect a great deal.

All said it was a good dinner. As the hotel staff cleared away the last of the plates I figured there was just about time for a last beer with a couple of folks on the rooftop terrace before turning in for a somewhat early night. With my health and fitness paramount, it was to be my last of the expedition and it happened to be an "Everest" brand beer, the can featuring a famous picture of Tenzing Norgay, the joint first summiteer of

Everest, standing on the top holding aloft his ice axe. Looking at the picture on the bottle I couldn't help wondering. Would I also one day stand there as he had done?

16

Hurry Up and Wait

It was pitch black when Mohan collected us and our duffels from the hotel lobby in the early hours of the morning, and before long we sped across a dim and quiet city in the same minibus as before.

There was a quiet reverence amongst the team, from a lack of sleep in part, perhaps, but also a sense of trepidation. The darkness, the abdication of responsibility, the unknowns which were soon to come; this trip to the airport through this unfamiliar land felt like a small microcosm of how our lives and our fates were soon to be decided. What was to come, no-one could know.

Harsh fluorescent lights outside the airport's domestic terminal starkly illuminated the small crowd which had already congregated, and I was now happy to abdicate responsibility to Mohan and the guides. Where I should go, and indeed the overall proceedings, were seemingly impossible to decipher. We stood waiting for quite some time in the ticket area and I passed the time by watching the pigeons which flew around *inside* the lofty terminal hall. It was weird. Mohan eventually reappeared, having checked in our duffels, and passed us each a boarding pass containing no airline name, flight number or departure time. Or our names! There might have been a single scribbled character on the paper although I'm not even sure of that. Only the airline's logo gave any information at all.

The departure lounge beyond the security check could be described as ragged. It was a large room with a low ceiling and walls covered in peeling turquoise paint, built for a passenger capacity long since exceeded. The center of this hall had a few rows of those super-uncomfortable plastic airport chairs screwed into the floor, and around the edges there was nothing but those scuffed painted walls. In one corner of the lounge was a small kiosk doing a brisk business selling vastly overpriced Styrofoam cups of strong Nescafe instant coffee and powdered milk. I bought one to kill some time and watched the lounge with paranoia.

Periodically there would be a surge of people towards the single departure gate located on the opposite wall. Flights to the Khumbu Valley arrived and left seemingly at random and everything was done in a rush to complete the daily schedule before the afternoon mountain clouds closed down the airport at our destination. If you were late the plane wasn't going to wait, and I don't imagine there is much of a "Final call for Mr X" in this particular place. As it was impossible to tell whether it was for our flight or not I kept a close eye on our guides, Andy and Mike, and they took the brunt of the pestering.

"Andy, is this us?"

"Mike, what about this one?"

And, of course, "Are you sure?" in response to every answer, every single time.

Those poor guys. I'm not sure they had much more idea about it than we did, but in true guide style they projected calm and control in the face of uncertainty. In any case, at least they had been here before.

I didn't know when our flight was supposed to leave so I guess "delay" is not the correct concept. Instead it was waiting, waiting and yet more waiting. Rush after rush surged until suddenly our guides indicated for us to make our way to the gate. We were up!

I unceremoniously muscled towards the front, a habit picked up from my prior travels in the subcontinent, and after a quick walk down a corridor I was speeding onto the tarmac. Nearby I could see our duffel bags being carefully loaded into the front and rear compartments of a small plane, each bag being weighed so the handlers could balance the plane to prevent it crashing. This was a little unnerving, but I had other priorities. Dashing up the mobile stairs I managed to snag a front row seat, a prize more than worth the effort. With no divider between the passengers and the pilot on this aircraft I could see right out of the front windshield! The full wonder and terror of this flight was now mine for the taking.

17

The Flight to Lukla

Our destination was Lukla, gateway to the fabled Khumbu Valley and revered as the most dangerous commercial airport in the world. By accidents per passenger that may well be true. I was about to experience a landing there and discover whether this fearsome reputation for crash landings was deserved or not.

The plane climbed rapidly above the steep terrain of the surrounding foothills, and as we gained altitude, new mountains were revealed to us, one layer at a time, with each higher than the last. Snow-capped peaks soon came into view yet it took 30 minutes or so before we were high enough to see the real giants. Still, the colossal peaks of Nuptse, Lhotse and Everest remained hidden.

Around this point of the flight my attention was drawn to the cockpit, where a display on the instrument panel was beeping and flashing bright red to warn that we were too low. To save time and fuel the planes skim a mountain ridge along the route rather than leaving a decent gap, and the trees cannot have been more than perhaps a hundred feet below us. This is not what you expect to see out of the window of a commercial flight. On the plus side, a panicking GPS does give you a nice little warm-up shot of adrenaline before the main event of landing.

Once over the ridge the ground quickly fell away and the plane slowly turned left into a vast valley flanked by huge mountains. The valley itself though was filled with a thin dull mist and our destination was obscured as we descended. Soon it was impossible to make out any features except the outline of a shining river running far below and a strange, short gray line on the opposite side of the valley. It was half way up the side of the mountain and at a weird angle, so I figured it must be some kind of road. But then we banked to the right and I realized the pilot was lining the plane up with this strange gray road. It was, of course, the runway, but it was literally half way up a mountain and pointing straight into a cliff!

Eventually, I could make out the white lines on the tarmac as well as a large brick wall at the end of the strip. I mean, why make it easier when you can make it more difficult. To make the situation even more precarious the thin air at 10,000ft makes for a fast landing and there isn't enough room to approach at a gentle angle. I was convinced we were going to crash, unable to believe how steeply we were descending, just how short the runway was and how quickly we were approaching it. The mountain and the wall eliminated the possibility to abort and try again. There could be no second attempt. I gripped the seat rests hard in those last few seconds, eyes fixed on the white lines through the windshield as the plane pulled sharply upwards at the last moment, its wheels thudding into the ground as small buildings zoomed past the window. The pilot immediately hit the brakes and with the last piece of momentum we pulled off the runway just in front of the wall to enter a small and blessedly flat paved area by the miniscule airport terminal.

We had arrived at Lukla.

18
An Aura of Tranquility

To step off that plane was to step into another world. Instead of Kathmandu's muggy dust and traffic fumes I inhaled a cold pure air which invigorated with every breath.

Everything here was different. Everything. Even the buildings. Every structure apart from the airport terminal was constructed from large, rectangular gray stones rather than bricks or concrete. Unbelievably, each one had been carved by hand in the local area as it was cheaper for residents to cut local stone blocks to size with a chisel than to transport pre-made bricks or concrete this far up the valley. After all, it was a five day walk to the nearest road. The "clink-clink" sound of hammer and chisel against granite was a common noise to be heard in almost every village along the trek.

The main path through Lukla was paved with cobblestones made of the same kind of shaped stones; no asphalt or gravel here either. Instead of cars the main vehicles were trains of dzos, a mix between a yak and some sort of ox, which was used to transport goods throughout the lower valley. Dzos were bred to be more suited to the warmer temperatures at these lower altitudes than a pure yak, but they still look the part, with thick, shaggy coats and large imposing horns. Each wore a cow bell and the constant "donking" sound was also ever-present throughout the valley. It was part of the soundtrack to my adventure and I soaked up every minute of this new and wonderful environment.

The people and culture were also markedly different from the lowlands. Hinduism had been replaced by Buddhism and its influence pervaded much of what I saw and heard. Great lines of colorful prayer flags had been strung high between the trees and buildings, sending their messages heavenwards with each flutter of the wind. The bright clear sound of tiny bells rang through the air as prayer wheels were turned by the faithful. Even the dress of the local people reflected the uniqueness of this place, an eclectic mix of down jackets and colorful traditional garments as the modern and the old danced in strange harmony. It was all a far cry from the more westernized look of buttoned shirts and trousers more commonly seen in Kathmandu, and the scene I now saw was far closer to the Nepal that I had originally envisioned.

We were met on the tarmac by Lakpa, a Sherpa who handled all things helicopter, plane and airport related in Lukla for IMG. He welcomed us before ushering our group to the arrival hall at the airport, which in reality was a single large orange-colored room with big roller doors on the side where the planes waited. The shutters were open and a couple of men stood checking the arrived bag labels before heaving them onto a large bench between the passengers in the terminal and the airplanes outside. The tiny size of the airport and the large amount of stuff - not just our luggage but general supplies for expeditions, shops and the like - made this process somewhat frenetic, but eventually our duffels were all present and correct. We stepped through the airport entrance and out into the village, which began right on its doorstep. Dodging airport workers was quickly replaced with dodging the horns of dzos as they passed through the narrow cobbled streets. I wouldn't have changed those moments for all the world.

19

Doggies and Dormitories

Our flight had indeed been delayed by the mist, and our guides now considered our next move. The original stop was to be at the village of Phakding, three or so hours walk up the valley, but it was decided that the best plan was to remain in Lukla for the night and make a bigger push the following day rather than get a late start towards our original goal.

We were ushered to our guesthouse, known as a teahouse in this part of the world, which happened to be right across from the airport entrance along a narrow cobbled path. Ironically this meant my first day's trek in the Khumbu was about 20 feet. Fortunately, there are rarely flights in the afternoon at Lukla and soon the last planes left on their final return journey to Kathmandu. Activity at the airport was now finished until the next morning's rush and tranquility quickly enveloped the valley.

Most teahouses in the Khumbu are a similar and wonderful affair. There is always a common area which is usually light and airy with many windows. They are almost always wood paneled and wood floored, and a wooden bench usually runs along every wall with a window, covered with thick woolen blankets. A wood-burning stove is located somewhere near the center of the room as at this altitude the night time temperatures are bitter the entire year. The stove is the epicenter of social gatherings as people sit close by to fend off the chills.

Buddhist imagery is seen in these common areas to a greater or lesser extent; usually greater. The Sherpa race, who come only from the Khumbu and a number of adjacent small valleys, are descended from people who first crossed the Himalaya from Tibet a number of centuries ago, and their ancestors brought Tibetan Buddhism with them. It makes for a wonderfully rich place to experience. Each teahouse, with its prayer flags, paintings and the smell of incense made me feel I was somewhere very unique and very special. It seemed as though you had put one foot in an ancient and magical past. Perhaps this really was Shangri-La after all.

I found our first dinner enjoyable. As is usual on my travels I gravitate to the local food, and Nepal was no exception. When in Rome, as they say. In the Khumbu that often means dal, a thinner lentil soup rather than the thicker variation often found in India and Pakistan, and momos, a Tibetan dumpling a bit like a wonton. Both are filling and tasty. The only western food exception I would generally make, and only if it had been a particularly arduous day of trekking, was a deep fried Mars Bar for desert. More Scottish than Nepalese, they are terrible for your health and amazing for your happiness.

After a time, our early morning start began taking its toll on the group, plus there was a long walk ahead of us in the morning, so it was time for bed. I walked outside and braved my way through the now freezing courtyard to the bedrooms which were located in a small annex adjacent to the main building.

Bedrooms in the Khumbu teahouses are also uniformly similar. Each is usually a small, unheated room with a low and wide wooden bench which acts as a bedstead. On that plywood platform lies the same kind of thin foam mattress almost no matter where you are in the valley. I wondered why these were always identical until I walked past some poor porter on a steep trail carrying about 15 of them on his back. Too awkwardly shaped to be carried by yak and too bulky for the helicopters, they are all carried there by people. Brutal. This mode of transportation makes bringing a heavy spring or foam mattresses extremely difficult and expensive and I never saw one. In any case, the thin ones aren't all that uncomfortable and I knew I would look back on them as a distant luxury once I finally stepped onto the mountain itself.

I was awake shortly before sunrise and was greeted by a gloriously clear but frigidly cold dawn through the small window pane. I was sharing a room that night with Thom, and I glanced across at the other bed only to discover that he wasn't alone. It seemed he had found a special friend the previous evening, and that friend had come back with him to our room. Lying next to him on the bed, with them both happily sleeping away, was the teahouse dog! It had clearly found a new best buddy and was going to make the most of this opportunity to get extra warm and extra comfy, rather than having to sleep on the floor as per usual. They were the sweetest picture of happiness, so I made the minimum of noise as I got dressed and crept out of the room to leave them both in shared slumber, at least until it was time for breakfast.

I think I was the only person up at that early hour, save for a couple of Sherpa and the owner of a tiny German bakery that was attached to the front of the building. With the stoves only recently lit it took a little while for coffee to emerge but eventually one was warming my frozen fingers as I stood on the teahouse steps and watched the airport across the narrow path slowly bloom into life. People and their luggage were soon arriving in a haphazard stream and after a time I heard the frantic feathering of propeller blades as the day's first flight arrived from

Kathmandu. This was the starting gun for the morning's turmoil. Partly to avoid the increasing commotion around the airport entrance and partly to test an interesting idea I walked the short distance along the path and round a corner until I stood atop the brick wall at the end of the runway. It was quite a unique experience to watch a plane land directly at you just 200 yards away. I'm not sure you could do that at Heathrow.

Back at the teahouse the morning was now in full flow and I joined the other climbers in the common area to order some Tibetan bread and jam for breakfast. Tibetan bread is a curious thing; part bread, part Indian roti and part donut. While the texture and taste takes a bit of getting used to, it is pretty good, especially alongside some hot milk tea. After eating we packed up our stuff and delivered ourselves and our two duffels to the courtyard. One duffel, containing day to day items like clothes and a modest sleeping bag, would accompany us on the trek and be available each night wherever we stopped. The other, containing our climbing gear, down suit, big mountain boots and the like, would be taken by yak directly to Everest Base Camp. Once it was gone I wouldn't see it for almost two weeks so it was important to sort through everything and make sure each duffel was correctly divided. With this task done and two huge mounds of bags piled up around us, our intrepid group tightened our hiking boots, put on our day packs and headed out of the lodge. We were on our way at last!

20

Put Your Best Foot Forward

A trek from Lukla to Everest Base Camp usually takes just over a week, but we were climbers so we were budgeting 12 days.

"Surely you super-fit climber types must be able to go faster?" is the common response when you tell them your schedule, and perhaps that is true. The simple reason for the easy pace is gentle acclimatization. As climbers our goal was not to save time but to arrive at Base Camp as healthy and altitude-acclimatized as possible. Bullet proof, as the guides often say. The road to the summit is long and it's certainly more like a marathon than a sprint, so by keeping the pace mellow and the acclimatization rests plentiful many difficulties can be avoided. As such, our mellow schedule had the village of Namche Bazaar as our destination for the day. After the prior day's delay it was to be a reasonable distance, about 7 hours or so, with a large hill to climb at the end. Officially it wasn't supposed to be too taxing.

It only took a few minutes to walk right through Lukla. Amongst the dzos and buildings a number of small children played on the cobbles and watched us with mild interest as we hiked through. With red cheeks from the sun and wind, dressed in well-worn puffy little jackets, these kids didn't have much, it seemed, but they looked pretty happy nonetheless. I hoped that was the case. At the end of the village we finally reached the old stone arch which spans the path and marks the official start of our adventure in the Khumbu Valley itself. Immediately a stone staircase, carved into the mountainside, descends away from the village and into the valley below, and it looks exactly what you would expect at beginning a mystical quest. I couldn't help a wry smile. It was like being in Lord of the Rings and I rued not bringing a Gandalf hat to wear on the trek.

Lush vegetation surrounded us as we walked and from every direction came the sweet, shrill calls of songbirds. Magnolia trees, with their large white flowers just beginning to bloom, lined the sunny trail and in the cool sweet air everything was just so fresh, like a forest after the rain. High above, the snowy mountains reminded us of where we were. This was truly a magical place.

We passed through numerous tiny villages along the way, each consisting of just a handful of buildings often separated with a small patch of land which seemed to be farmed for subsistence crops. Each plot was separated by a stone wall, and it felt a bit like old rural England but without the drizzle and a vastly improved backdrop. Most of these villages also had a monument called a Chorten. A Chorten is a collection of large stone tablets carved with Buddhist prayers, and must always be passed on the left. This meant they generally were placed in the middle of the path, allowing travelers in either direction to receive a blessing. There was also usually a tiny shed-like building at one end of the chorten with a wide opening facing the passing travelers. Inside these small shelters stands a prayer wheel with a large circular handle along its base to allow it to be turned. Each rotation rings a small bell and I rarely missed an opportunity to rotate the wheel and listen to the high pitched ring echo across the landscape. I could probably use the prayers for what was about to come.

After a couple of gentle hours we reached a suspension bridge which crossed the main river at the village of Phakding. There are many such bridges along the route and all of them are a little nerve wracking, being generally over something scary and fatal, like a raging river or a 500ft drop. Or both. They are also a little wobbly and often you also have to time your crossing to avoid any dzos or yaks coming the other way. These beasts take up the entire width of the bridge, especially if they are carrying a heavy load, and their huge horns don't move for anyone. More than one tourist has been gored over the years I am told. Part of me wished they hadn't replaced the original rickety, Indiana Jones style wooden slat and hemp rope bridges with these more modern steel ones, but that was before I crossed one. Subsequently I was *very* happy they had been replaced.

After a cup of tea in Phakding we ascended from the village before crossing an even longer and much higher bridge which marked the start of the long unending climb up to the village of Namche Bazaar. It's a gain of perhaps 2,000 vertical feet on this one section alone and it's no cakewalk at this altitude. The guide's estimate of "not too taxing" seemed optimistic as for long hours we ascended the unrelenting dirt path between the trees and over tree roots, onwards and upwards forever.

At about the halfway point, the narrow switchbacks of the trail opened into a small rest area; just a little clearing in the trees at the edge of the ridge. We dropped our packs on a low stone wall and stretched our backs for a brief rest, which was well earned I thought. There was more reward to come though, when Andy beckoned us over to the far side of the space.

"There! This is the first place you can see it. Look!" he urged, and pointed through the small line of sparsely arranged pine trees along the small ridge where we stood.

Gazing up the deep valley, past the branches and the distant mountain spurs, in the far distance I could make out what seemed like an icy mountain plateau. Behind it rose a small dark pyramid.

Still thirty miles away as the crow flies it took me a second to fully realize what I was looking at, but then an enormous grin grew across my face as I stared up towards this peak. And I do mean up. Our current altitude was close to the top of the highest ski lift in Europe and yet the summit of Mount Everest was still another 5,500m / 18,000ft *higher* than where we currently stood. We were barely one third of the way up from sea level. I was already a bit knackered from just half a day's trek and again I sensed the difficulty of what we were trying to do. I can only imagine what went through the mind of Sir Edmund Hillary all those years ago when he must have stood where I now stood and looked at the same sight as I now saw. I'm sure he felt that same sense of awe and the same sense of apprehension. To climb this mountain seemed impossible. The big difference was that when he stood there, it still was.

21

A Village in the Sky

Soon it was time to tear myself from this grand sight and continue grinding upwards along the forest path. Eventually, the gradient of the trail lessened and we began to traverse a flatter path which clung to the right-hand wall of the mountain face. Soon we reached a wooden building alongside the trail, which was the main trekking permit checkpoint. Our guides fished out our permits and soon we were around the next corner to see a village perched precariously inside a steep hemispherical bowl. Finally, Namche Bazaar! In no time we were among the narrow cobbled streets, winding our way between equipment shops, souvenir stalls and assorted bakeries to reach the Khumbu Lodge, one of the oldest and most historic of the teahouses in the village. This was to be our acclimatization base for the next few days, and for both the location and the rest I was thankful.

Perched at 3,450m / 11,350ft Namche Bazaar is one of the highest villages in the world. It is the largest in the Khumbu, but it was still relatively small and intimate. I liked it. Yes, it's undeniably touristy, with those coffee spots and trinket shops, but for me it still manages to retain a sense of authenticity. Maybe it's the potato fields on the unbuilt terraces within the lower part of town, or the trains of menacing yaks which intermingle with the locals and tourists as they make their way through the streets. Perhaps it's the local market which caters to the needs of the people who live in the valley, or maybe just Namche Bazaar's improbable location on the side of a mountain. It has a sense of isolation, a sense that you are in a place which requires effort to reach and which wants to reward you for that determination. Perhaps I was fortunate to see the village before the main throng of trekkers arrived a few weeks hence and maybe then some of the magic is lost as the horde descends. In my few days there, however, it was a fabulous place to relax and enjoy all that natural splendor.

If Namche Bazaar was a cake and the scenery the icing, then the Khumbu Lodge was the sprinkles. I think it was the common room that did it for me, with its panoramic view out across the valley towards the towering face of a vast mountain massif on the opposite side of the valley. The scale of the Himalaya is evident and that stirs something deep inside. I will never get bored of sitting in the Khumbu Lodge, looking out at the ice and rock while drinking a pot of coffee and eating a plate of steamed momos. Never. Forget the retirement home on the golf course, *that* is where I want to spend my summers when I'm old and grumpy.

22

Lama and Lavazza

After a couple of days in Namche to acclimatize it was time for our expedition to continue on once more. Namche Bazaar lies at a great curve in the valley, and after a short but rigorous climb out of the bowl in which it sits for the first time you see the upper part of the Khumbu. It is only at this point that the true behemoths of the Himalaya come into clear view, rather than the glimpses we'd been limited to. And it is magnificent. To the left, the steep sides of Cholatse and Pumori. To the right, the dramatic towering spire of Ama Dablam, known as the Matterhorn of Nepal, while beyond rise the even higher summits of Baruntse and Makalu. Still further away, the south face of Nuptse and behind it the great peak of Lhotse. Then, finally, above all the foreboding pyramid of Everest. It is quite something to see, this view of such colossal scale and contrast. It is truly awe inspiring.

From the top of the bowl the main path must soon return back down to the river in order to cross to the eastern side of the valley. With several thousand vertical feet lost, you cross the steel suspension bridge above the raging torrent and immediately begin to ascend until reaching the monastery at Tengboche, one of the highest in the world. The continual and severe elevation changes makes for another strenuous day of walking, but the compensation of both the destination and the journey itself more than make it worth it. The smell of warm pine envelopes the senses as you carefully hop over tree roots down towards the river, while juniper and rhododendrons scent the air as you labor upwards in the bright afternoon sun. Eventually, though, you make it, tired and relieved, and immediately understand that all the toil was more than worth it. Surrounded by snowy Himalayan peaks the Tengboche monastery looks exactly like you hoped it would. Made of thick stone walls and sturdy wooden beams, the ornate stone lions guarding the archway entrance show a place which belongs in an age long past. I'd found Shangri-La at last!

Phinjo, our Sherpa guide, was well known at the monastery so we were invited inside by the monks and allowed to sit in the main prayer chamber for a few minutes. It is a cold, dimly lit room encompassed in Buddhist imagery, and a large golden statue of Buddha is located at the back wall. Several rows of low, wide benches run across the room, making platforms on which a number of monks, dressed in their dark maroon robes as always, were meditating. It is an authentic, tranquil place and there is a great sense of calm which I found quite spellbinding. It was like being inside a great cathedral and I felt very much at peace. My only regret is not spending a few more years there to calm my soul.

Outside, just a stone's throw from the monastery, there are a couple of low buildings which make up a small teahouse. They also contain a café and a small bakery, of all things. I'm not sure it's quite in keeping with the theistic atmosphere of the monastery but I highly recommend it anyway! The counter had a decent range of delicious cakes, including the aptly named Crazy Wacky Cake, and they even have a proper espresso machine with which to make genuine Italian Lavazza coffee, as evidenced by the large metal drums of coffee grounds underneath the counter. Evidently a shard of the modern world has reached this far flung outpost of humanity, and in some ways it was a little disappointing. It is to be expected, of course, and after a long day's trek it's hard to deny yourself these little creature comforts along with a teasing exclamation of "Ohhh, go on then." The benefits naturally go both ways, and such seemingly minor services have become an economic boom for the locals. They have realized that plenty of trekkers will quite happily pay US$2 for a real latte - made with yak's milk no less* - and the same again for a large slice of cake. In a country where the average person's income is around US$16 a *week*, the simple task of making a few cups of coffee brings immense riches on a relative basis. In a single day a popular café can bring in the equivalent of the median Nepali *yearly* income and I can hold no grudge against that.

* PS Asking for yak milk in the Khumbu will draw giggles from the Sherpa as no such thing exists. Yaks are male, whereas the females are called naks. Ask for nak milk!

The trail now descends steeply from Tengboche but only for a short distance before flattening out into another tiny village. It was here we stopped for the night at a teahouse aptly named Rivendell, after The Lord of The Rings I am sure. Given its mystical location and superb views of Ama Dablam I couldn't argue with the choice. The nights here were even colder than in Namche and the bare concrete walls and floors of the bedrooms didn't help in that department. Perhaps we were slowly being toughened up in preparation for the weeks ahead, but I was unwilling to let go of partial comfort quite yet. I was glad to spend most of my time in the common room where the stove was constantly lit, and after dashing to bed in the evening I repeated the reverse quick dash back the next morning, quickly ordering some tea to warm my bones.

It was times like these that the use of showers became a real challenge for me. Some of the tea houses have a propane heater and you can buy a hot shower for a few dollars, but I always felt so guilty about the effort required to bring those heavy fuel tanks so high into the valley. In any case, many teahouses in the upper valley don't even have that option, and as the average temperatures got colder so did the water. You'd often have to wait until the afternoon for the water pipes to unfreeze if the teahouse even had pipes, as usually the water was just kept in a large plastic barrel in some corner of the bathroom. In these situations the "shower" was the plastic jug which floated in it. Throwing ice water on my naked body is not my idea of fun even if it is 120°F outside, so at 20°F I generally resorted to the main alternative weapon in the battle for cleanliness - baby wipes! Along with merino wool underwear and thermals I could keep the dirt and general yuckiness at bay for quite some time, and with surprising effectiveness. Or at least that's what I told myself! Every couple of days I would surrender and have a real wash with this ice water for the sake of my teammates, but limiting these torture episodes was generally a priority.

Our next destination beyond Rivendell was a visit to Lama Geishi. Ah, Lama Geishi. Originally from Tibet and 85 years old the first time I met him, he lived in the village of Upper Pangboche, isolated by a small detour from the main trail. As far as I understand he was actually third in succession behind the Dalai Lama! For some reason, probably hidden by the mists of time, it is now traditional for climbers to pay a visit to Lama Geishi on their way to Base Camp and receive a blessing ahead of their expedition. This is something that few trekkers did, likely as most are not aware of this possibility as he was happy to bless all and everyone as far as I understand it.

His house was a small, nondescript building constructed with hand-carved stones, as all the houses in Pangboche are, located up a short side alley at the very top of the village. We entered the small dirt yard behind the house and left our packs by the wall before entering. Stepping through the doorway was like entering the fairytale dwelling of a wizard. The cold air inside the dimly lit narrow corridor was hazy, and the smoky scent coming from the wood-burning stove in the kitchen pervaded everything. Light entering through the few small windows high on the walls shone as white shards across the space before ending brightly on the bare wood paneled walls. Despite the numerous people who now crowded the small area there was a hush and a stillness, as though no-one wanted to disturb the sense of reverence which hung in that smoky air.

We waited briefly in the corridor before being led to the main room of the house. Here, the wooden wall panels were more ornate and one wall was completely covered in small photos of climbers pinned amongst the Buddhist paintings and scrolls which hung at intervals along its length. On one side of the room ran a long wooden bench and a line of windows along its entirety. In contrast to the dimness of the interior, the windows revealed a bright and majestic scene. Beyond the small rooftops of the village below, the pine-covered slopes of the valley rise dramatically to become snow covered peaks. Everything shone closely and brightly beneath a bluebird sky; it was just the most perfect mountain view you could imagine. In the far left corner, between two tables covered in papers and scrolls and with one side of his face illuminated in the sunshine, sat Lama Geishi himself.

A somewhat portly man it seemed, he was dressed in the maroon robes worn by monks here in the Khumbu. A thick pair of spectacles hung at the end of his nose in stark contrast to his hairless head. With eyes closed he performed the ritual, his deep murmuring voice barely audible despite the quiet of the room.

Soon it was my turn to be blessed. I approached the Lama and he smiled, calmly gesturing to the chair in front of him across the corner of the table. He asked my name and shook my hand. There was a sense of balance about him. I had been a little nervous, not knowing what to expect or worried I might do something wrong, but those thoughts were soon banished. It was a real privilege to be in his presence.

I passed Lama Geishi a traditional blessing scarf along with a small donation. These thin, silk-like scarves are commonly offered as good luck blessings and it is usual to accumulate a few from various people over the course of an expedition. During the blessing the Lama places it across your shoulders, and after the chants he ties a brightly colored string around your neck.

"You must keep that on until it falls off naturally," advised Phinjo, one of our Sherpa guides. Looking down at the indestructible yellow nylon microcord I figured I would do my best. Old age might get me first, and in fact it nearly did; I gave up after wearing it after two years straight after which it had barely even faded, let alone started to wear out.

Receiving this blessing under the gaze of the Himalaya connected me to the mountains and this place in a way I hadn't been before. For some people perhaps it doesn't have much impact, but for me the experience was quite profound. I felt in some way closer to the culture, as though through this blessing I had now been accepted into it in some tiny way. Seeing Phinjo and the other Sherpa guides also receive the same blessing only reinforced that feeling of commonality. Perhaps there was also the knowledge that in general only climbers received this privilege and I was now somehow closer to that fraternity as well. Whether I believed in Buddhism or not didn't matter. Participating in this ancient ritual performed by a revered ancient monk in this magical place was an honor, and one I will remember forever.

23

Touching Heaven

Above Upper Pangboche you begin the penultimate major ascent on the trek to Base Camp. This part of the journey takes you above the treeline, where the lush forests of the lower valley morph rapidly into bare ground and brown tundra as you enter a land of ice and rock. At the top of this climb you reach a wide, gently ascending valley at the confluence of three rivers. It is a barren vista of immense scale and it is hard not to be impressed with the utter desolation of the place. Gone is the carefree wandering of the lower valley; here the harshness of the high mountains can be seen and felt in all their glory.

Soon after cresting into this higher valley you reach the small village of Pheriche. It's a ramshackle, one road kind of village with low stone buildings surrounded by low stone walls which are mostly there to demarcate small paddocks where the yaks are sent to rest each night. There doesn't seem to be much to redeem it to the casual observer, yet look closely and there are a couple of things which make it far better than it may appear.

The first is the Himalayan Hotel. It doesn't look like much from the outside, although the courtyard entrance arch is an elaborate arch in the style of a temple entryway. Inside though is a different story. Snuggling up on the bright woven rugs covering benches beneath the windows inside the ornately decorated common area while looking out across the wide, snow covered valley, with yaks walking past and the peaks beyond, is a real treat. With such a stark contrast between that cozy warmth inside and the harsh environment beyond it has become perhaps my favorite place to stay on the entire trek. Really the only downside is that they seem to play the same soft rock CD on repeat, year in, year out. If you can't stand "sultans of swing" by Dire Straits, don't stay there.

The second redeeming feature is that Pheriche hosts the first of two clinics run by the Himalayan Rescue Association (HRA), the other being at Everest Base camp itself. During the climbing season they provide care services for the local people as well as deal with the inevitable ailments suffered by climbers and trekkers. It's a prestigious posting and the competition to spend three months in arduous conditions, unpaid, is fierce. These doctors, tucked away in harsh conditions with limited resources are paradoxically an elite group of professionals from all over the world.

Each day at 3pm one or more of the doctors conducts a short, free talk for any and all who care to join. The topic is altitude sickness and it's well worth the time. The doctors walk you through the various symptoms and treatments for altitude related afflictions. I'd done a fair amount of research on the topic, but I learned some new things and refreshed my old knowledge. It's important. Hundreds of people are treated for altitude sickness each season and nearly one a day must be evacuated by helicopter down to Lukla or even Kathmandu for the worst cases. An average of one trekker a year dies from altitude sickness, in addition to the deaths of climbers. We'll get to all the insidious effects of altitude on the human body a bit later on, and they are frightening and grim. I was motivated to ensure I didn't fall victim to this silent enemy and I only wish more trekkers and climbers would go to these HRA talks.

I spent a rest day acclimatizing, listening to three lifetime's worth of Dire Straits and drinking milk tea in the common room before it was time to get going once more. Several of the guide companies now integrate a training climb into the expedition prior to clients stepping foot on Everest, in order to give climbers a better sense of the Himalayan environment and a first look at things they may not have used before, such as ascending on fixed ropes. I'm sure it also gives the guide company a better sense of how everyone is doing and if anyone needs extra assistance. IMG subscribed to this philosophy and had chosen a peak called Lobuche East, located about a day's walk before Base Camp. At 6,100m / 20,000ft this summit would offer my first taste of proper climbing in the Himalaya and it was to this mountain that we were heading to next.

IMG's camp at the base of Lobuche wasn't much to look at, just a small group of tents in a small meadow in a small flat-ish depression a few hundred feet above the Khumbu Valley floor. Two midsized marquee-type tents were erected at one end of our camp , one as a cook tent and one as an eating and gathering place for the clients and guides. No Lavazza coffee or slices of cake here.

We stayed in camp for three nights for some more acclimatization, and on the afternoon of the fourth day our team made the two-hour ascent up to a higher camp on the mountain flank. This advanced camp would be the jumping off point for the summit bid. It was more of a scramble than a climb for the most part, although there were some rock slab sections which required some significant effort. The Sherpa had put up some fixed ropes in a few of these parts and it was plenty enough work at this altitude to haul ourselves up while being careful not to slip.

Although I'm certain we could have reached the summit straight from the main camp in one go, separating the ascent into two parts had a couple of benefits. First, it better replicated summit day on Everest, when we would sleep just a few hours on the South Col before continuing on for the summit push. And second, this upper camp helped with acclimatization and make the overall exertion level to climb Lobuche a bit lower. Remember, the aim here was to train and arrive at Base Camp bulletproof, rather than broken. There would be plenty of time for that later.

I was excited for the climb and aghast at the wakeup time. I abhor getting up in the middle of the night, no matter what the reason. At some primordial, reptilian level my subconscious resents being torn from its warmth and slumber to an outside world so cold and dark. I think my reaction is a result of my metabolism, which is either on or off. When it's on I'm a furnace. T-shirt in the snow? No problem. When it's off I'm a block of ice. When I sleep it's usually off and I often wake up freezing to the touch. Sometimes this oddity has actually been an asset. I remember one night at a less than salubrious hostel in Mexico when everyone else in the dorm room was ravaged by bed bugs, but in my frozen stasis I remained untouched. Usually, however, it is a hindrance. When trying to crawl out of a protective cocoon into frozen air it becomes a burden which only a herculean effort will overcome. The shock of hunting around in the cold to find the right clothes is second to none.

At the appointed time I heard a rustle outside the tent. The rustle got louder until I heard the shrill sound of the zipper on our tent being swiftly drawn up and a face, illuminated by a head torch, thrust itself through the fabric. Great clouds of steam billowed through this beam of light from two mugs of hot milk tea he was passing through the opening towards us. Oh the joy, the rapture! I was a happy bunny to be given the antidote to my frozen state and felt guilty at such good treatment. Not guilty enough to decline this wondrous gift, though!

I eventually dressed and crawled out of my tent before making my way to the nearby kitchen tent where our cook was already making a surprisingly complex breakfast given it was 2am and we were at 5,250m / 17,200ft on the side of a mountain. I remember thinking it seemed like a lot of effort when personally I would have been happy with a packet of oatmeal and a few spoonfuls of Nutella. Still, today an omelet, toast and coffee would be very welcome.

The other climbers were for the most part already there. There was plenty of inefficient faffing about as we each brushed the cobwebs off our individual climbing preparation routines. Eventually, though, we were on our way.

I felt strong and so did the others it seemed. I think everyone shared a sense that today we would be making a big step towards our potential success on Mount Everest and we all wanted to do well. The pace was sharp as we scrambled up the dark rocky slopes, taking care over the sections covered with a thin dusting of snow, and as the dawn glow began to compete with the beam from our head torches we had already reached the start of the snowfield beneath the summit. Conditions were absolutely perfect. The snowpack was solid but not icy, while the air was cold and completely still. Above us the early rays of sun shone through a cloudless deep blue sky.

We briefly munched on a snack and attached our crampons. Everyone was in fine fettle and I felt there was a sense of camaraderie building amongst the team. As warm dawn colors bathed the high snows on Ama Dablam on the opposite side of the valley I felt good. I was having fun climbing with this impressive group of people. So far so good.

The route now traversed the snow field before climbing steeply for several hundred vertical meters to the summit. This was my first taste of fixed rope climbing and the Sherpas had already put in place a rope from this part of the slope up to the top. I duly attached my ascender to the line. This is a one-way ratchet device which allows you to move up the rope, but it catches if you fall back or pull. It's pretty straightforward to use on these moderate slopes, although climbing the fixed lines wasn't as straightforward as I supposed it would be. Even though these ropes are made of non-stretchable material, it still jerks and wobbles from the movements of other climbers above and below. With each pull on the ascender you are never quite sure what will happen. Will the ascender engage rigidly or would it move down as you pull against someone else above you on the line? Would it be still or heave side to side with the movement of others. Will someone step at the same time you pull, causing a sudden surge in an unexpected direction just as you were delicately balanced? You never knew, and I found it mightily awkward. In the end I learned to treat the rope as a safety backup rather than something to pull myself up with, which meant switching focus to climb almost exclusively with my legs. It took a while to figure this all out, especially on the steeper sections, and I was relieved to practice this skill before I was on Everest itself. In the end, for me the fixed line didn't make the climb all that much easier. But it did make it a lot safer.

Four hours and five minutes after departing High Camp we crested the final lip of the snow slope to reach the small plateau of Lobuche's eastern summit. The route had ascended the south face of Lobuche so this was the first time we could see over the mountain towards the top of the Khumbu Valley. Ahead we saw Pumori, looming high above Base Camp, with Nuptse beyond and Mount Everest towering over everything in all its glory. It was magnificent. We could see the jet stream still blasting snow from its summit, very much in stark contrast to the completely still air in which we stood, and as always, climbing that mountain seemed inconceivable.

There were hugs all round, especially with my guide Andy and with Brooks, who arrived alongside me at the summit. Ellen, an impressive climber and athlete on our team, had reached the summit a few minutes before the rest of us, so we sat down next to her to soak in the experience.

The group had been uniformly impressive I thought, and at 6,100m / 20,000ft none of us appeared to be suffering from the altitude, aside from Ben who had a bit of a minor cough. Personally I felt fabulous. Our climbing time had smashed expectations by several hours and there was a rumor that we might have beaten the unofficial IMG client record. I finally had my first benchmark and I knew that if an average Everest climber had a decent chance of summiting then, logically at least, all of us now standing on the top of Lobuche did as well.

24

Arrival at Everest Base Camp

We descended all the way back to Lobuche base camp in one go, and ten hours after leaving High Camp for our ascent we arrived. It had been a long day and I was fast asleep before sunset. The next morning we were soon packed up and leaving camp, retracing our footsteps back to the main trekking trail, and after a couple more hours we reached the village of Gorak Shep, the last proper village before Everest Base Camp itself.

Gorak Shep is a tiny little place which exists only to service the trekkers and climbers on Everest. In the winter it is basically abandoned and mostly acts as a place to store equipment, especially the heavier pieces like stoves and tents which last a long time and are needed every year. During the trekking season, however, Gorak Shep bustles with activity. The couple of teahouses there do a brisk business, and having a milk tea while looking at the view is really quite good. I believe there is also accommodation there as trekkers are generally not permitted to spend the night at base camp itself.

Soon it was time for the final leg, so tea was finished and packs shouldered for the last time. Base camp was a little over an hour from Gorak Shep on the rocky moraine ridge to the left of the glacier as you ascend. For the last 10 minutes the trail dives steeply down and crosses onto the Khumbu glacier itself. Although on ice, the path is gravel-strewn, as the majority of the glacier is at this point, but there are still crevasses to navigate around as it weaves towards camp. And then finally you are there.

A great pile of rocks, adorned with an even greater number of prayer flags and a makeshift sign marks the entrance to Everest Base Camp. Most people add a stone with their name or expedition written on it, and so the marker grows during the season. Throughout the day there are almost always people there, usually trekkers taking pictures of their final destination, but then sometimes also a couple of porters taking one final rest before delivering their cargo, or perhaps a yak herder picking up the stragglers of his herd with a loud shout and the deft throw of a large stone. My advice is not to get reincarnated as a yak.

The main irony of the entrance to base camp is that you can't actually see the summit of Mount Everest from there, or in fact from anywhere on the glacier once you reach it. It is hidden by the shoulder of the lower mountain so if you continue on the path the next time you see the top - if you are fortunate - is about 50ft from the summit itself. Still, that doesn't matter. If you are a climber and you make it to Base Camp you have at least made it to the start of the race.

Base camp itself is 2 *miles* long, distributed along a single path which is rerouted each year as the ice moves and melts. The far end of base camp, its northern end, is closest to the start of the climb and the most densely populated part of this temporary metropolis. Some teams prefer to set themselves up in this area to reduce their access time to the mountain, plus this is where the medical center, the main helipad and various other functions are located. This area is known as downtown. The medical tent was, in my view, the limit of its advantage, whereas the big disadvantage of downtown is that it's crowded. Very crowded. Every possible undulation on the ice seemed to have been leveled off and a tent pitched on top. The occupants are also right next to the main path through camp; a path walked by yaks during the day and both Sherpa and climbers at night. Was downtown ever without the penetrating whir of a gasoline generator, a snoring neighbor, the loud blast of helicopter blades, the snorts and cowbells of yak, the shuffle of footsteps, the clink of equipment or the talking of climbers? Probably not. Some of the tents were even located right at the edge of the helipad and I remember watching one literally get blown away by the rotor downdraft as a helicopter took off. This was not prime real estate, at least in my book.

IMG always located its camp far from downtown, much closer to the Base Camp entrance, where there was significantly more space and infinitely more peace. I preferred it. Even the 20 minute walk through camp at 3am to reach the start of the climb felt like a benefit rather than a disadvantage; time to get both my brain and my body warmed up and primed for the work to come. I couldn't understand why everyone else didn't move down here as well, but I was very happy they didn't.

25
A Proper Expedition

Building base camp is a real undertaking. My expectation was a few randomly scattered tents. Instead, there was an entire village complex. Around the edges, on ledges chipped flat by the Sherpa, were the client tents. This year there were two rows, one above the other, and I was quick to get an upper tent for no reason at all. Towards the center were the communal tents. Two large yellow tents, similar to those marquee tents at Lobuche base camp, were erected next to each other as the eating tents for the different groups of clients. Each had a set of plastic picnic tables arranged as a single long central table, with a row of plastic chairs on either side that allowed the tent to seat perhaps 16 people at a time. Every table had a plastic red and white tablecloth, and arranged in a near continuous line along the length were all the condiments, drink powders and snacks a climber might ever want. There was also a thermos or two of hot water at all times, so you could make tea or coffee whenever you wanted, partly to keep warm and partly to keep hydrated, which was critical in the absurdly dry air.

Near to the client eating tent was the cook tent where the Sherpa would create miracles with our meals. Wide stone benches were constructed from rocks around the camp to create both a plinth on which the chef could work and a place to stand the violent gas burners they used to cook with and boil water. From 6am to nightfall there was always the gentle roar of a burner, the faint smell of kerosene exhaust and the steam from a giant aluminum water pot to greet a visitor.

Most days and nights in Base Camp followed pretty much the same routine. I was usually awake just after dawn, perhaps around 5.30am and would wander to the Sherpa kitchen and wait for the day's first batch of milk tea to be ready. Clients aren't really allowed in there, but as no one else was awake the cooks were always happy for me to perch on the end of the stone bench in the tent and watch the world. They were a fun bunch and the tent was warmer than outside, so I'd usually stay in the tent for that entire first cup before getting a refill which I would take outside. Usually, I'd make my way to a small ridge at the edge of camp and watch the light move down the mountain flanks towards us. It was nice just to stand there in my fluffy down trousers and enormous down jacket and observe the comings and goings. Even at that early hour the first trains of yaks and loaded porters were arriving. It was nice to know they were nearly at their destination for the day. More of our Sherpa would emerge from their tents during that next hour and make their ways to get some tea, and I'd usually have a quick chat with the ones I knew. It was a lovely way to start the morning. Soon enough the kitchen tent would be a hive of activity and the day would begin for real.

When I'd run out of tea and was getting chilly I'd make my way toward the client eating tent. Sometimes it was as early as 6am, but usually it was late enough that a couple of other climbers were already there. If I was lucky, our cook had already delivered a thermos flask of hot water and that meant coffee! There was a pour-over coffee filter maker device thing which lived on the table in the mornings and whoever arrived first or was sitting closest when the water was delivered was generally responsible for the first brew. I had zero complaints with the setup, especially as they provided us Nepalese-grown gourmet coffee called Himalayan Java, and in a place like Base Camp, with its monotony and stresses it was the simple things and the pleasant moments which kept you sane as the days dragged on.

Breakfast began promptly at eight; the first of our three solid meals each day. Each mealtime was preceded by the banging of a frying pan by the cook, a universal sign to slowly saunter towards food. The first thing which greeted us each mealtime was a member of the kitchen staff carrying a pot of steaming face towels. Total luxury at 17,500ft! Removing the grime of the night or day was a wonderfully refreshing moment, and as my singular moment of pampering each day it was something to be treasured. During those moments Base Camp life was quite a lot better than at home!

Breakfast was usually an omelet and toast, or sometimes porridge. Very occasionally, if I had been a good boy, they would serve us tsampa, the Nepalese version of porridge. Maybe I liked it because it tastes just like ReadyBrek, a brand of breakfast porridge I used to have when I was growing up in the UK. Tsampa just brought back those good associations, plus I could mix Nutella into it. Nutella is the ambrosia of the gods, and nothing you can say will change my mind. I sometimes think I go on expeditions solely to justify eating it with a spoon straight from the jar. Adding great dollops of it to Tsampa just makes this behavior more socially acceptable.

Lunch and dinner were more varied, and dinner was usually the most varied and involved. The first course was always soup, and each evening great pots of bubbling liquid would be carried in by one of the staff, with another ladling us each a generous portion. It was invariably very good and probably my favorite thing to eat in camp, apart from tsampa and jelly beans from the enormous tub on the table.

The main course was usually western-inspired fare. Both Kaji and Purna, our two main client chefs, were excellent and had developed a skill for cooking at extreme altitude. It's not as simple as you might think. At Base Camp the low air pressure means that water boils at just 81°C / 180°F so all the ingredients behave differently and all the cooking times go haywire. So far from civilization on a glacier in the middle of nowhere it was an amazing feat and sometimes I felt genuinely guilty at the effort the Sherpa and the expedition had expended just to please us. Some poor soul had even carried a small pizza oven to base camp so that we could occasionally enjoy the comforts of freshly baked, hand-made pizza! It was totally unnecessary and utterly remarkable!

26
A Step into the Unknown

Outside of meals there wasn't all that much to do apart from go on short walks or just rest in our tents. Still, as a way of both training and something to pass the time our guides set up a couple of climbing practice areas on some nearby ice. One of the aluminum ladders used to cross crevasses on Everest had been found, but instead of spanning a bottomless crevasse our guides had suspended it horizontally about a foot above some flat ground. It was certainly worthwhile practicing the crossing, as locating the spikes of a crampon to match the rung spacing could be tricky. Setting the ladder at different angles also helped us get an idea of the traction levels, as some of the inclines could be quite treacherous to deal with. Sometimes my crampons would get stuck or slip on the metal rungs, causing me to lose my balance and hop off the side. Knowing how to avoid this was a vital skill; one I'd rather learn here before trying it in the dark over a 200ft drop.

After a week or so of acclimatization in base camp it was nearly ready for my Hybrid team to set foot on the mountain itself. This foray would be a mini trial run, a small taste of climbing to get us ready for the longer climbs ahead. In our path was the Khumbu Icefall, the most dangerous part of our climb.

The Khumbu glacier actually starts high above base camp in a great bowl ringed by the peaks of Nuptse, Lhotse and Mount Everest. Accumulating here over many years the ice slowly flows through this bowl until reaching the valley edge and tumbling down towards the main Khumbu Valley far below. This vast waterfall of broken ice is the only reasonable route up the mountain from the Nepalese side and so the maze of teetering ice blocks and crevasses must be negotiated in order to progress to the higher camps. The ice is constantly moving and the icefall is treacherous. Many climbers have lost their lives here and it is not a place to take lightly.

To facilitate the climb, a group of Sherpa known as the Icefall Doctors are tasked each season with first finding and then maintaining a route through this maze. Each year the route is different and it can change quite significantly during the season as ice vanes tumble, crevasses widen, snow falls and the ice melts. It is only when the fixed ropes and ladders are all in place that climbers are allowed onto the mountain itself. This was the event we were now all waiting for, and after a week in Camp we got news that a route had finally been found! It wouldn't be long now before I would have my first foray onto Mount Everest itself and I could hardly contain my anticipation. One of our Classic teams would be heading a short way up the mountain the next morning for their first look at the icefall and the day after it would be our turn to go.

27
A Terrible Tragedy

6.04am. I had already collected my tea from the cook and moved to the client tent to write a little in my journal and hopefully keep my fingers partially defrosted until the warming sun rose above the mountains. I'd been sitting in the tent for a few minutes, tapping away on the little tablet screen when I heard the unmistakable rumble of an avalanche. I wasn't overly concerned. It was a sound we were all becoming acquainted with and barely a day went by without hearing a big fall somewhere on the mountains nearby. Usually, they came down from the slopes of Nuptse, high above us but on the other side of the glacier, and despite sounding worrying close by they were still a couple of miles away or more. The location of base camp had apparently been chosen for a reason. As I heard the deep echoes reverberate back to silence this particular avalanche seemed the same as all the others before it, no more and no less, and I quickly put it out of my mind.

Five minutes later, as I randomly stepped outside the tent to take a break from typing, was when I noticed something was amiss. Unusually for that time of the morning, all of the guides were up and walking around the camp, and I could hear a lot of chatter on the radios they each carried. A steady stream of people were making their way up to the expedition's central command tent, located at the highest point of our camp, and few seemed to be leaving. Eventually one of the guides came down, and as he zoomed past I asked him what was going on.

"There's been a big avalanche in the icefall," he replied. "We are trying to figure out the situation. It could be pretty bad."

Yikes. Straining towards the icefall, with my naked eyes I could just about make out a couple of black specs high on the route. They appeared to be making their way down. From our position at the far end of base camp it was a long way away, and as the upper section of the route was hidden behind the flank of Nuptse it appeared that whatever had occurred had happened beyond our sight. We would have to wait for news.

It was only several hours later, when that first group of IMG clients returned from the icefall itself, that we finally learned something concrete. And it wasn't good.

"There was a massive avalanche from the West Shoulder of Everest," explained one of the guys as he sat in the client tent nursing a plastic mug of tea. "The whole massive sheet just came right down and landed right on the icefall. It happened a few hundred yards ahead of us. We got hit by the blast, but I think there was a whole group of people who actually got buried."

As the morning progressed I watched from a nearby vantage point as helicopters from the lower valley arrived and flew up towards the affected area. A number of Sherpa had been badly injured and were being brought back down to be treated by the doctors. Soon though, rather than return with an injured Sherpa each helicopter brought a body; a corpse hanging from a rope beneath the machine. Each an unmistakable outline, arms and legs dangling lifelessly in the air. The helicopters would then take off once more and return a while later with yet another body. By early afternoon the bodies of 13 Sherpa had been recovered. Three remained missing, frozen within the ice and never to be seen again.

28

Of Mountains and Men

The mood in camp for the next few days was deeply somber as you would expect; days of mourning and of concern. Most Sherpa had been given permission to descend back down the valley to their villages for several days, and I remember watching a long line of them crossing the glacier and the short moraine wall to continue down the trail. It was a poignant moment; to see these proud, strong people leaving our endeavor hammered home the seriousness of what had happened and the enormity of the risks we all took in this cruel place.

On day three or four we began to see them return, usually in small groups of just two or three. Once again there was heightened activity at our camp, in contrast to the flat and somber atmosphere of tragedy. As life in camp returned to what passes for normal, thoughts turned to the obvious question. What happens next?

It is still hard to write about the week which followed, and I shall try to present the situation as objectively as I can. I care about those affected in the disaster and it was a tragedy for the Sherpa and for everyone, no doubt about it. I was there. I talked with the Sherpa. I saw the bodies. I did what little I could in the moment to help, and my only regret that there wasn't more I could have done.

Emotions were raw, boiling beneath the surface without spilling over. You could feel the tension around the tents. The Sherpa community is a small one, and brothers, cousins, fathers and sons all work on the mountain to provide for themselves and their families. Many of the Sherpa in camp had lost a relative or friend in the disaster.

Yet amongst the expedition leaders, the climbers and Sherpas there was a decision to be made, an unavoidable choice which impacted everyone. Should we continue to climb the mountain that season? The decision was going to change the direction of our expedition, the other expeditions and the lives of everyone involved.

And there was no "right" answer. And for the record I take no position on what "should" have happened.

Do you cancel the season? Many think this is the only answer, the "right" answer, but it is perhaps not so clear cut. Some of the climbing Sherpa make 10 times the average yearly wage for Nepal in just 7 weeks. How would staying or leaving affect them, now and in the future? Canceling the expeditions would not help the porters who made the majority of their yearly income by carrying supplies to base camp and were paid by the load. No loads meant no income, and their families and children would likely suffer as a result.

For some climbers this expedition was a once in a lifetime dream, and many had poured their life savings into this one shot. Some would never get another chance to come back. Obviously it was not the primary concern, but it was still a factor. You are not heartless and evil for recognizing that. Perhaps it all comes down to the original question about climbing Mount Everest in the first place. Is it right to pay someone to help you climb that mountain in any circumstance? You are asking people to risk their lives for money. Is that ethical? Many of us might quickly say it is not, but much of society is built on this exact tradeoff. You pay a pilot to fly the airplane when you go on vacation, and every time they take to the sky they risk their life to provide that service to you. It's the same for millions of jobs around the world, from coal miners and fishermen to taxi drivers and boxers. People die in work-related accidents every day. Who or what determines what an acceptable risk is, or what appropriate compensation should be? Like I said, it's not so simple.

There were arguments to continue climbing and arguments to cancel the season. In any case, in the midst of the debate the Nepalese Maoist party got themselves involved. This was not an omen of happy, productive compromise, and as might have been expected, a long list of both related and tenuously unrelated demands were drawn up. The Minister of Tourism made a visit to Base Camp to address the Sherpa, a somewhat comical affair as he arrived by helicopter breathing from a large oxygen cylinder clutched to his chest. Flying directly to 17,500ft is rarely a good idea, but I applaud the gesture and the effort. Almost everyone in base camp attended, myself included along with all the Sherpa, and at the meeting he essentially agreed to their original terms. At that point he was then handed an envelope containing an additional and hitherto unseen set of new demands on top of the ones he had just conceded.

Businesses were threatened with arson. Clients were threatened with broken legs if they tried to climb. These were not jokes and certainly not empty threats, as the Maoists have murdered more than one tourist in Nepal over the preceding decade or so. After several more days it was clear that the negotiations and general situation had become untenable. Those physical threats to the climbers themselves were probably the last straw for the expeditions tasked with their safety. Greg called everyone around one afternoon and outside the kitchen tent told us that we would not be climbing the mountain that year. The mountain would be closed to climbers from the Nepalese side for the rest of the season, and that was it. This day was to be our last at Base Camp and we would be leaving the following morning.

Lives lost, livelihoods imperiled, dreams shattered and little accomplished. An unmitigated disaster.

There were a couple of bottles of whiskey floating around camp in preparation for our summit victory and as the sun set that night they were opened. Travel speakers were turned to full volume and most people were determined to have a good time on their last night in camp.

I wanted nothing to do with it. In the falling darkness I climbed to a nearby vantage point, away from the music and commotion, and just stared up at the mountains and the stars. I felt the tragedy as acutely as anyone, but I also now felt that politics and greed, rather than compassion and reason had robbed me of this unique opportunity. Closing the mountain may well have been the right decision, but the way it was decided was all wrong. It all just left a bitter, bitter taste. Frankly I didn't really know how to process it, other than to feel immense anger about the tragedy which had happened and at society's inept response to it.

I don't remember how long I stood there, shivering violently in the frozen night air. I didn't want to stay, but I couldn't face returning to the world either. I don't remember if I went back for dinner or what time I went to sleep. Time didn't register in my mind, only the cold outside and the rage inside.

All I knew was that I would not let other people determine my fate from this day forward. From now on I would try to forge my own path.

29

The Long Walk Home

By the next morning I had calmed down somewhat and was slowly coming to terms with the situation. Our remaining time here was now short and I eventually resolved to enjoy it, at least as far as I could. After all, I might never return. After an early breakfast we packed up our tents and watched as Base Camp was dismantled around us. While it was disconcerting to watch this physical embodiment of our dream's end, the speed at which it was deconstructed was distracting. These people don't hang about up here without a good reason. We'd packed our climbing duffels before eating and gave them to a couple of porters who had arrived that morning, so by 8.30 everyone was ready to head back down the valley.

I say everyone, but it was just the few remaining members of the team who had decided against taking the helicopter back to Lukla. I suppose it was just an artifact related to the type of people who generally sign up to climb Everest. If you can afford US$50,000 for an expedition you can probably afford US$2,500 for a 14 minute helicopter flight. In fairness to them, a good number of my teammates were heading back to work, and for the surgeons and CEOs in our group the day or two they saved more than paid for the helicopter. I had no job to go back to so I was happy to make the experience last as long as I could.

Myself, Thom, Brooks and Ben were joined by Phinjo and a couple of the IMG guides who had also chosen to accompany us. It was a genuinely fantastic group of human beings. We were to walk 26 miles to Namche Bazaar on that first day and make an early start the following morning on the remaining 13 or so miles to Lukla. Today was undoubtedly going to be a long one.

It was a beautiful morning and we set a brisk pace. Still, it is a long way on rough, mountainous terrain at high altitude, and it was already nearly 5pm by the time we arrived at the Tengboche monastery. We decided to take a quick break before tackling the last few hours and stopped off at the adjacent bakery. I ordered a coffee and as we took our seats one of the old monks, dressed in full robes as always, entered the small room. Phinjo greeted him warmly. Prior to being a guide, Phinjo had actually spent several years at this monastery. He and the wise old monk took a table next to us and Phinjo ordered them a drink each from the counter, soon returning with a couple of cans of Everest beer! It was incidentally a Friday, and so at 5pm on a Friday evening here were two old friends catching up over a beer. I found it such wonderful symbolism; yet another confirmation that while we may all live in very different countries and cultures, dress differently or even look a bit different, deep down we are all human and very much the same.

From Tengboche we descended into the thick forests of rhododendrons. Spring had arrived during our short absence and the flowers were beginning to bloom, filling that late afternoon air with a wonderfully uplifting fragrance. In the soft light everything felt calm and gentle, a soothing balm for the mental injuries sustained by all of us during the prior week of uncertainty and pain. We continued on as the sun ended its swoop below the horizon and for the final part of the walk we were guided only by our torches and the starlight.

It was 9pm by the time we stepped across the threshold and into the Khumbu Lodge. Fortunately, the owner was expecting us and had set a couple of tables aside for us at the side of the common room. Dumping our packs in the middle of the room, we ordered some beers and relaxed our sore legs. It was my first drink since I'd arrived in the Khumbu and it was worth the wait.

It was a memorable evening after a memorable day. Everyone was in good spirits, assisted by a combination of thicker air and beer, and we even managed to persuade the owner to keep the place open a little longer for us. We even had a drink with David Breashers, a celebrity in these parts from his IMAX film work in the early days of Everest expeditions, as well as the subsequent charitable work he has done in the valley. It's amazing who you meet in this place!

Next day we arrived in Lukla and checked into the same teahouse as before. Immediately we ran into a number of our team members who had taken the helicopter. Every climber and guide from every expedition was simultaneously making his or her way back to Kathmandu and there was a demand for plane seats which far outstripped supply. Unable to get on a flight they had been stuck in Lukla ever since arriving. I did find it a little amusing. That helicopter ride was the best US$2,500 I never spent.

As luck would have it, the next day we got on the same plane as everyone else. Ha! Before I knew it we were back in Kathmandu and at the Hotel Tibet, sitting on the roof patio with an Everest beer in hand. It was as though the expedition in some ways had never happened. I was bitterly disappointed but also in one piece. There had very nearly been a much worse outcome for me and I felt grateful that I had lived to fight another day. Others had not been so fortunate.

I now wondered what on earth I was going to do with the rest of my life.

30

The Non-Wonder Years

The next few years were tough. I wanted to start a company, primarily driven by a desire to take control of my own fate, and I also wanted to move back to California for both personal and professional reasons. My frustrations with all the bureaucratic hoops during that process reminded me why I enjoy the simple life of the mountains. I decided to try living in Los Angeles. I figured the weather was pretty good and I wondered why all the "beautiful people" had moved there.

I hated it. Maybe it just wasn't designed for people like me. An imposing concrete jungle where I struggled to connect with people who generally cared about such very different things than I did. I had handled it for a year, but I realized that soon all my clients would be people I disliked. The thought of having to suck up to them for the next 10 years seemed unbearable. Still, it was a big move to change everything once again, but as often happens fate intervened to make up my mind.

That weekend I'd taken a drive north and made a winter ascent of Mount Whitney, the highest peak in the continental US. That sounds a lot more impressive than it is. The hardest part by far was finding the trail in the snow. I'd been a bit laissez faire about the whole thing and rather than leave camp on the mountain at 2am to begin the climb, at 6am I was still in the nearby town of Lone Pine because I wanted to get a bagel and hot coffee on that cold morning. In any case, I eventually arrived at the trailhead and began an enjoyable climb through the day. It was late in the afternoon when I summited, which was not best practice by any means. But I knew my strengths and limitations, plus I had the right gear if it all went a bit sideways. The risks were well within my limits so I wasn't concerned. With the sun beginning to slide behind the distant mountains I began my descent from the summit along the ridge. I figured I was alone on the mountain, but to my surprise I soon came across two people just sitting at the side of the trail. One of them looked to be in pretty bad shape and it was clear she had altitude sickness and was already hypothermic. With darkness coming and the cold really starting to bite this was not a good situation, not by a long way. I gave the girl most of my clothing and her boyfriend slowly fed her a little bit of a snack bar to get some sugar into her bloodstream. We both tried to get her warm and after a few hours she had recovered enough to be able to stand. I now began to short-rope her down the mountain. With a steep drop on the side of the thin icy path this was not a fun experience, but at least we were making some slow progress. We managed to descend a few thousand feet, at which point her altitude symptoms subsided somewhat, and from there on we knew she would be OK. It took 12 hours to get back down to the car park rather than the usual 4, but most importantly everyone was back safe and sound. A life had been saved!

On Monday morning I arrived at my coworking space in downtown LA and randomly got talking with a couple of the people I knew there. They asked how my weekend had gone so I gave them the 30 second synopsis about saving these people's lives.

"Oh well done," one of them replied. "But seriously, did you see what Lady Gaga wore to the Emmys this weekend? OMG!!!"

And so began the 15 minute conversation about Lady Gaga's outfit. Now, I am more than aware that people have different interests to me and what I find interesting might not actually be interesting in the slightest. However, a 30:1 ratio in caring between a) the person they know and are talking with who saved two lives the previous day, and b) a dress worn by someone they don't know at an event they weren't at... well, it puts everything into stark contrast. Each to their own, I guess, but I knew these were not "my people" and that they never would be.

Time for a change. I still wanted to keep the dream alive so I decided to move north, back to San Francisco. I had friends there and figured if I did a different business idea it would be a fresh start. I'd resolved not to let others dictate my life; I'd just never appreciated quite how difficult that was going to be.

After this first business failure my confidence was at rock bottom. I had to do something to get that confidence back and at this point I was frankly worried about the state of my mind. I was physically out of shape, at least by my standards, pretty unhappy and definitely burnt out. I was at such a low ebb that I found it hard to make eye contact with others. I felt ashamed and a failure. Sure, I was starting a new business, but I had minimal confidence it was going to work. I needed a goal whose achievement was within my control, at least to some extent. Despite money pressures I thought about climbing Mount Everest once again. Maybe it was the combination of escapism and challenge that I needed, a fixed goal in time and space which would get me back on track.

It was time to tackle some unfinished business.

31

The Death Zone

I knew I wanted to go back and actually get on the damn mountain for real this time. Understanding why I wanted that is easy. Far more interesting is why this time I decided to try without bottled oxygen.

As I've mentioned, a core driver of Everest climbers is to succeed where success is hard; to compete and win, against the mountain, against themselves and against others. To climb Everest using bottled oxygen is still extremely hard work, no doubt about it. There is significant risk, and success does give you membership to a small and unique club.

Yet that was no longer enough to stoke the fire inside me. From my first attempt I now had a sense of how my abilities stacked up. I'd seen the strengths of other climbers considered strong and I'd seen how I compared. I now knew, rather than hoped, that with bottled oxygen I had a good chance of reaching the top, notwithstanding factors outside of my control. It was that knowledge which removed some of my motivation, as though I decided it was now doable rather than impossible, and that wasn't enough. I needed more.

To climb without using supplemental oxygen would offer the next level of challenge.

I also felt quite drawn to the purity of the concept as well. Mano a mano, just me and mother nature toe to toe. This time I could tackle the death zone "without cheating", quote-unquote.

Ah, the death zone. Coined during one of the early attempts of an 8,000 meter peak, it generally refers to altitudes above the symbolic 8,000m altitude, around 26,000ft. Above this height there is insufficient oxygen to be able to fully acclimatize, and if you stay long enough you will die with 100% absolute certainty. It is within the death zone on Everest that things get really serious.

Climbing with bottled oxygen lowers the effective height of the mountain by making the air you breathed more sustaining. The impact is so dramatic that a climber using the standard flow rate of oxygen from the bottle may never actually experience an effective altitude above 8,000m at any point on the climb, not even at the summit. In essence, you would never experience the death zone, at least in a physiological sense.

To meet the challenge of climbing without Os, as it is commonly known, to experience the death zone for what it was, to find out how good a high altitude climber I actually was; these were the thoughts which now bounced around in my mind. I knew that if I stood on the summit using oxygen and wasn't at my absolute extreme limit I would *always* wonder whether I could have made it without using it. Perhaps that's a neurotic characteristic of mine. I would regret not trying it the hard way and that knowledge would gnaw at me. If success was even remotely possible then I had to try.

Did I have a chance of success? Forgoing supplemental oxygen was a different ball game with a very high chance of failure and I didn't want to go back for a third attempt. It was time to get some opinions.

I called Thom from the first expedition for his advice. He'd spent more time in the high mountains than most, and if anyone could gauge my chances it would be him.

"Thom, you've been high on Everest, you've seen what it takes up there and you've seen me up there as well. So I have an idea I want to run past you."

"Yeah I've seen a fair bit up there, not sure I'd call myself an expert though. What's the idea?" Thom asked.

"So I want to head back to Everest in a year," I continued. "I was looking at the folks we were with and how they stacked up against most people who have a good chance to summit. And I feel good about my chances."

"You were strong up there, no doubt about it!" Thom replied. "We had a strong group."

"We did! So here is what I was wondering. I'm trying to figure out where a no Os attempt is something I can consider. It appeals to me a lot, and I think I have a half-decent shot. But I wanted to get your thoughts."

"Usually I'd say no," was his considered response, "BUT in your case I think you could do it. You were strong up there. I know that it's a lot more difficult, though. I remember Konrad saying it was pretty brutal, a hundred times more difficult. And that's Konrad Anker talking!"

"Cool!" I replied. It was more positive than expected. "I'm no Konrad, obviously, but maybe with enough support it is possible? I want to figure out how to try the attempt without Os and then if it appears I can't do it then revert back to putting on Os. So I can kind of have my cake and eat it."

"That sounds like a great idea!" Thom remarked. "I think you have a decent chance without the Os, but having the backup makes it way smarter. Go for it man!"

And that was it. It made me fearful for my life and yet I was more excited about living than I had been for a long, long time.

To force myself to train without excuses, to face a true challenge, to experience something genuinely unique. And as you know by now, I'm all about those kinds of experiences.

32

What Could Possibly Go Wrong

However you cut it, climbing Mount Everest without using supplemental oxygen is one hell of a risk.

Let us start at the beginning, assuming of course that the climber has made it to Everest Base Camp. Even that is not a certainty, with accidents and sickness claiming victims with alarming frequency. On my first expedition, one of the IMG climbers in another phase broke their ankle while descending Lobuche and never even made it to the main event.

Beyond Everest Base Camp you enter the Khumbu Icefall where avalanches and ice tower collapses are random, unpredictable and common. Deep crevasses must be crossed on those narrow ladders lashed together with thin rope. People fall. People die. It just takes one moment of carelessness or bravado or bad luck. I myself saw two big ladder mistakes. One person fell but was fortunately tied to the safety rope. The other very nearly fell, and was not. He is lucky to be alive.

Once above the icefall, you cross the crevasse-filled Western Cwm where the Khumbu glacier begins. Beyond, each climber must then tackle the Lhotse face, a 3,000ft, 45 degree sheet of rock-hard blue ice. This also holds potentially fatal consequences for the unlucky, careless or unprepared. Even the most minor slip can rapidly escalate into a fatal tumble down the face. Tomahawking head over heels while leaving a red streak as you go is punishment for the smallest of errors, and it happens at least once almost every season.

At this altitude, harsh weather at some point is a certainty. There are only a few days a year when the summit winds are low enough to reach the top and if you get your timing wrong or delay in poor conditions you risk death. Each climb is a race against time and it's not a race you are guaranteed to win.

Death from hypothermia is a real risk. Temperatures on summit day can easily fall to -40°C / -40°F and as low as -60°C / -75°F when you include wind chill. One climber I spoke with summited when it was -54°C / -65°F. In these temperatures keeping warm is both critically important and a genuine challenge. The lack of oxygen reduces your ability to generate heat and you struggle no matter how thick your down suit is. You are also moving exceptionally slowly and can't warm up by working harder. Lose your core temperature and hypothermia will set in, along with confusion and delirium. People have been found frozen to death, naked, with all their clothes neatly folded beside them. In the last stages of deep hypothermia your body flushes blood to the capillaries in a last ditch attempt at warmth, a response which simultaneously draws cold blood to your core and accelerates your demise. The flush makes the skin feel hot, burning almost, and the confused victim tries to cool down by removing their clothes. Folding may bring some order to the situation in their disoriented mind. That's pretty wild to think about, and not in a good way.

Frostbite is yet another huge worry. If your hands or feet get cold your body cuts off the blood flow to these areas to conserve core warmth. Perhaps you took off a glove to open a stubborn chocolate bar wrapper or to take a photo. Perhaps you left your boots in the tent vestibule overnight and they froze, forcing you to climb wearing two ice boxes on your feet. With reduced blood flow no heat can reach the tissue to rewarm it, and it continues to cool. Eventually, ice crystals will form, smashing your cell walls from the inside out as the tissue solidifies. Capillaries freeze and crack, turning your fingers, nose or toes black. If you get it badly wrong then your whole hand or foot will be lost, and even if you are subsequently rescued you could still die from gangrene or septic shock when the tissue is defrosted.

Beyond the risks of the terrain, weather and cold, the altitude itself is an insidious killer. Human beings are not designed to function at these heights.

The first and surprisingly common ailment is a pulmonary edema. The low air pressures cause the plasma fluid in your blood to start leaking into your lungs from the inside, like water soaking into a dry sponge. Slowly they fill with fluid and each breath crackles with bubbles as you inhale. High on the mountain you die by drowning. Red blood cells come along for the ride and it is not uncommon to see pink splodges on the ice as you climb, deposited there by sick climbers who are spluttering, spitting and dying as they pass.

Equally frightening is a cerebral edema, where the fluid leaks not into your lungs but into your brain stem. As it swells you suffer all manner of psychological issues, from dizziness to disorientation before progressing towards a profound impairment of your rational thought. You forget where you are or what you are doing, and understand nothing of what you are told, ignoring the very commands which would save your life. Oh, and crazy people don't know they are crazy so it's hard to self-diagnose and hard to believe that it is happening to you.

At extremely high altitudes your blood becomes thick and gloopy from all the extra red blood cells your body creates as it acclimatizes. This can easily combine with acute dehydration, which is a common occurrence when working hard for hours in the dry air. It is actually kind of amazing to see just how thick and goopy your blood can actually get. I once accidentally cut my hand a little bit in Base Camp and it didn't even bleed. Squeezing the cut merely extracted a scarlet red gel. Literally a gel. Jam for blood is dangerous as it can easily clot and cause a stroke, and if this happens on the mountain you are finished. Pumping such thick fluid is also hugely stressful on your heart which has already been weakened by the hypoxic conditions. The result can be a heart attack, not just on the way up, but even when you are sleeping in your tent.

Exhaustion and collapse is also common. Summit day is long and brutal for all climbers whether using bottled oxygen or not. You push as hard as your body can tolerate for up to 24 hours straight. Unable to digest food in such thin air your glucose levels fully deplete resulting in hypoglycemia and exhaustion. If you collapse and can't somehow recover the strength to continue you will probably die where you fall.

Your sight is also at risk. Lose your sunglasses or goggles and the UV radiation at such extreme altitudes will burn your retina and temporarily blind you. I am told the pain from snow blindness is excruciating. Temperatures are also so low that the surface of your eyeballs can actually freeze, something which actually happened to a friend of mine. This also causes temporary blindness. The damage to your sight can be permanent, which you then have to worry about even if you can somehow make it down the mountain without being able to see where you are stepping.

The death zone is where all of these risks are by far the most acute. Using supplemental oxygen adds back a little cushion to your chances; choosing to climb without supplemental oxygen obviously does not and the statistics back that up. The majority of people who attempt Mount Everest without supplemental oxygen are professional mountaineers yet for every 37 individuals who make an attempt only about 4 will actually reach the summit. One will die.

But what the hell, I thought. No-one ever said life was safe.

33

Be Careful Whose Advice You Buy

It now was June, which gave me until the following March to train. This time, half measures could be fatal. This time, no excuses. But what did I need to do?

There are lots of training ideas. Some actually work. On my first Everest expedition I had seen proof that some do not. One of the climbers had hired some hotshot personal trainer in his native southern California, and as this trainer was based in a gym he decided to train our climber the way he trained everyone else. To a hammer everything is a nail, so for this chap the aim of the game was strength.

You know that leg press sled machine in the gym, the one where you sit nearly on the floor and push a sled loaded with plates up at a 45 degree angle? This climber told us a story of his last training session which included a one rep max workout on this particular machine. The wisdom of doing such an injury prone workout just prior to the expedition seemed daft in the extreme, but hey, what do I know.

"We were going for the one rep max!" the climber proudly told us as we sat around one evening in Base Camp after dinner, discussing our preparations for the climb. "I managed over 1,000lb. I couldn't believe we'd got there, you know, we'd worked so hard with my training. I might have even shed a tear!"

1,000lb! Lifting such a weight is amazing to me, an unbelievable achievement. I'm a weakling with a max of maybe 250lb and I'm in awe of people who are that strong. I could only imagine the immense weight he could carry on his back. And therein was the problem. Maybe he really could carry hundreds of pounds on his back for a short distance, but we'll never know because it is an unnecessary skill for high altitude climbing. You rarely carry more than 40 or 50lb up the mountain on Everest and usually it's closer to 25lb. What *is* important is the ability to carry that more modest weight fast and to carry it for hours on end. And unfortunately training for strength and training for endurance are two different things.

On the morning of that conversation in Base Camp I'd done a hike to keep myself active on the rest day, up to the advanced camp on Pumori. Like everyone else I was still early in my acclimation and so set a measured pace; enough to give me a good workout but not overdoing it by pushing the redline. Despite a big wrong turn and some precarious boulder hopping to refind the route I reached my target in about one hour 15 minutes; a decent performance.

At dinner it turned out that our super strong climber friend had done that same climb that same afternoon, so I asked him how it went.

"It was pretty tough but we just kept pushing through, you know, so we managed to get up there in under four hours!"

In my shock I might have blurted out something similar to "Only 4 hours?!" Oops. I immediately felt terrible as I always try to be a cheerleader for people in their efforts, expert or beginner, but it was just an involuntary reaction. I just found his statement somewhat unfathomable. In fairness to him I had no actual idea what to expect on Everest itself, not having set foot on it yet, but his performance at this stage seemed some distance below what would probably be required. It wasn't him, though, it was his training.

I was determined not to fall into the same trap, not with strength necessarily, but in guessing what plan to follow. I was unwilling to let a random personal trainer run the show as I'd seen how that could turn out. Instead, I decided to learn everything there was to know about high altitude training and make my own judgment. It was the only way to be sure.

34

The Oddities of Altitude

What makes you a high performer at high altitudes? This question is surprisingly hard to answer. Most of the studies carried out at Everest-like altitudes have focused on how the body works at altitude rather than how training affects performance. To answer it we must extrapolate what we know about the body at high altitude and what we know about training at sea level, and hope they both apply. I believe they do, at least to some extent.

Two metrics stand out as key to your potential at altitude - your aerobic capacity and what is known as your VO2Max.

Aerobic capacity measures how efficient your body can use fuel. Ultimately it measures how easily your body can burn fat for energy rather than sugar. Fat is turned into useful energy using oxygen, while sugar can be turned into energy either with or without it. Unfortunately, sugar is far less efficient than fat and your body has a much smaller supply of it. If you go long enough you will eventually run out of this fuel and "hit the wall". A higher aerobic capacity means burning more fat and sparing your sugar, and on Everest this means climbing faster for longer.

To burn all that fat, though, you need oxygen. This is where VO2Max comes in. This is a measure of your body's ability to absorb oxygen from the air and deliver it to your muscles. Basically it's how hard you work when your heart and lungs are going as hard and fast as they can. At sea level this metric is important for sprinting, but at high altitude it becomes relevant for even the slowest of climbs. Research has found that everyone's V02Max limit is genetically determined, in part because you can't grow your lungs and heart bigger than your ribcage. However, training *can* help you make the most of what you've got.

Beyond these two metrics, it turns out your performance is also closely linked to how much you train at the exact sport you are focused on. Training muscles turns out to be even more specific than you might think. Cross training is for amateurs, sport specific is for the professionals.

In the same vein, strength is less important. Yes, climbing Everest does involve some upper body strength, predominantly in the icefall where there are a good number of steep slopes and plenty of ladders to climb wearing a moderate pack. As with my super strong friend, though, developing strength beyond that point is a waste of your training time. Enough is plenty.

Slowly a training plan was born. Lots of running to increase my aerobic capacity. Steep hill sprints to increase my VO2Max and train my climbing muscles. Plus a full body workout at the gym a couple of times a week so I'd be strong enough! I also tried to replicate some mountaineering, at least as far as possible. Fortunately, there is a mini-mountain not too far from San Francisco and I'd climb it pretty much every weekend. At 800ft I would load my backpack up with rocks that lie around near the path before climbing the steepest trail to the 2,750ft summit as fast as I could. At the top I would empty my backpack to save my knees on the descent and jog back down to the starting point to refill my backpack for a second and third lap. Starting at 20lb I was carrying 70lb of rocks by the end. If you ever go to the top of that mountain there should be a 1,500lb pile of rocks at the summit as a lasting legacy of my efforts!

I'd work out twice a day, running in the morning and often going to the gym in the evening. There are plenty of people in the world who train that much and I respect their dedication all the more having done it. I found it difficult but by March I felt good. I was still slowly improving and I didn't know if I was ready. But perhaps I was ready enough.

As before, there was only one way to find out.

35
Kathmandu Déjà Vu

Déjà vu. I flew from San Francisco to Kathmandu via the UK, where I collected a few bits of Everest gear that had spent the previous three years gathering dust at my parent's house. It turns out that outside of an 8,000m mountain or Antarctic expedition there isn't much need for a down suit. It was also a chance to visit my parents before I headed off to what I hoped wasn't my doom.

I'd managed to keep the "without bottled oxygen" nature of this climb concealed from my mother until this point, but now it was time to tell her. She wanted to follow along with the expedition and the blog I was writing was titled "Everest Without Oxygen", making hiding this aspect a little tricky. She was quite naturally worried about my Everest exploits, perhaps more so because she understood the dangers from her own mountain upbringing, and I hadn't wanted to amplify her worries. In any case, she'd told me once before that she only wanted to know what was happening after I was safely back home.

It took a while to pluck up the courage but tell her I did. After all, it wouldn't be fair for her to find out by deduction. She took it better than expected, I must admit, although I'm sure deep down it didn't help her stress levels. At least I'd spared her a couple of months of anxiety.

Once again I said my goodbyes as she stood in her dressing gown on the back step of the house. Was I more apprehensive this time than last? I can't be sure. The first time I was worried because I didn't know what to expect. This time I was worried because I did. My dad took me to Heathrow, and as I watched him drive away I wondered, not for the first time, whether I was doing the right thing.

The flight to Nepal was uneventful and after what seemed like a lifetime of travel we eventually began our descent into Kathmandu. This time I'd flown via Oman rather than Turkey and this alternative flight path denied me a view of the Himalaya. In any case, there was a thick, impenetrable haze across the entire sky. This time Everest was keeping its secrets.

As on the prior expedition I had assumed that someone was coming to meet me at the airport, but as before I didn't actually know. I'd once again neglected to ask and now wondered if I had been a little overconfident for the second time in a row. Would anyone be there?

"Mr James! Mr James!"

Déjà vu. Mohan came striding toward me, his enthusiastic smile unchanged since the last time. It was lovely to see him. Again a welcoming wreath of wonderful fresh golden marigolds was placed around my neck and another faux-silk scarf was given as a blessing.

Rather than a minibus, this time we took a car, but the banging, crunching and swerving along our journey into the city was identical. The sights and smells and vibrancy were once again music to my soul, as though part of me which had been locked since leaving had been opened. I was free once more.

There had been quite a lot of turnover in the staff at the Hotel Tibet since my last visit, according to Mohan, at least, but from my perspective it was hard to tell. It seemed much the same as I had left it a thousand days beforehand. There were only two differences I could identify. They had redone the bathrooms in the upper rooms, making them modern looking. Oddly though I preferred the prior charm of the dodgy tiling and exposed piping. The other difference was that there were no other climbers in the hotel. My no Os attempt meant I had arrived several weeks before everyone else, ahead of even Greg and the guide staff. This time I was in a team of one.

And that was a very big difference indeed.

36
The Gateway to Hell

The first order of business in Kathmandu was the gear check as now was not the time to fall into the deep trap of complacency. Everything was emptied onto the bed and I ticked off each item against the IMG checklist I'd printed out at home. Yes I'd also done this before I left, but one can't be too careful. I had indeed been diligent and the only thing I needed were some Buddhist prayer flags to hang over my tent in Base Camp. And some people say I have no sense of style....

It was time to brave the dusty streets of Thamel. There were only about five thousand places to buy them and so avoiding being ripped off was the only challenge. I probably still overpaid but nonetheless rewarded myself with a pizza at Fire and Ice, a well-known restaurant in Thamel that our team had visited on the first night we met in Kathmandu on my first expedition. Once back at the hotel I headed for the rooftop patio, where there was time for a final Everest beer before I went teetotal for the remainder of the expedition. It seemed strangely fitting to replicate the actions of the previous expedition, althoughI hoped this one would turn out better.

Once again it was dark when Mohan and his driver arrived at the hotel to pick me up in the early hours of the morning. I knew the drill and I was already in the lobby, duffels stacked by the ornate entrance. We arrived at the airport in good time and Mohan once again did a superb job of navigating the bureaucracy. Soon enough my duffels were whisked away by the airline staff and Mohan gave me my boarding pass. We hugged and then I was ushered through a metal detector towards the same departure lounge as before. It hadn't changed a bit. The boarding pass once again showed a total lack of flight boarding information, but this time I had to figure it out for myself. With a cup of still-overpriced Nescafe from the same kiosk as last time I monitored each chaotic rush towards the single departure door and each time waved my ticket at the lady who manned the gate, only to be ignored with disdain. On one flight though she finally nodded and this time it was time to board. Success!

A serene dawn broke through the Kathmandu mist as our airplane lifted itself into the sky. Fluffy low clouds surrounded us as we climbed, but eventually we rose above them to finally witness the Himalaya in the bright morning light. My face was glued to the window as we flew, wondering whether Everest would be revealed as I'd not seen it on the prior flight. It was only once we had passed the low ridge and entered the Khumbu Valley itself did the magic begin.

Far, far away a black pyramid slowly emerged from behind the foreground peaks. It barely looked like a mountain now; it was too distant, too vast and too high. I was acutely aware that I was looking up at this summit from inside an airplane. Its dark peak seemed ephemeral, a momentary bridge between this world and a world beyond. Yet this was no home of the Gods; instead I stared at an entrance to Hell. My mind embodied it with a presence in some way; there was a soul of foreboding malice which somehow radiated from it. As I stared towards that forbidden place I felt wonder mixed with a deep hopelessness derived from the only thing I now knew for certain.

For me, this climb without supplemental oxygen was impossible.

I stared unblinking at the dark pyramid until it disappeared, once again hidden behind the curtains of lesser peaks as our plane descended towards the improbable runway of Lukla airport. I had once again secured a prime seat to watch my fiery dismemberment, and the sense of relief as the wheels touched the tarmac as intended was again palpable. I had arrived in Lukla once more.

37

A Living Legend

I climbed down the narrow airplane steps and stood on the tarmac looking lost. Looking lost is my standard tactic in such situations, working on the assumption that the right person was more likely to find me than the other way around. I need not have worried; standing literally right next to the plane was Dawa, my guide for the trek and on the mountain itself.

It turns out that Dawa is a climbing legend, quite literally. At 57 years old he was older than you might expect for an elite Everest guide, but his experience and abilities put him in a tiny and special group. Dawa's first Mount Everest expedition was in 1978, before I was even born, and he had guided the mountain 20 times with 13 client summits. He'd also made many successful ascents of Cho Oyu and Makalu, both 8,000m peaks. In short, if anything bad happened when I was up there, Dawa had been there, seen it, done it, and lived to tell the tale. I quickly felt I was in good hands.

We picked up my duffel bags from the same rudimentary baggage reclaim as last time - it was still a man and his table - and this time walked the short distance around the runway to a teahouse located on the opposite side of the airport. The Paradise lodge was a place which I hadn't seen on my last expedition.

Walking through the Lukla streets and then through the teahouse door into a traditional wood-paneled common room gave me just the widest smile that a man can smile. I noted all those little things which meant I was truly in the Khumbu once more. The cool, thin air and bright sun, the sight of prayer flags fluttering from the trees, the clank of the cow bells as the dzos cantered through the village, the faint smell of incense and burning firewood. I felt grateful that I had been given the opportunity to return to this place, regardless of the outcome of my climb. I'd never before understood why people returned to climb Mount Everest for a second or third time. Now it was clear.

We took some tea as a porter sorted out my duffel transportation while Lakpa, still IMG's man on the ground in Lukla, was there to organize. Dawa then vanished somewhere to do a final errand. I was more than happy to sit there with that pot of tea and just soak it all in. Rather than stay in Lukla, Dawa had decided we should make a little progress and sleep in the tiny village of Monjo, about half way to Namche Bazaar. By mid-morning our backpacks were shouldered, our boots tied and our trekking poles ready. It was time to begin our quest.

After the short walk through town we passed beneath the stone arch and descended along the stone trail past the magnolia trees. Their fragrant white flowers were not yet in bloom and I could clearly tell I had arrived in the Khumbu earlier in the season than on my previous visit. After a couple of easy hours we reached the river and the village of Phakding, a nice spot for a brief pause and a snack, before continuing the relatively short last section to Monjo.

The village was so small I walked right through it; just a few buildings placed either side of the narrow trail a short distance from the official entrance to the Sagarmatha National Park, in which much of the Khumbu Valley technically lies. Monjo was peaceful but otherwise somewhat unremarkable, for the Khumbu at least. And that was OK by me. I was just happy to be in the Himalaya once more.

38
Round and Round We Go

As with my prior expedition, a slow and steady acclimatization was the key to success. To become capable of survival at nearly 9,000m takes many weeks and the process is perhaps not quite as obvious as you might think.

The most obvious solution to adaptation would be to continually climb higher every day. Unfortunately, at extreme altitudes that plan fails. Not only would you be living in some pretty impossible conditions for a long, long time, the continual stress at extreme altitude prevents your body from repairing and adapting itself. Instead, the best method is generally considered to be more like going to the gym - periodically overstress your body and then give yourself plenty of time to recover and grow. In mountaineering terms, that means climbing high, staying at extreme altitude for a short time of hours to days, and then returning to Base Camp to recover in its relatively thicker and more nourishing air. Each of these trips up and down the mountain is known as a rotation.

Clients with IMG generally do two rotations before making their summit attempt. It is a tried-and-tested schedule with plenty of success. In my case, however, the acclimatization needs for a no Os attempt were even more acute and Greg thought that an extra rotation would be the right place to start. As climbers all summit around the same time that meant starting my trek into the Khumbu several weeks before everyone else. The plan was to trek up the valley with my Sherpa guide and meet the rest of the expedition when they arrived in Base Camp a few weeks later. To trek nearly alone in the Himalaya and get the unvarnished cultural experience; well, I was excited at the prospect.

39

A Stranger in Familiar Lands

There was just one other group of trekkers at the teahouse in Monjo that evening. These spring nights were still bitterly cold even at this altitude so the common area was soon rearranged into a ring of plastic chairs huddled around the toasty warm stove in the center of the room. It was an eclectic group of random folks who had joined a locally run trek. They were generally young and most were traveling around the world for various lengths of time. I liked them, but despite our many commonalities I felt strangely distant.

This expedition already felt different to the last. It felt more serious. On the surface I was happy and enthusiastic, but beneath that positive demeanor ran a constant current of stress. In two months I could be brain damaged, dismembered or dead. These were not hypotheticals or distant risks but significant real possibilities. That knowledge created a constant subconscious tension which was impossible to shake off, making it difficult to relax sufficiently even to just "hang out". Every moment of doing nothing felt like a waste, a missed opportunity to do *something* which might improve my chances of survival in the not too distant future. Logically I knew there was nothing more I could do, but subconsciously my brain did not.

The trekkers asked why I was there. I stalled, avoiding a direct answer. I inferred it was for the same reasons that they were. They asked why I had my own guide rather than traveling in a group. I dodged and deflected as best I could while struggling to explain Dawa's presence without looking like I needed hand holding on the trek. I guess everyone has an ego about something. Still I remained vague, obscuring the reason for my trip. They undoubtedly locked their doors that night with concern, worried about the evasive and decidedly sketchy Englishman with the shadowy motives and the private guide.

Why didn't I tell them my story? There are a number of reasons I suppose. Base Camp trekkers account for 98% of visitors to the valley and I was acutely aware that for some of them this journey might have been the most difficult, most audacious and most physically challenging thing they had ever attempted. Reaching Base Camp was their own personal mountaintop and I had no desire to lower someone's own sense of achievement through comparison with what I was trying to do.

I also felt like a total imposter. I was sitting next to a veritable mountaineering legend whom the travelers had mistaken for a trekking guide. Yet Dawa had been humble and quiet. It only reinforced my desire to withhold talking about my climb, especially until I'd earned the right to do so.

I also knew that explaining my trip probably wasn't even worth the discussion. Over those next few weeks there were a couple of occasions when I had let slip my reason for being there and it made each conversation worse, not better. I was doing something so unique that for most people, even those trekking in Khumbu, it was too far beyond their experience to fully understand and thus to fully empathize. It makes for an awkward dynamic.

I remember this same strange phenomenon from my travels in Mexico a long time ago. That time I rode a bicycle from Alaska to Argentina and on the way the locals would naturally ask where

I had come from previously. Sometimes I'd pick a town which I had passed a few days beforehand, and invariably they would throw their hands up in the air with shouts of "Dias Mia!", marveling how someone could undertake a bicycle trip of *two hundred miles*! But if I told them I'd ridden from the USA, some 1,000 miles distant and there would barely be any reaction at all. They would look at me, smile and say "Oh that's nice. So how was your breakfast today?" Saying I'd ridden 4,000 miles from Alaska on a bicycle was even more disjointing. I'd sometimes just get blank stares and no response at all. These were distances so vast and places so alien that many people could not comprehend the journey, not least on a bicycle. It was so far outside the framework of their own experiences that it somehow just didn't compute.

For most trekkers in the Khumbu, climbing Mount Everest without bottled oxygen was similarly difficult to extrapolate from their own personal experiences. It is such a different world even from conditions on the trek that for most it just didn't register. Even now I am asked "How much did climbing Everest cost?" far more often than "What was climbing Everest like?" I've always thought that was weird. I guess money is something people can relate to. Climbing a Himalayan mountain in the darkness at minus forty Celsius while barely able to breathe is something most cannot. Indeed, one of my hopes for the rest of this book is to give you, my treasured reader, that experiential sense of what climbing Mount Everest is actually like. Especially as I've already told you how much it cost!

40
Phortse

The next day we left Monjo at half past eight, which was to become our usual start time each morning. There was no need to depart at the crack of dawn as our trekking distances each day were fairly short. The benefits of a no Os acclimatization plan thus seemed to include time for a third cup of coffee.

The walk up the long hill to Namche Bazaar didn't seem anywhere near as tough as the previous expedition. Perhaps it was because I knew what to expect or perhaps because we'd split the distance in half with our stop at Monjo. Or perhaps I was fitter than before? It was impossible to tell. In any case we were at the midway rest area in no time and it was time to look for Mount Everest. I went to the spot and despite some clouds I could just about make out the summit rising behind the ridge of Nuptse. As before it was still threatening and still very far away.

It was wonderful to finally return to the cobbled streets of Namche Bazaar and walk into the entrance hall of the Khumbu Lodge. A home away from home, or at least it felt that way. Dawa and I spent two days resting, drinking tea and eating momos, which at the Khumbu lodge can be ordered either steamed or fried. Both are excellent. On the second day, for a bit of exercise and something to do we went on a short visit to the Sherpa museum. Located at the top of the village there are two main parts to the museum. The first is a replica of a traditional Sherpa house, complete with artifacts used in everyday life before us westerners arrived and changed the place forever. It was interesting; from the paper windows to the traditional wooden furniture and woven baskets. The second part of the museum was more modern and introduced visitors to the history and culture of the Sherpa people. In one large room the walls were covered from top to bottom in framed portraits of Sherpa. This was the climbing Hall of Fame.

Starting to the right of the door, where the oldest photos were located, I began looking through the pictures just to see. Many were faded and old, developed with camera film from an age past, but that just added to the sense of history. Suddenly one picture caught my eye. It took me a moment to recognize the person in it as the photo was of him as a much younger man. Yet it was unmistakable. It was a picture of Dawa! I turned to look at him and he just smiled back. I guess he really was an official legend. Near to his picture I found those of Ang Jangbu and Funuru, brothers who organized the majority of the IMG expedition in Nepal and whom I would meet when I arrived at Base Camp. These folks were some of the heavy hitters of the high altitude climbing community and I was in their care. A most encouraging thought!

That evening a dusting of snow fell gently across the valley, reminding me once more that it was still March. Woken by the piercing cool light of reflected dawn rays through a clear sky I opened my bedroom window wide and huddled beneath the heavy warm covers for protection as I gazed across the pristine white views. It was a joy to marvel at such tranquil peace and for the longest time I just lay there in pure relaxation. I'd missed this place. By breakfast though those same rays were making quick work of the snow and by the time we left the lodge a majority had already melted from the path. Climbing the same switchbacks as the previous day we crested the ridge by the museum and soon arrived at a fork in the path. I remembered this junction from the first trek. Virtually everyone takes the right fork, descending to the river and then up to the Tengboche Monastery. Today we were to take the left option and make our way to the village of Phortse.

This tiny picturesque hamlet is one of the highest permanently settled areas of the Khumbu and a stark contrast to the bustle of Namche Bazaar. Back in the original days of Everest expeditions many of the Sherpa who worked on the mountain came from Phortse and many Sherpa who work on the highest parts of the mountain still do. Dawa, Ang Jangbu, Phinjo and Funuru all came from here, as do others on the IMG team. Several of the Sherpa owned small teahouses in the village and Dawa was one of them. It made infinite sense to spend the night at his teahouse and I was looking forward to seeing Phortse after hearing so much about it.

By early afternoon we were climbing steeply and crested onto the shallow slope of the plateau which contained the village. I could see a few buildings spread out on a small, inclined array of terraces which had been carved into the angled plateau. Hand built, chest high stone walls created a maze of paths around the tilled soil of the terraced fields. Most of the fields were bare during this part of the year, the barley just having been harvested and the potatoes soon to be planted. Those fields not awaiting crops acted as pens for a few yak which grumpily huffed around inside. We made our way into the village by zig zagging around the fields until we reached the home of Dawa.

It was a simple and pleasant place. The spacious common room faced south with views down across the village plateau and the hazy blue mountains beyond. The dimly lit kitchen was located opposite the common area and a long corridor connected those with several basic bedrooms at the other end of the single story building. I was introduced to Dawa's wife and she took me to my room as Dawa began to tackle a few of the chores which had accumulated during the few days he'd taken to chaperone me from Lukla. Once settled in I kicked off my boots and lay on my bed to rest my body for a few minutes. The village was peaceful and a shaft of sun angled in from the central window like a warm ray of pure calm. There was no rush to unpack.

Bang!

A loud noise rang through the building, quickly followed by as strange a noise as I have ever heard in my life. And then silence. The sound had been both near and far, clear yet indiscernible. Startled, I sat up in bed and listened intently. Nothing. I was perplexed as to what could possibly have made that noise, but still, I was not unduly concerned. Things were surely under control and with no reason to assume any differently I closed my eyes and lay back into the patch of sun.

A minute or two later I heard a soft knock on the door of my room, so I shuffled across the bed to unhook the small latch, and then sat up to open the door. Standing outside was Dawa's wife, her eyes glistening with tears. She spoke no English, but beckoned that I should follow her. I obliged.

As we walked down the corridor I could feel my body tingle as the adrenaline began to surge. Why did she need me and why would she be crying? We turned into the common area and my eyes followed her as she approached the bench by the window to the left. A man lay there, his body twisting in pain and his breathing shallow.

It was Dawa.

41

The Strength of the Sherpa

"James!" he called out in a strained voice. "James, I fell. My back, my hip. I think they are broken!"

Dawa had been fetching some climbing gear from a storage area in the small attic above the kitchen. In a most unfortunate accident he'd tripped on one of the rafters and fallen backwards through the trapdoor, straight down to the solid concrete floor at least 10ft below. He was conscious but in serious distress, his body contorted with pain.

For a moment I was stunned. I'm not a medical professional, not by any stretch, but I had done a little wilderness medical training some time ago, just in case something went wrong on an expedition. I regretted not doing another course before I had come to Nepal. In any case, it was too late for all that now and I just had to rely on what I could remember.

I decided the first task was to make sure his wife went and told others in the village so we could get some help. As a stranger in a remote village high in the Himalaya I was at a loss at what to do next. Did they have a telephone? I didn't even know that. The feeling of impotence was appalling. "Get proper help" was about all I could do. Dawa's wife set off to a neighbor's house and I began to assess the seriousness of Dawa's injuries, primarily to ensure we didn't make him worse. Rule one, don't make it worse. I did an ABC check and for feeling in his extremities.

"Dawa, can you breathe OK?" I asked.

"Yes. But it is difficult," he replied, with shallow but otherwise controlled breaths. That was a start.

"OK Dawa. Now I'm going to check to see if I can tell what you have done, see if we can find out. Can you wiggle your toes?" He'd mentioned his back, so I checked the feeling in his feet. He was still able to wiggle his toes, which was good. With his wife now returned we rolled him gently to the side so I could see his back, where he told me it hurt. I could already see a large lump forming in the center of his lower back.

With nothing much else I could do I gave him ibuprofen for the pain, which was the strongest thing I had. Fortunately, it was only another 5 or 10 minutes before Funuru arrived. Excellent!

"Hi James, how are you! Sorry we are meeting like this again! Ah, Dawa!" said Funuru and moved across the room to take a look at his friend and colleague.

He acted quickly and calmly, a real professional. He'd done all the courses, including having worked as a mountain guide in Canada. I told him what I'd seen, and he was quickly on the radio, calling around to various people across the valley. Quickly we discovered it was too late in the day to arrange a helicopter. Damn. Dawa would either have to wait until the morning or somehow be taken to the nearest hospital, which was located just outside Namche Bazaar, right back along the mountainous path I had walked just a few hours before! He would have to be carried there on a stretcher by the Sherpa.

Over the next 30 minutes a number of young men gathered at Dawa's house. One brought with him a rigid, bright orange plastic stretcher, the type they use to move injured climbers down the mountain. We carefully maneuvered Dawa onto the stretcher, while simultaneously wrapping him in blankets and tucking him into a sleeping bag as best we could. Funuru helped to strap him securely onto the stretcher and then it was time for the team to go.

Funuru, along with six or seven other Sherpa set off into darkness, taking it in turns to carry part of the stretcher as each became fatigued. They were carrying an awkward, 160lb combination of sled and Dawa along a steep, narrow and now icy mountain path, a path which had taken me four hours to walk that morning. I didn't see how it could be done in any kind of reasonable time frame, and with the bitter cold and utter darkness amongst the trees I was terribly worried about what might happen.

"It's better if you stay with Karma Sherpa, up the hill," Funuru told me before leaving. "Can you pack your things?" I did so immediately, and a short time later I was escorted through the village to another, slightly larger building further up the plateau. This was the teahouse of another of the IMG Sherpa who I think I had met briefly on the previous trip. He was standing behind the little counter in the common area, next to the wall. At the side of the room was another, more familiar face.

"Fura!" I exclaimed as a young man rose to greet me. Fura had been the junior Sherpa on my previous expedition and had endeared himself greatly to the team. Even now he was barely 20 years old. Thom especially was a big fan of this kid, and it was great to see him again. He seemed to be doing well, a small ray of light in an otherwise terrible evening.

"Terrible, I heard about Dawa," said Karma Sherpa as he brought me a mug of milk tea to calm my nerves a little. "Don't worry, though, they will take him to the hospital. He is very strong, he will be OK!" I wished I shared his optimism.

Two hours later we got a message.

"Dawa has arrived at the hospital and is being checked by the doctor," Karma Sherpa told me. "We will know more later, but it seems he will be OK."

I was relieved and astounded. Barely two hours had passed since they had left the village and at that moment I understood why the Sherpa people are held in such high regard by the climbing community. This display of comradeship and strength was more impressive and more meaningful than any summit of Everest could be. Their response and their abilities in this rescue left me in awe.

An hour or so later there was another update.

"He has an injury, but they think he will be OK. They have made him comfortable for the night and tomorrow he will go to Kathmandu by helicopter," Karma Sherpa told me. We'd know more the following day, but for now he was stable. It was a relief, although we all remained concerned. I hoped that the doctors in Kathmandu wouldn't have a different, or at least more ominous, opinion. Still, for now the prognosis was good.

42

An Old Acquaintance

Karma Sherpa was another climbing legend who was also in the Hall of Fame. For each successful climb of an 8,000m peak in Nepal you are given an official certificate from the Nepalese Ministry of Tourism and he has a whole room of them. Literally a whole room. Hung in a horizontal line, they covered over half the perimeter of the substantial common room. Everest, Cho Oyu, Manaslu, they were all there, multiple times for each; more than twenty successful summits in all. I also saw his certificate and medal in the Everest marathon. Known as one of the hardest races in the world, the trail from Everest Base Camp to Namche Bazaar is a brutal test and people come from all over the world to participate. It had been Karma's first ever marathon and he'd placed second. The Sherpa really are made of something different from you and I.

The next day was a rest day, as originally planned. I got a message from Greg telling me he'd heard about the situation and they were working on getting me another guide. For now I was just to stay with Karma Sherpa. In two days I was due to resume the trek, but who now was going to accompany me on the journey? I woke up fairly early in the morning on day three and wandered into the sunny common area to get some breakfast. There, sitting by the window in the corner, stirring some sugar into his tea, was Phinjo.

"Phinjo!" I called out, somewhat surprised to see him. "What are YOU doing here?"

"James! I'm taking you to Base Camp!" was his reply. Ah wonderful. With Phinjo and Fura both in the room it was like getting the band back together!

We set out shortly after breakfast.

"James, we must stop at my house, I have to collect a few things before we leave," said Phinjo and pointed to a sizable two story house at the top of the village. It seemed like he was doing well and that was great to see. Phinjo invited me inside, and I briefly talked to his wife while he assembled the rest of his backpack, and soon enough we were on our way for real. It was a little over an hour to reach Upper Pangboche from Phortse, and Phinjo confirmed that we would go and receive our blessings from Lama Geishi. This time I hoped it would be more effective.

This visit was even more magical than the previous occasion. We were invited in for a cup of Sherpa tea in the kitchen while we waited for the Lama, and I sat next to Phinjo on a low wooden bench in the smoky room as he chatted with the two elderly folks who worked there for the Lama. Rough wooden panels covered the walls and rays of morning light shone into the room from the two small windows high in the wall, their panes darkened by smoke. Flickering flames from inside the small metal wood-burning stove helped to further illuminate the shadows in the surroundings not reached by the sunlight, but overall it was dim and cozy. It felt exactly what I imagined a woodcutter's house in medieval Europe would have been like.

Sitting in that place as I silently cupped a hot glass of milk tea was the experience of the Khumbu that I had hoped for. I was a fly on the wall, an invisible observer to that small slice of real Sherpa life. Obviously I couldn't understand a single word they spoke but that mattered not a jot. For those moments I felt I had been invited in as one of the family and got to see a little of what real life here was like. With enough tea I could have stayed there all day.

Moments like these made this expedition different from the first. In normal expeditions there is a spectrum of interaction. At one end of the spectrum are the clients. They are generally just along for the ride, and most of their interactions are with each other and the home-country guides, by which I mean the guides who are employed by the commercial operation from their base location. They eat together, follow the same schedule and are fully integrated as a unit. Unlike the clients, however, the guides have a much wider set of relationships across camp, especially with the local guides and the Sherpa support team.

There is also a set of senior Sherpa guides who accompany the clients and the home-country guides. These guides generally hang out with the other Sherpas and eat with the Sherpa, but are free to come and go between the two sets of people. This makes them a major bridge between the support team and the client group.

In a similar strata are the head cook and the folks who run and organize camp - and to a large extent the whole expedition. You see them quite frequently, but they don't climb with you and the interactions can vary. Some you hardly see and conversations are usually need-based. Perhaps you have a question about a rotation or a problem with your tent. Maybe you get an early morning cup of Sherpa tea from the kitchen tent. But that was about it, at least from my experience on that first expedition.

Finally on the spectrum are the porters and the other Sherpa in camp. With these folks it is pretty rare to interact, just like you don't talk with many of the staff at a hotel. There just isn't much cause for your paths to cross, and overall the upshot of all this is that you always have a somewhat peripheral interaction with most of the Sherpa. As such, you don't really get to look "behind the curtain" all that much, so to speak.

This expedition was proving to be quite different. It was just me and the Sherpa now, and what a privilege that was turning out to be.

43
The Wall of Victory

It was time to meet the Lama. We left the kitchen and opened the small door a little way down the corridor to his study. At the far side of the room, in the corner at one end of the window, sat the Lama in his dark red robes. His thick glasses still hung from his nose and it seemed as though he hadn't changed one bit. In fact, it seemed as though hadn't moved from that very spot during the intervening three years. Everything appeared to be the same with the exception of one small photo pinned to the wall amongst the others that hadn't been there on my last visit. He told me to look for it, and after an age of scanning around that wall I finally saw it, near the left edge of the wall about 2ft from the ceiling. It was a picture taken in the dark, and was a little grainy and hard to make out. But I knew exactly who was in it. There, in Lama Geishi's room was a picture of my friend Thom, illuminated by a camera flash as he stood in the blackness at the summit of Everest.

Despite his climbing pedigree, until 2016 Thom had never actually had the chance to summit the mountain; the downside of being a paid cameraman is that you go where you have to film, not where you want to go. That year he had joined another expedition but only on the condition that he could have his own summit bid this time. And what a summit bid it was. What should have taken 10 hours took five; so quick that he summited at 2.40am. It must have been a strange, ethereal experience to stand there in the middle of the night, just him and his Sherpa, alone with only the stars and the moon to illuminate such a grand vista. A wonderful experience indeed.

As before, I was blessed by Lama Geishi and received another indestructible string necklace. It wasn't long before we were back in the bright morning sunshine, making our way up towards Pheriche on the main path once more. In a few hours I was stepping through the ornate archway into the Himalayan Hotel. Nothing seemed to have changed since my last visit, not even the 80's rock CD which had somehow survived its 10,000th repeat and was playing when I walked in, I kid you not. I took a seat by the sun-drenched window and relaxed as the yaks walked past outside in the chilled air.

With all the Phortse drama and my probable over-eagerness were already a couple of days ahead of schedule. Base camp wasn't even under construction yet so there was quite some time before I could even arrive there and this created somewhat of a dilemma. Nice as it was, I had no desire to spend a whole week in the Himalayan Hotel and I also didn't want to spend them all in the village of Lobuche, a tiny little village between here and Gorak Shep. It seemed to be a bit of a waste. As we sat on the benches in the ornate common area and drank some tea I asked Phinjo what our options might be.

"Yes, I agree, it is pretty boring to stay here for so long," he mused with a chuckle. When Phinjo spoke you often had a sense that a laugh or a chuckle was only a sentence away. He seemed to take everything in his stride and looked on the upside from what I could tell. A wonderful guide to have.

"We could go up to Chukhung village," he continued, after a sip of tea. "It's only a few hours from here along the other valley." And then he had an even better idea. "We could perhaps climb

Chukhung Ri for some extra acclimatization when we are there. It's not too high; a trekking peak. Does that sound good?"

"It does!" I replied. Did it ever! "Let me check with Greg on the email, and if he says it is OK then we should definitely go," I continued. I was quickly on my computer, as these days most of the lodges have Wi-Fi. I sent Greg an email asking for his thoughts and he was fine with the plan. From my perspective it was a great idea. I hadn't gone into that valley on my last visit so this was all going to be new. It was time for a mini adventure.

44

Keeping Up with the Phinjos

If you ever tackle the trek to Mount Everest I recommend a detour to Chukhung. The trail veers right from the main path, taking a tributary valley along the southern flank of Nuptse. Several hours up the valley, the village of Chukhung is located towards the northern wall in a vast bowl of nearly unfathomable scale. The setting is unquestionably quite something. Behind you to the North rises the great mass of Nuptse, while to the West tower the giant peaks of Makalu and Baruntse. To the South, directly across the valley, the improbably steep faces of Ama Dablam. You walk through a valley surrounded by giants; a view of such mass that the world may not have its equal. Even the view at Base Camp is not nearly as imposing. In the center of this bowl you can also see Island Peak, a mountain whose name always confused me until I saw it rise alone and isolated in the center of this great cul-de-sac. Although in itself a 6,200m / 20,300ft peak, far higher than anything in the Alps, it looked tiny in comparison with the mountains around it.

There seemed to be just the one teahouse in Chukhung and fortunately it was pleasant enough, especially with its stone courtyard that seemed purpose-made for gazing at the view. There were only a few trekkers staying there when I arrived, plus a German fellow who was there to climb Island Peak. It is a popular ascent, being mostly non-technical and is considered an excellent introduction to Himalayan climbing. The view up there must also be amazing. For us, though, it was still too early in my acclimatization, plus all my technical equipment like crampons was in my second duffel bag located somewhere on its way to Base Camp. Rather than Island Peak, our goal instead was the peak of Chukhung Ri, located on the ridge right behind the town. Rising to 5,500m / 18,000ft it was still a substantial climb from the village. Most importantly there was no snow on the summit, so we could climb just fine in our normal boots. That said, with my acclimatization in the early stages, I expected a stiff challenge.

We set off early, and although the climb itself wasn't hard, keeping up with Phinjo was. He's a big guy who doesn't outwardly look all that athletic but has the agility and speed of a mountain goat. The pace didn't seem all that fast so I was trying to look like I wasn't trying, which wasn't as easy as it sounds. Breathing calmly when you would rather gulp for air is not so pleasant. Still, I never once heard Phinjo actually breathe and I didn't want to be the only one panting. After a couple of hours of this we reached the summit and sat on a narrow pile of rocks to take a break and admire the view.

From our high vantage point I could now marvel at the grandeur laid out before us. Behind, a new panorama of Ama Dablam, and beyond we could really appreciate the long valleys and the fierce rivers of the Khumbu as they thundered down to the lowlands of Nepal and India beyond. In front, the full brutality of Nuptse's south face. No longer partially masked by Chukhung Ri, we could see the entire height of this incredibly steep and massive wall of ice and rock rising from the glacier below as a vast shield ahead of us. It was something to behold. And, of course, above this all stood my ultimate goal, still 11,000ft higher than where we now sat.

Turning to Phinjo I asked him how I was doing. I was keen to get some feedback as until now I'd had no indication of my performance since landing in the Khumbu. Phinjo's reply was short and simple.

"You are strong!"

I was overjoyed. From a Sherpa with the climbing caliber and experience of Phinjo that was high praise indeed. For a moment I dared to dream. Perhaps I had some small cause for hope after all. For now, though, I wasn't going to get too carried away.

45

The Hill of Despair

The descent was uneventful, as was the next day of rest. The best thing was watching a little stoat-type creature, all white and fluffy, bouncing around the rocks as it tried to find a Pikka, an extremely fluffy and cute mouse-type animal, for its lunch. It was absorbing to watch both little animals scamper around and I couldn't decide which I was rooting for.

The next day took us back through Pheriche and up towards the village of Lobuche. There are two routes along the valley as I understand it, and we took the upper. The first part of the climb on this route is significantly steeper than the other, extending into a wide stone staircase until you reach the top at the Thokla pass.

It is here the path takes you through the Everest memorial cemetery.

Dozens of small stone monuments are distributed on a narrow, flat plateau. Some are bigger than others and most have a plaque of some kind memorializing those to be remembered. Expeditions from across the entire world seem represented. Most prominent is probably the memorial to Scott Fisher, who lost his life to the famous storm in May 1996. It is covered in prayer flags, and it is poignant to stand there and think of all the tragedy which has fallen on those who have challenged the mountain and lost. These were sobering, somber moments.

From the cemetery you soon cross the river at Thokla, where we took a quick tea in the small yet busy teahouse just above the water. It wasn't flowing too hard at this stage of the season, but you could tell from the size of the boulders that by summer it would be raging. From there, it is a long steady climb to Lobuche village, where we checked into the ambitiously named Eco Lodge for our final rest day. Taking my first hot shower for two weeks was undoubtedly the highlight of the stay, and five dollars well spent. I would set out on the final leg to Everest Base Camp clean and fresh. It was day seventeen since I landed at Lukla.

I had grown stronger as the days had progressed, no doubt about it, yet I was dreading the upcoming section of the trail which took climbers over the terminal moraine of the Khumbu Glacier itself. It had been such a struggle during my first expedition that I'd privately given it the moniker "The hill of despair". In the context of the climb to come this was clearly a vast exaggeration, and nothing compared to what I expected on the mountain itself, but on the prior expedition I vividly remember it being by far the most exhausting part of the entire trek to base camp. That time I was completely knackered when we reached the top of the moraine ridge and it took a solid rest and some serious snacking before I was happy to continue.

We reached the base of the slope a few hours after leaving Lobuche. It rises dramatically up from the modest path you are walking so it's pretty hard to miss. With a breath and a quick mental note to summon my resolve I began to ascend. I was expecting my lungs to burst and my heart to explode like last time, but instead, nothing really happened. It was hardly warranted a mention. Perhaps Phinjo's declaration that I was strong was close to the mark after all.

This time we didn't even stop at Gorak Shep for tea and before long we were stepping from the moraine onto the ice of the glacier itself. Soon we would arrive at my home for the next two months.

46

My Very Own Base Camp

IMG's site at Base Camp was in a similar place as it had been three years before, located at the southern limit of the wider camp.

As expected it still looked sparse. The Sherpa cook tent had been built at the top of a small ridge and a Sherpa eating tent constructed directly opposite, but other than that there wasn't much to it. The eating tent was a fairly large, marquee-type affair, with a bench built from nearby rocks running around the entire internal perimeter. Foam pads and a few thick blankets had been thrown on top to make sitting on it a little more comfortable. Another pile of rocks formed a long, low table in the center. This was covered with a red and white checkered plastic tablecloth to complete its transformation. A cluster of extension leads and plug sockets were arranged at one end, the cable rising to the roof and fed around the tent to the solar panel outside. There were usually a few of the Sherpa's mobile phones plugged in and charging, especially during the afternoon. Technology had most definitely arrived in the Khumbu.

The rest of the camp was still under construction. Equipment and supplies were still packed in their boxes, which were themselves wrapped in coarse white rice sacks, and a great pile of these were arranged in the center of camp. The pieces of a large storage tent sat next to it all, awaiting construction once a platform had been fashioned. This involved a fair bit of rock clearing and ice chipping with a large pickaxe that some unfortunate porter or yak had carried to camp. Another, even larger platform was also needed for the two communal client tents. Paths across camp still needed to be built as well as channels to drain the pools of meltwater which would eventually start to accumulate as daytime temperatures rose in the days and weeks ahead. Clean drinking water had to be found nearby and the toilet facilities constructed. There was still much left to do.

The Sherpa had set up a temporary tent for me on the opposite side of the camp, primarily to keep me out of harm's way until they could build my proper home. Several times a day I made the short walk across camp and joined the Sherpa for each meal. I ate what they ate and I very much enjoyed the traditional Nepalese food which we always had. Most commonly we were served dal bhat, along with some vegetables and a little meat. Sometimes it also included curried potatoes, which were especially delicious.

As a final touch to all this good food, the head Sherpa cook made a small plastic pot of homemade chili sauce as a condiment. It was absolute dynamite, both in taste and spiciness. The Sherpa were in awe that I actually put it on my food and even more so when I began requesting it. An Englishman eating the Sherpa hot sauce? What kind of Englishman was this?

Only one dish unnerved my palette and my senses. It was fermented…something. I can't even remember the name for it and my research uncovered exactly zero English language recipes for it. That came as no surprise. Having tried it I am not shocked that no-one wants to know how to make it. Even the smell was nauseating. I did force myself to taste it a couple of times just for the experience and each time found it tasted marginally better than it smelled. Marginally. They must know the westerners can't stand it, as the few times it was served I was simultaneously given a bowl of Rahman noodles without even asking. I'm sure it's like Marmite, an English breakfast spread made of… something. If you grew up with it you probably like it. If you didn't… Well, let's just say it's fun to give it to my American friends just to see their reactions of disgust.

While everything in camp was very civil and pleasant in those first few days, I will admit the atmosphere was a little awkward for everyone. It was rare for a client to eat with the Sherpa and I could sense they were all being on their best behavior. I'm sure they didn't enjoy having to be "good" and I certainly didn't want them to act any differently merely because I was there. I tried my best to break down the barriers, but it wasn't easy. Luckily a few comic moments helped a great deal. The hot sauce was one, while another was the "haircut incident". PK, an immensely strong Sherpa with a wonderfully warm and outgoing personality, shaved a lightning bolt into the side of Mingma's head during an impromptu haircut one afternoon. It was awesome; a fine job done only with a razor. The Sherpa rightly found the result hilarious, just as did I, and our common reaction seemed to break the ice a little. Eventually, they realized I wasn't judging their every move, far from it, and began to see me a little more as a person and a little less as a client. By the end of the week it seemed they had realized that I was nothing to worry about, and seemed more talkative and back to normal; a situation I think everyone much preferred.

47

In the Company of Climbers

My seventh day in Base Camp was auspicious. Today was the day that Greg would arrive. We'd talked on the phone and on the radio a fair bit since I'd arrived in Kathmandu but now the chief would be there in person. You could sense there was a change in mood within the camp since the previous day. Not that the Sherpa were slacking in that first week, but the pace of progress and the rate of work seemed to rise up a few gears. A lot of progress was made in the final day before his arrival and Greg seemed happy with how camp was evolving.

"I need a proper toilet though," was his one main gripe, and you could see the Sherpa scrambling through the piles of equipment to build one. There are various stages of toilet design at camp. The most basic is a barrel positioned in the ground between some rocks with a couple of planks of wood over it and a tarp screen for a modicum of privacy. The complexity escalates with a bit more effort until there is a proper 6ft high tent with a zipper, and a purpose built stone platform with a proper plastic toilet seat secured over the barrel beneath. Although the setup sounds a bit raw, shall we say, as average temperatures are below freezing it's not all that terrible. Most of the time you don't even notice it is there. When each barrel is full it is sealed up and taken down the valley for safe disposal.

The main tent platform was worked on hard, and by day nine of my stay it was full of tents. After breakfast that day I had my pick, so I chose one towards the far left near a small path. That way I could avoid tripping over any of the tent guy lines when walking around at night. I'd just finished moving my stuff inside my new home and was stringing my prayer flags along the top of it when I heard some activity in the newly constructed client eating tent. The first climbing team had arrived! I was looking forward to seeing them; not just to meet the team for the first time, but also because I was in need of some company. I'd been in the Khumbu Valley for 27 days by now, and I admit I was getting a bit lonely. Waiting for the group's arrival that morning felt like waiting for people to arrive at a party you are hosting. There was that endless anticipation until finally you hear noises outside as the first guests arrive! Unlike a party, however, I was infinitely more excited to see them than they were to see me. None of them knew who I was and after I'd made my introduction it was apparent that frankly none of them cared all that much either.

It honestly felt a bit disconcerting, but I should have expected it. It is easy to forget that ultimately everyone on this expedition was in it for themselves as I mentioned previously. Yes, you are in a team, and you do develop friendships with the other climbers, but there is no "team" as with other group endeavors. Indeed, anyone outside a specific group, like the Classic Phase 1 or the Hybrid team, seems doubly exorcized. Even many weeks of sharing this expedition with the other climbers I still felt a thin and invisible barrier remained between us. I didn't trek to Base Camp with them, or discover the Khumbu with them, or climb Lobuche with them. Most of our climbs on Everest itself were also separate. Indeed, even our ambitions and aims on the climb were different. Our lives were intertwined for a while, but like oil and water shaken together we were combined but never truly mixed. We got on very well for the most part, and I enjoyed their company. I respected them all immensely. Yet even amongst that closest of crowds I remained in a group of one.

The one person I felt perhaps more of a connection to was Dallas, the guide for the Classic Phase 1 team. He'd completed some really hardcore physical challenges and ultra-endurance events in his life and that gave us some common ground. As a guide he had nothing to prove, and I felt that allowed him to accept what I was trying to do a little easier than some of the others. As I would spend a fair amount of time on the expedition in the same places on the mountain as his team, Dallas became in some ways my surrogate guide, my "man on the ground" so to speak, in comparison with the senior guys at the other end of the radio. I enjoyed his company and trusted his judgment as much as anyone.

Despite all this, though, it was still nice to have good people around and to have some proper conversations again. I stopped eating with the Sherpa and life switched to a more normal base camp setup. The only difference remained my unwritten early-morning Sherpa kitchen privileges which I maintained during my entire stay there. None of the other clients ever joined me in the Sherpa kitchen or on the little ridge just above it to watch sunrise with my cup of tea. It was like living a double life. 5.30am to 8am was one kind of base camp, 8am onwards was the other. And that was fine by me.

48

A Second Blessing

All the IMG climbers were in Base Camp but there was no climbing of Mount Everest to be done just yet. The route through the icefall had not yet been found, and equally importantly from the Sherpa's point of view, our team had not had its blessing.

Many teams on the mountain hold an event called a Puja, which is the ritual blessing of the expedition by the local monks. A Lama from the monastery came up to Base Camp and set up next to an impressive stone shrine which the Sherpa constructed on a high point of our camp somewhere near its center. In the early afternoon, each person in the team, client, guides and Sherpa alike, places an object on or next to the shrine to be blessed. Sometimes it's a personal item like a necklace, but we are also invited and encouraged to put some items of climbing equipment there as well. Plenty of us have ascended the mountain wearing holy crampons and boots! I guess if the boots are protected, so are you by extension. By the time the Puja really gets going there is a great mound of gear and paraphernalia covering the shrine. Name tags are recommended!

The entire team gathers for the ceremony, which begins with much chanting and burning of juniper. The monks sit cross-legged in a line beneath the shrine and read through the sacred texts which are written on long horizontal wooden boards that they slowly work through during the ceremony. This part lasts for perhaps an hour, after which the Sherpa raise a tall flagpole in the center of the stone shrine. Once done, they string great lengths of prayer flags from the top of the pole all across camp. Once the chanting and blessings have reached a certain stage, it is time for the singing, dancing and rice wine. Yep, rice wine! Some poor yak had carried an entire barrel of locally brewed rice wine up to our camp, and several of the Sherpa were liberally distributing it from large aluminum kettles to anyone whose cup seemed to be getting empty. It's an acquired taste, but after a couple of cups it is certainly a taste you acquire! It is a wonderful bonding moment for the entire team. At one point the entire expedition, Sherpa, guides and clients, link together, arms over the next man or woman's shoulders, and we sing and dance in a line. It was a poignant cultural moment for us westerners to experience.

With the team now blessed, the Sherpa are willing to set foot on the mountain. For IMG that meant the climbing could now begin. Tomorrow, hangover or not, blessed boots and all, I was finally heading up the mountain itself.

49
The Labyrinth

It was -15°C / 0°F when my alarm went off. Ordinarily my aversion to such cold would subconsciously guide my hand to the "off" button before returning to the land of slumber, but today there was a Khumbu icefall to be climbed. I was soon awake enough to drag myself out of my sleeping bag and into my thick down jacket and mountaineering boots. Urgh. After much self-persuasion I took the plunge and unzipped the tent fly, before stumbling over to the kitchen tent by torchlight. A couple of folks were already sitting just inside the door on the stone bench, each holding a cup of hot tea as Kaji the cook heated water by the light of the single incandescent bulb hanging from the tent roof. Karma Rita, one of the Sherpa guides, was there and to my surprise so was Greg. He is a man who doesn't sleep much on expeditions. I drank a quick tea with them, stashed the small goodie bag of snacks which Kaji had assembled, and then Karma Rita and I were ready. Head torches on, backpacks shouldered, a shake of the hand from Greg and into the darkness we went.

The path through towards the icefall was more complex and harder to follow in the dark than I expected. So early in the season it was still being formed and trampled down by porters and yaks as they brought endless loads of supplies to each expedition and it was somewhat difficult to make out by head torch. I would have taken many a false turn but fortunately Karma Rita was a seasoned pro and knew exactly where we were going. Around the rocks, over small meltwater streams and across patches of gravel-covered ice we walked, until Karma Rita informed me that we had finally reached Crampon Point.

Crampon Point makes the official boundary of a Mount Everest climb on the main Nepalese route. Until this point you are a trekker. Beyond you become something else entirely. To pass this invisible threshold requires two things - a permit to climb Mount Everest and, somewhat obviously, crampons. Although the path to this point had been a relatively flat walk with a few bits of ice to scramble over, from here it would be frozen water almost all the way to the top.

This season the trail beyond crampon point began with what can only be described as a glass slide. I've never seen anything so strange in the mountains. A natural U-shaped channel of smooth ice ascended upwards into the icefall, perhaps 15 feet wide with sharp bottom corners and vertical frozen walls on either side. It looked like a giant had carved a fairground slide into the glacier. Several small sections were more than steep enough to need a rope and the hard blue ice was tricky to grip even with my newly filed and exceptionally sharp steel crampon points. Only a few people had so far ascended the icefall this season, and the surface showed none of the steps which would eventually appear as endless people kicked away at the ice during the coming weeks. Despite the difficult terrain, with our way illuminated by the bright moon and the beams of our head torches we climbed quickly, aiming to keep our time in the icefall to a minimum.

The route through the icefall had changed substantially since my last visit. The catastrophic avalanche that year had broken away from the West Shoulder of Everest and to avoid a repeat of this tragedy the Icefall Doctors had shifted the fixed lines to the right of the valley, closer to Nutpse. This decision was not without its own risks. As we climbed we saw small avalanches billow towards us from the high flanks of Nuptse only to stop while still above us and it was clear that there was no safe solution to this most dangerous of puzzles. Success would require both tenacious speed and a large serving of luck.

At this point I have a small confession to make. It is controversial, and most of the people who have been there will disagree. Despite the serious risks and a history of tragedy I loved climbing though the icefall. Just loved it.

Why? Well, for me there is just something undeniably special about it. It is a maze like no other, as dangerous as the minotaur's labyrinth and equally tortuous to navigate. Yet this maze was made not by Daedalus but by mother nature herself. It is spectacular, with its teetering walls of blue ice, deep crevasses and endless complexity. Perhaps it was that grandeur which in some way calmed me as I passed through and I never felt afraid. I remember one of the guide's incredulous disbelief when I told him that, and to this day I am sure he thinks my statement was either intentional lying or insane bravado. Yet it remains genuine and true. There was no adrenaline and no drama as I climbed, just a heightened sense of awareness. I understood what can and does happen in this place, yet once I was climbing quickly and carefully there was nothing more I could do about it. There was only the binary choice of continuing ahead or turning around. Instead of stress I found the icefall a serene, calm place of wonder and mystery, where the Gods suspend the sword of Damocles high above each person who dares to pass through their realm.

Watching the sunrise from within the Khumbu Icefall is also a staggeringly beautiful event. Shadows of the higher summits lay across lesser peaks below, creating a band of dark indigos and violets both above and beneath the warm colors of sunrise. In essence, the sunrise emerges as a band of color suspended in the middle of the sky. As dawn emerges this band expands with the coming sun, its light reflected around the mountains by the brilliant white snow, and if I was lucky I would catch the exact moment when the bright rays of alpenglow first hit the very summit of Pumori on the opposite side of the Khumbu Valley. In those brief moments the snow glows with a vivid pink. As I watched, the sunrise would brighten and morph into flames of orange as the extent of the light progressed down the mountainside, punctuated by the blue of dark crevasses and gray of weathered rock. It was a glorious thing to see and worth pushing back momentarily on my guide's protestations that we needed to keep moving.

My aim for this first climb was to re-familiarize myself with the ladders, reacquaint myself with the terrain and brush away the climbing cobwebs. To wait until the first proper rotation to Camp II before stepping back onto the mountain would be ill advised; much better to realize something doesn't work while within easy reach of help or retreat rather than to push ahead and invite disaster. With that in mind our goal for this dry run was to reach the so-called "football field", a well-known location about half way up the icefall. It is a common resting point on the route, being an area with fewer ice towers and positioned somewhere between the avalanche-prone walls of Everest and Nuptse. We hoped to reach this area in about two hours, so after about an hour and a half I figured we must be almost there. With Karma Rita Sherpa leading the way we'd successfully crossed ladders, walked around truck sized ice blocks and passed below giant seracs as we followed the fixed line through the maze. Passing around one particular ice block, though, he came to an abrupt stop. I paused behind him and looked forward, my gaze rounding his shoulder to follow a finger which now pointed at the ice a few yards ahead.

"That's it," he said, before turning back to highlight where he was pointing. "No more rope."

And indeed there wasn't. The red rope we were holding just disappeared into the ice a few yards in front of us. Where the route should have been was an enormous jumbled mass of ice the size of many houses. Ten thousand tons of debris now blocked our way.

A towering ice serac had evidently collapsed right onto the route and buried the path, fixed line and all. As the route through the icefall is repaired each afternoon we must have missed this particular collapse by mere hours, so with bad luck we would have joined the rope in its icy tomb. As I stood and looked at the vast white landslide in our way it was hard not to dwell on what might have been. It was a sobering thought.

"So what do we do now?" I said, asking the most obvious of questions.

"I will radio in, and we can ask Greg. But we cannot continue from here so we will have to go down."

Karma Rita radioed back to camp and explained our situation to Greg, who was following our progress as he always did. With no fixed rope and the route blocked Karma Rita was certainly right; there was now no safe way to make further progress and there was no compelling reason to continue up much further in any case. No matter. We had nearly reached the football field and had certainly progressed far enough to call our test run a win. We had also narrowly avoided being crushed to death, so I considered it a double win. Success on Everest involves speed, skill and luck, and that first morning had given me a blessedly cost-free reminder that all three would be important.

50
Visiting Zeus

Twice a day, towards the end of both breakfast and dinner, the team would usually get a visit from Greg. It was a chance to hear the latest news about our expedition and the general state of things on the mountain. Greg's most important information at this stage, however, concerned our schedule, and each update was greeted with enthusiastic chatter amongst the climbers.

The schedule for each group's climbing activities was affected by a multitude of variables. The route condition, the fixed lines, the weather, the number of people at each camp and your rest days are all factors. Even the number of loads the Sherpa had previously taken up the mountain had an impact. Sometimes they are unable to climb or forced to return back to camp due to the weather or the route, and these delays sometimes create a domino effect. After all, people can't stay at Camp II if there are no tents up there. While there is a general sense of the overall plan, each day affects the next, and combined with the weather forecast it means you generally find out that you are heading up the mountain with just half a day's advance notice. Sometimes, if the weather was particularly unstable, the timetable was determined just hours ahead. IMG received twice-daily weather forecasts and the second of which usually arrived at 4 or 5pm local time. After an hour or two to digest, discuss and plan with the guides, Greg's announcement at dinner would confirm the go/no go decision about your departure in 6 hours time.

Being the only climber with my specific schedule gave Greg a little more flexibility with my expedition; after all, one extra climber in Camp II doesn't make all that much difference compared with ten. It also meant we could afford to personalize my plan based on how I was feeling and performing. In that spirit, every couple of days I'd stop in at the operations tent for a check in.

Greg and Ang Jangbu - the same Ang Jangbu whose photo hangs in the Sherpa Museum's hall of fame - lived and worked in that tent, which was located at the highest point of our base camp to give the best radio reception towards IMG's camps further up the mountain. With its slightly out-of-the-way, elevated position and the processional entrance staircase built by the Sherpa it was nicknamed Mount Olympus, despite Greg's multi-year grumblings about the name. I think he disliked the elitist connotations, and he certainly didn't think he was omnipotent against the foe of Mount Everest. Still, it felt like visiting the gods. It was the same feeling as making the journey to the top floor corner office for a meeting with the big boss.

Those discussions about my performance and current plan were always informative and interesting. For me it was not just about hearing the latest information and planning the climb, it was also a chance to learn from the very best. I loved those visits. I'd give them the update on how I was feeling and float a few ideas that I may have had during my ample time to think. Sometimes they were good ideas, sometimes they were not. Both Greg and Ang Jangbu always had good insights, and it was always a productive chat. It also helped to keep me calm; there are a lot of new things to absorb and subsequently worry about when you are on an Everest expedition, and it's a soothing balm to hear that you are doing just fine. In a place where the demons in your mind can be hard to dislodge, positive feedback can work wonders.

51

Thunang And The Plan

I'd been up to Mount Olympus a couple of times since returning from my dry run through the icefall, and although we'd discussed the plan and timing it had been too early to make a fixed conclusion. At breakfast that day, though, Greg asked that I come and visit during the morning, so around 10am I duly made my third visit. This time the discussion was different.

"James, hi," said Greg as I pulled back the curtain on the marquee tent. "Come on in."

"I want you to meet Thunang. He is going to be your Sherpa guide as the replacement for Dawa," he continued and gestured to the man standing next to him.

"Pleased to meet you," I said, turning to Thunang with my hand extended. "I'm excited to be climbing with you."

"Me also," said Thunang, shaking my hand. "We are going to try very hard to get you to the summit."

He immediately struck me as a thoughtful kind of guy. He appeared to be in his thirties, of average height and build but with a very athletic poise.

"Thunang is one of the strongest Sherpa we have," noted Greg. "He's got a lot of experience with climbing the 8,000m peaks and has several summits of Everest. He's a good guy to pair with you I think." I certainly couldn't disagree with that.

"Fantastic. Glad it is all sorted out. So shall we figure out what the next steps are? Any thoughts on when I will be heading up the mountain?" I asked Greg.

"Well the Sherpa are taking some gear up the mountain this morning, so if that goes well there should be enough gear up at Camp I for you to stay there," Greg remarked. "We'll plan for you to stay there for a night, or maybe two with this blackout day. And then up to Camp II."

"Great!" I replied. I was excited to get going. "Uh, what is the blackout day though?"

"It's commemoration for the disasters in 2014 and 2015. So no climbing that day for anyone, not even the Sherpa," Greg answered. "So we'll just have you stay that extra night up there in Camp I. No problem."

To be honest I was more than happy about it. It's not often you are forced to relax for a day on the slopes of Mount Everest.

"Alright. Thunang, let's make it happen!" I remarked. "I guess I will see you early in the morning," and with that I took my leave of them, stepping back outside into the sunshine with a smile. Tomorrow would be my first climb with Thunang and he seemed like a solid, low drama kind of guy. I was confident our time on the mountain together would be just fine.

That evening Greg confirmed our morning start so by 2.30am I was geared up and once more in the kitchen tent for a cup of tea and a small climbing breakfast. As always, Greg was there to see me depart.

"Good luck on this one," he told me as he shook my hand, "We'll be on the radio with Thunang and we'll chat as needed. See you when you get back down."

The butterflies were definitely jangling around in my stomach now. It had taken so much effort and I had endured so much disappointment and pain to get to this point. Now, finally, I could take a step into uncharted territory.

52
An Abyss of Darkness

The fixed lines had indeed been rerouted around the ice collapse I had previously encountered, and we reached the football field without incident. We took a brief pause for a snack and sip of water, and as the sun began its colorful emergence above the clear Himalayan sky we began our ascent of the upper icefall. Here, the nature and construction of the terrain began to change. The seracs seemed both more orderly and larger than lower on the route, no doubt a consequence of the continual collapse and mangling which occurs as the ice flows slowly into the valley below. This greatly increased the sense of exposure. Huge vertical walls of smooth blue ice, many meters high, seemed to stretch right across the valley and there were no simple routes around these cliffs. The route thus took us further left, nearly beneath the hanging glacier on the West Shoulder of Everest itself. It was here that Thunang took a moment to point out exactly where the avalanche had fallen in 2014, and right now we were pretty much in its path.

"We must push now," he remarked, "This is not a good place to be." I couldn't agree more. It was not a place to linger.

Towards the top of the icefall the nature of the route changes. Until this point you are often climbing through the valleys between the seracs. Now, as the valleys narrowed, the route climbed up one of the vanes and traversed along the tops in a dramatic zig zag. Sometimes only a few feet wide with a precipitous vertical drop on each side, the path was precarious to say the least.

Occasionally the fixed line crossed between these vanes and several ladders tied together were needed to span the distance between them. To cross one you picked up the safety rope which was usually anchored by both ends of the ladder, clipped your safety carabiner into it and pulled it both tight to give your movement a little more control. Often there were ropes on each side, making this position a little more symmetrical and stable. Slowly but assuredly you could then locate the points of one crampon on a pair of rungs, the metal between the spikes spanning the rungs like its own tiny little bridge. This requires balancing on one leg, and if the ladder is at an awkward angle or wobbly, or if you misplaced a crampon point this is not a fun moment. Metal on metal didn't give much traction, and you can acutely feel that slipperiness with every step. It takes an assured yet slow movement to bring your back leg to the front, and it is a temporary relief to feel the spikes engage correctly between the next rungs ahead.

In the middle of the bridge I'd sometimes take a second or two to look down between my feet and marvel at the chasm below. After all, it was a unique perspective and despite the drop and my tenuous position I was never really scared. Except once.

There was one particular crevasse, high in the icefall just below Camp I, which was in a different league to the others. It seemed nothing out of the ordinary as you approached, but stepping onto the ladder bridge was far from it. Looking down revealed… nothing. Below was an endless abyss, a bottomless pit from those ancient myths. Sheer smooth walls continued down until vanishing into darkness below, depths from which there could be no return. Falling in would mean doubly-extra-certain death compared to the certain death of falling into the other crevasses on the mountain. With this crevasse, though, you would disappear from the face of the earth, never to be seen again. To step onto that ladder was to walk across a real bridge of doom and oh boy did it feel like it.

Beyond this point the crevasses became narrower and by the time we crested the glacier's edge at the far left of the valley most didn't have ladders any more. Instead, you had to just jump across. Each was still tens of meters deep so these crossings were as exciting as the ladders, if that is the right word to use. Eventually even these became less frequent and the route now turned right, away from the wall of Everest towards the center of the glacier. Each step took us further from the dangerous West Shoulder and with it came an increasing sense of relief, knowing that we were now reaching a place of relative safety. I might have even allowed an extra big smile to cross my face. We had made it through the icefall and for the first time I stood in the Western Cwm.

53
Whispers In the Silence

We soon left the main trail, and continued our traverse towards the center of this immense hanging valley slightly on the downhill side of it. Ahead I could see little red flags sticking out of the bright snow, each made from a piece of tape stuck to the top of a thin bamboo stick, similar to those you find in your garden holding up the plants. These flags marked out a small area on the ice which IMG had reserved for our Camp I. Each team competed for the flattest and safest spots at each camp and I felt IMG had once again secured a good spot. It was some distance from the main tent area and occupied a small ridge with fabulous unimpeded views of Pumori on the other side of the valley. The only downside was the crevasse that ran through the middle of our site. Pointing towards our tent it closed up scarcely six feet before reaching us. Literally six feet. I wondered if this was a good idea, as being swallowed by the ice or falling in during a midnight bathroom break was not the way I had envisioned my demise.

The only other downside of our location was the wind. Away from the shelter of Everest's west face and the icefall itself we were greeted by gale force winds which tore down the western Cwm and threatened to both blow us and our camp over the edge and into the blue sky beyond. Setting up our own tent in these conditions would be challenging, so with no time pressure we decided to wait out the storm inside the single tent which had already been set up by the Sherpa. It currently contained all the equipment that they had stashed so far, and fortunately there were lots of the thin foam sheets which are used as sleeping pads inside the tents. It took some squeezing but we managed to wedge ourselves in. With so much foam beneath and around each of us it felt cozy, especially as the sun rose above Lhotse and bathed the tent in a warming light. We must have spent a couple of hours there, napping and munching on some cookies which Thunang had found buried in one of the bags he was laying on. It was the best of times.

Eventually the wind had died enough to make assembling our own tent a little easier. We crawled out of the vestibule and in the sunshine we got to work. Thunang immediately started banging an aluminum stake into the ice even closer to the crevasse than the first tent.

"Hey, is that going to be OK?" I asked as I pointed to the large and very obvious crack in the ground.

"Sure, it will be fine!" was his response. Those sounded like famous last words to me. Still, he had done this a lot more often than I had so I acquiesced to his superior judgment.

We pushed the tent poles through their guides in the fabric, and I held the resulting shell as Thunang hammered some additional wooden strips into the compacted snow surface. Occasionally the aluminum ones were used, but mostly the tents were held down with long bits of thin wood. I was skeptical they would be strong enough but I was proved wrong. They were in fact excellent - and biodegradable, which was the best part. With our home for the next 48 hours held in place we threw in some extra foam padding from the equipment tent, muscled our backpacks into the vestibule and climbed inside. Now blessedly out of the cold wind once more we got settled in for the remainder of the day.

We dozed a bit, chatted a bit, and generally lounged. There's not much else to do. Later in the day Thunang made dinner, an event which became the now-infamous spicy Rahman noodle incident.

I'd selected a couple of packets of spicy instant noodles to bring, and it turned out they were already very hot, a fact which Thunang had perhaps underestimated. Assuming they needed some more pep he had brought a little bag of the Sherpa hot sauce with him as he'd noticed I had enjoyed it at base camp and figured he'd bring some along. Unfortunately, he had underestimated the heat of that as well. He made the noodles on the camp stove in the vestibule and stirred a great dose of the sauce into the broth.

It was like eating lava soaked in burning jet fuel. Immediately he knew his mistake but by then it was too late. With all the effort to melt the snow and our limited food rations, it's not the sort of place where you can just start over again. With our mouths burning we ate them slowly, both knowing what he'd done but neither wanting to acknowledge with words how painful this meal was turning out to be. We both did manage to finish and for the rest of the night had a good laugh about it, especially once the burn subsided. It was an evening which neither of us will forget in a hurry.

As night fell I slipped into a deep sleep, which was an encouraging sign. A common and early symptom of altitude sickness is difficulty sleeping, either in falling asleep or waking up due to something called cheynes-stokes breathing. The altitude lures your body into thinking it has more oxygen than it does, only for it to realize its mistake. That initiates a bout of violent gasps, waking you up in the process. It's quite worrying to watch someone suffering from it, but in itself cheynes-stokes breathing is relatively harmless. The main ill effect is disrupted sleep, given you wake up every few minutes all through the night. Tonight though, in our tent the only thing waking me up was Thunang rolling over in his sleep and squashing me into the sidewall fabric. It wasn't particularly comfortable but overall our night at Camp I had been a fair success. I was still sleeping when Thunang began to heat some water for oatmeal and coffee as dawn broke. It was another meal to remember but for good reasons this time. It's amazing how nice a cup of hot coffee makes you feel when it's minus 20 outside.

By 9am we were dressed and outside, stretching our legs. The sky was bright and the wind had vanished, making for cold but otherwise pleasant conditions. Given the rush of the previous day it was the first time I really had the chance to look around at the Western Cwm. And what a place it was.

On the left rose Everest. Although the shape of the mountain still obscured the actual summit I knew it was there, hiding behind this colossal mass of rock and ice still some 9,000ft higher than where we had already reached. On the right rose the North Face of Nuptse, even more imposing than Everest as it rose steeply and unbroken to the sharp summit ridge 6,000ft above us. To stand below such an imposing mountain face was quite something. Between these two mountains I could see the long valley of the Western Cwm and the Khumbu glacier which continued steadily upwards until it terminated at the headwall beyond. From there, the mythical Lhotse Face rose high towards the summit of Lhotse, itself the fourth highest mountain in the world.

From where I stood the Western Cwm looked like a vast arena, the greatest stadium of mountaineering on earth. And indeed, walking into that place the day before had been like entering a stadium. I'd always wanted to see the Western Cwm for myself and I was not disappointed.

We were alone at Camp I with no-one else to ruin the magic and the solitude of this special place. As I stood there and contemplated life, the universe and everything, I eventually noticed something strange. It was the sound, or rather the lack of it. In that still air the Western Cwm was phenomenally quiet. Surrounded by snow on the encompassing mountains, all the noise was deadened and was now so quiet all I could hear was the ringing in my ears. Standing there I understood the cwm's enduring colloquial name.

Welcome to the Valley of Silence.

54

One Born Every Minute

Our only job that day was to assemble the remaining tents for the other IMG clients. Thunang laid out their prospective positions, and to utilize the flattest ground he'd placed them all about a foot back from our crevasse. Definitely not a good idea to exit these tents using the wrong vestibule, that was for sure.

We were assembling the second tent when I looked up to see a single lone figure emerge along the path from the icefall. The figure was moving extremely slowly so I would occasionally take a glance to check his progress as he moved further into the cwm. It must have been at least half an hour before he got close enough to make the turn towards our camp.

Such a slow approach created an odd conundrum. When do you say hello? If you wait until he's right with you it would appear that you were ignoring him. If you start the conversation when they are some distance away then there's a good chance the entire conversation will be over before they even arrive. If that happens, do they complete the walk towards you just to say goodbye? I'm pretty sure there are no right answers and despite 30 minutes to think about it as we waited for him to arrive I still couldn't decide. Fortunately, he solved my dilemma by speaking first.

"Hi there!" he shouted at us in a thick New Zealand accent from a medium, shout-a-bit-but-not-too-much distance. I might have mistaken it for Australian except for the large silver fern I could see on his black climbing jacket.

"Hi," I replied. "What brings you up here today? Are you alone?"

"Yeah, just me." This took him quite a long time to say, as every other word was held up by his need to take a large breath.

"My Sherpa said yesterday he would put up a tent for me," he continued. "Any idea where it might be?"

The logical reply was to ask where his Sherpa was. The response was unexpected.

"So my Sherpa didn't want to come up today, so it's just me."

"Do you have a radio?" asked Thunang.

"No." he replied.

Great.

Firstly, today was the blackout day. Frankly he had been lucky, as the Sherpa have been known to "overreact", shall we say, to such transgressions. This guy had also climbed alone through the icefall. Now I've tackled a few solo climbs over the years, but even I knew that the Khumbu Icefall was a different beast. Can you climb it alone? Yes. Is it a good idea? No. If he was an elite professional with experience that would be one thing, but he most certainly did not look like it. His pace was dangerously slow and surely altitude sickness (or worse) was a real risk in his current state. No-one would be there to assess his situation or assist him in returning down the mountain if the worst happened. No-one was coming to rescue him because he couldn't radio his condition, and no-one knew exactly where he was either. Hell, *he* didn't know where he was.

He also didn't know where his tent was.

What happened if he couldn't find it, or it had been damaged by yesterday's wind, or there had been a mix up and it didn't exist at all? All three were possible. If he couldn't find it, he would have to descend the icefall in the afternoon, a very dangerous proposition in the sun as our training climb's rope burial had proven. The alternative of sleeping in the open at 20,000ft was an equally poor choice. He would need to rely on the charity of strangers i.e. us, to keep him alive. We would have helped, of course, but that is a dreadful climbing plan based on luck. Five minutes ago he had no idea if anyone else would even be at Camp I. As I've noted previously, luck is not a strategy.

Very fortunately for him, Thunang had been one of the Sherpa who had delivered a load to Camp I the previous day and had seen another team assembling some tents a few hundred yards further up the route on the opposite edge of the Western Cwm. We sent this chap to take a look and told him to come back if he got stuck. At his sub-snail's pace it took him 45 minutes to approach the area, whereupon a snow ridge blocked our view. From that moment on we never saw him again. Maybe he found his tent, maybe he fell into a crevasse. Who knows.

This whole shambolic episode was troubling. This was the first climber I had met on the mountain and he was an idiot. I thought the idiot factor might be a risk on Everest and now this had been confirmed. Clueless about safety, clueless about the risks, no idea what was happening on the mountain and poor altitude performance. Right now he was a danger to himself and everyone around him. I prayed he would be the last moron I met on this climb, but something told me this was a wish that would not be granted.

55

The Edge of the World

By 7am the next morning we were ready to depart for Camp II. It looked like pretty flat terrain and with under two miles to cover I was puzzled why we had to leave quite so early. I quickly found out.

I had been deceived by the mountain. It was in fact "Nepal flat", meaning not flat at all. Before us lay an undulating set of wide crevasses with flat floors of compacted snow. The white snow at each ridge top had blended together in the harsh light to trick my eyes. Passing each crevasse now involved a 30ft rappel down to its floor, followed by a 50 to 100ft walk and a strenuous climb back to the lip, all to merely regain your original height and a tiny amount of progress. This new evil was exceptionally demoralizing.

The first half a mile took nearly two hours and if the scenery hadn't been so spectacular I might have been a bit grumpy. It was an infinite relief when we finally cleared the last crevasse and I could see the main body of the glacier inside the Western Cwm. Quite some distance ahead, perched on a rocky outcrop at the left side of the valley, I could see a few tiny dots of yellow. The tents in Camp II looked so close, but the scale of this place had deceived me once again and it took nearly an hour to reach them.

What to say about Camp II? It is an odd place, and my initial impressions were mixed. The first thing you notice is the mess. Bringing trash back down the mountain involves carrying extra loads through the icefall, a burden the Sherpa are keen to lighten if they can. Part of this is achieved by throwing trash into the narrow crevasses which criss-cross throughout the camp. My sense is that recent government policies and penalties designed to encourage trash removal rather than just throwing it away are making a difference, especially via the more responsible teams, but I also wouldn't be surprised if there was still some significant cheating. In addition to the steady buildup of everyday rubbish, Camp II is also still littered with a lot of debris from the earthquake tragedy in 2015. That year everyone was evacuated by helicopter and the remaining tents and equipment were abandoned. Everything was pretty much then destroyed by winter storms. Fragments of fraying nylon tent fabric and bits of rope are now buried several meters below the ice, and you can even see them emerge beneath the surface when you look down on the crevasse walls. It's not a pleasant sight.

Fortunately, IMG's location was at the very top of the camp area so we were spared the worst of the mess. I quickly became used to the sight and aside from the debris I actually quite liked it there, although I'm not really sure why. The best views are obscured by the mountain faces on three sides and the climate is extremely harsh. As soon as the sun set behind Nuptse the daytime temperatures would rapidly plummet from perhaps 5°C / 40°F down to -25°C / -20°F, forcing you to scamper back to your tent and put on more layers. Eventually, most of us just gave up layering in those temperatures and wore our full down climbing suits to dinner. Even then it wasn't particularly comfortable. Combined with the thin and extremely dry air which cracked lips and made throats sore it was not a place you would want to stay for long periods.

Ultimately I suppose it wasn't the place itself which I liked but what Camp II represented. It is a place where few people have ever been. It was a place of adventure and a genuine outpost at the final frontier. It was the final gateway to the summit of Mount Everest. Mount Everest! Even at Camp II I still couldn't really believe that I was actually climbing it.

56
The Hungarians

It was still early when I dragged my chilled corpse into the Camp II Sherpa cook tent. I poured some tea from a thermos to restart my body as Mingma - a different Mingma from the one at Base Camp - made us some wonderful hot noodle soup. Old but reliable kerosene burners continually worked in the kitchen to heat the pots of water which were always being boiled and my sunglasses would fog in the steamy atmosphere every time I drew back the fabric door and walked inside. Sometimes the fumes within the tent got a little unpleasant but that didn't matter; just to sit with the Sherpa in those cold mornings and be part of that "authentic" experience once again, to watch the comings and goings of the various people now working up at this camp was worth it. Usually, most of the Sherpa left camp well before dawn to fix ropes on the Lhotse face or to ferry equipment and oxygen bottles to Camp III, so I usually only met the Sherpas arriving from Base Camp with their heavy loads, even at that early hour. These folks sure climbed fast.

On our first morning there, once the sun rose high above Nuptse, Thunang and I took my first walk beyond Camp II. Our goal was to stretch our legs and take a closer look at the Lhotse Face, which began where the Khumbu glacier peeled away from the mountain. It was about an hour's stroll along a mostly shallow incline to reach the bergschrund, which is the name of the ice cliff which forms when a glacier breaks away from the back wall. Above this bergschrund began the icy slope of the Lhotse face itself. After the moderate terrain of the upper Western Cwm this was where the climbing undeniably began, and where things once again became riskier. Even approaching the bergschrund isn't safe; anything falling down the ice face is doing a fantastic speed by the time it flies off the end. Rocks, equipment or even people, unfortunately. Even tiny rocks are a major hazard; I remember one coming past and it made a sound like a bullet ricochet as it flew past, just like in movies I kid you not. There are also big rocks. On that walk a boulder the size of a small house fell down the face of Everest just to our left and it was the oddest thing to watch. It seemed to fall in slow motion, so far did it fall in this immense landscape, and made a strange whirring noise it made as it rotated through the air. It was a surreal sound, like spinning helicopter blades but slower and deeper. At the base of the wall it impacted into the glacier with a great thud, making a small crater in the ice. Seeing this rockfall made me realize just how much higher we still had to climb and just how dangerous that climb might be.

We fortunately returned to Camp II without further incident, and as I relaxed outside the tents with a cup of warm juice I had the good fortune to meet two other climbers who had set up their tents nearby. Both were from Hungary and they were attempting to become the first Hungarians to summit the mountain without supplemental oxygen. Both were professional climbers and both looked the part. With the appropriate roughness of grizzled beard, sufficiently wild hair and wearing bright red jackets covered with sponsorship badges, they fitted the stereotype of what you think professional alpinists *should* look like. From the quantity of badges I figured they must be pretty good, and I was intrigued to see how they would progress as the days went on. Alone on my quest I still had no real benchmark for comparison, and it was only the assurances of Greg and my indirect performances which gave me hope. Now, with the Hungarians on a similar schedule I could finally find out where I stood, at least against the best. I just hoped I wouldn't be ridiculously far behind.

Those few days in Camp II were otherwise pretty boring. There was no-one to talk to, and, with the exception of repeating the walk we had just done, there was nowhere to go as every other direction was either a rock face or crevasse-riddled glacier. The most interesting occurrence during those days was the opportunity to help construct the other cooking and eating tents for the clients. The task involved carrying a lot of rocks around for a morning in the sunshine while being plied with endless tea. This was a good deal in my opinion and I felt good to be useful for a change. With the Sherpa working hard it was amazing how quickly a flat platform was pickaxed out of the ice and covered in suitable rocks. Although sad that I would soon be leaving the Sherpa kitchen I was relieved when the first team of IMG climbers stumbled into camp. They would be here for a couple of days before returning back to Base Camp and I looked forward to the company.

The next day our newly arrived team set off on the same little walk to the bergschrund I had previously done, so I went with them for the exercise. It was their first full day at this altitude so I expected the pace to be slow, but wow, slow really meant slow. Agonizingly slow. I'd become conditioned by Thunang to climb fast, to push quickly past the dangers, so I very much struggled to hold back against my programming and not speed ahead. I was cognizant of being a good boy, though, and wanted to show that I was part of the extended team so I walked with the group. It was a leisurely morning from my perspective, to say the least.

We made it about two-thirds of the distance to the bergschrund before stopping. A few folks were definitely struggling at that altitude and it was clear that this would be the limit of our foray that morning. After a decent period just lounging in the sun on the compact snow we turned back down towards lunch.

As we approached camp I noticed two figures with large backpacks and trekking poles making their way along the path towards us. Both would move a pole and leg in synchronization as though climbing to a slow rhythm. A really slow rhythm. Their progress looked even slower than ours had been, which was saying something. In fairness they looked to be carrying quite a bit of weight, but still, on this relatively easy terrain I was surprised at their lack of pace. I wondered who they were. As we neared I could eventually make out a collage of sponsor patches which covered both their red jackets. It couldn't be! But indeed it was.

The Hungarians were breathing hard as we passed and neither of them even raised their heads to acknowledge us. Both were focused on their feet and deep into a zone of concentration. I saw that one carried a tent, which puzzled me as the Sherpa teams were still on the mountain and the Lhotse face was closed. Perhaps they were just stashing gear on the face but I still found their journey supremely irritating. Why should I play by the rules, sitting on my bum at Camp II while others continued their acclimatization unimpaired? Not that I blamed our team, of course, which was doing things correctly. Instead, I blamed the selfishness of other expeditions on the mountain. And unlike the clueless New Zealander, this time by people who should have known better.

We arrived back in Camp II shortly after 10am and with nothing to do until lunch I went back into my tent and watched a movie on my phone. With the solar charger I had carried to camp there was still limitless opportunity for first world time wasting using the wonders of technology. At midday I heard the customary banging of the pans and wandered over for a leisurely lunch. It was the usual affair, and I made sure to drink plenty of warm juice to keep hydrated in that fantastically dry air. With nothing else to do after lunch I went back to the tent and took a nap.

I woke up shortly before 3pm. The sun was still shining brightly and the air was still, combing to make our tent stifling despite covering the roof with our sleeping bags to ward off the worst of the rays. I was restless. Having seen the Hungarians continue up the mountain a part of me thought I was somehow falling behind. The walk that morning had done nothing I felt, and although I couldn't climb the face I wondered instead if perhaps I should do the same walk again but at a challenging pace this time? It was a relatively safe walk with no surprises so I let the cook know where I was going and set out alone towards the bergschrund for the second time that day. My pace was solid, enough to get the heart and lungs going without overdoing it, and 45 minutes after setting out I had reached the ice wall.

What I saw there amazed me.

Scarcely above me were two people making their way up the fixed lines at the bottom of the Lhotse Face. They had climbed the single aluminum ladder the Sherpa had fixed up the short ice cliff and were now climbing in a slow, rhythmic motion up the ice. "It can't be!" I thought, not for the first time that day, but once again the sponsor patches and red jackets gave them away.

I now had my fitness benchmark. In the time the Hungarians had taken to climb to a point barely above where I now stood I'd walked back down to camp, watched a movie, had a leisurely lunch, taken a nap and then walked back up to their current position.

As I looked at them inch up the face for the first time I knew, really *knew*, that the summit might be in reach. And that was an encouraging thought.

57

Closest Point of Contact

That night we learned the Sherpa fixing team had been successful in fixing lines up to Camp IV on the South Col. Fantastic news! With ropes now in position the Lhotse face was open for businesses, legally this time. While the Classic team was due to descend back to Base Camp the next morning I had a different task. It was time for a touch-and-go to Camp III at 7,320m / 24,000ft. For a successful no Os attempt this milestone was one I absolutely needed to achieve. Success would mean I was on track, failure… Well, I didn't want to contemplate what failure would mean. This climb would be a personal altitude record for me, and I was now moving into the unknown.

Unlike the lower camps, which are chosen for their relatively safe locations and ample available space, Camp III is literally and figuratively carved into the side of the mountain. Small terraces must be hand cut into the ice face, as without them there is no chance to pitch any tents at all. It is slow, backbreaking work at that altitude and as few tents as possible are carried up. As each camp must be built from scratch anyway, IMG shunned the usual site on the Lhotse face and chose instead to create their own Camp III about 250ft above the other groups. It involved additional work, as the slope here was even more unforgiving, but the relative isolation from the other climbers meant more control over our destiny. The higher location also meant a shorter haul up to Camp IV on the second day, plus the view was also fractionally better. The team leaders didn't care about that last part, obviously, but I certainly did!

We set off in the dark as always and reached the bergschrund as the pastel colors of sunrise lit the lower valley far behind us. Even using the ladder the Sherpas had assembled on the cliff face I found the short section a challenge. The rungs didn't quite reach the top, and it required a bit of brute strength and bravado to surmount the slightly overhanging bulge on the lip itself. With the rope cutting into the snow your ascender is useless so you have to go freestyle, pulling yourself up this small section without any protection from a fall. A couple of big moves, a surge of adrenaline and then suddenly there I was, standing on the Lhotse Face at last! It was a dream to have made it this far.

Everest has somehow acquired this reputation of being an easy climb. Some parts are but most parts are not, particularly in the early season before any kind of indentations are kicked into the surface as climbers pass over. At the base of the Lhotse face you look up at a 50 degree surface of hard blue ice; endless, unrelenting and imposing. Anyone who says Everest is easy hasn't spent hours on the Lhotse Face trying to kick crampon points into sheet ice at 7,000m / 23,000ft.

I found the slope to be a particularly awkward angle, lying between the best angles for the two main crampon techniques. When climbing vertical or near-vertical ice your footholds are made by kicking the front two points of your crampons directly into the wall, a skill unimaginatively known as front pointing. If you do it deep enough the next two points just behind the front spikes also touch the ice, giving some additional traction and stability when you stand up. The only problem is that front pointing is hard work and so is difficult to sustain for long climbs at altitude.

For moderate slopes the technique changes to what's called the French technique. At these angles the most efficient way to climb is to get as many points of your crampons as possible in contact with the ice. Maximum grip for minimum effort. On shallow slopes this is easy, but as the gradient increases so does the foot contorting needed to make good contact, and with my inflexible ankles I find it awkward. I found the Lhotse face to be right between both techniques. It was too long, sustained and shallow to front point at this altitude, but I found the contortion required to get a good contact at these angles was equally strenuous. Balancing on shallow front point indents to maintain each foothold I found was tough going.

Thunang would have preferred to go faster, but he *always* preferred to go faster, so to motivate me he'd race several meters ahead, stop, and then wait for me to *almost* reach him before racing ahead once more. I found it infuriating for more than one reason.

The first was the climbing method. On Everest there seems to be two general philosophies for making progress up the mountain. The first is what I would call the "sprint" philosophy. These folks are the hares. The climber takes a number of quick steps ahead, followed by a short rest to recover before sprinting ahead again. This was the dominant method I saw on the mountain and almost all the Sherpa used it.

The second philosophy was the "Everest shuffle", where each individual step is followed by its own micro rest but it continues without a long break. This is the slow-and-steady approach, the tortoise method. It should, physiologically at least, be the more efficient of the two methods, and I was surprised that most of the Sherpa seemed to sprint, including Thunang. Each to their own, I suppose, and ultimately your choice of philosophy is just a preference. The problem comes when climbers of different philosophies meet on the same route.

If you are a tortoise like me, climbing behind a hare is demoralizing and annoying. They zoom ahead and stop, resting until you *almost* catch up before zooming once more, making them annoying to follow. Worse is that they are difficult to pass if you happen to be a faster climber overall. By the time you reach them and start your attempt to move past they have recovered just enough to accelerate and thwart your overtake, putting themselves once more out of your reach.

If you are a hare the problems are reversed. There is always a person in the way as you begin your sprint and you always are being held up. If you can't pass then you are stuck there, forever snapping at their heels. That must also be demoralizing.

As passing a climber is quite difficult, everyone is forced to climb as slow as the slowest person. High on Everest that is often very slow indeed, and so a mix of climbing philosophies can make everyone's climb worse as the route becomes a literal traffic jam. On the steeper sections progress can grind to a complete halt. Waiting as you feel the deep cold slowly and insidiously seep into your fingers and toes is diabolical and I detested those situations, as did everyone else.

I was a tortoise and Thunang was a hare. I usually prefer to be the follower on a climb - less expectation to set the pace - but after a while I just couldn't take it anymore. It was becoming distracting and half way up the face I found myself focusing more on this frustration than on the placement of my crampon points. That was not a good situation to be in, so I made a change.

"Hey Thunang," I called out to him as we reached an anchor point, "I'll go first."

He nodded and I clipped around him into the next section of the fixed line. I knew how quickly I wanted to climb and I wanted to take back the responsibility to execute on my plan. Thunang fortunately seemed fine with our position swap; I imagine it isn't a common client request but maybe he was getting frustrated with my constant tortoise lagging. In either case, climbing out front felt SO much better for me. It felt so good that we kept that order for the majority of the expedition.

58
Up To Camp III

From Camp II it took us 2 hour and 45 minutes to reach Lower Camp III at 7,150m / 23,450ft. It was located in a small area of the slope with slightly less steep ice. It was sheltered enough to warrant a proper break in any case, the first stop we had since leaving camp. As I chewed through the tasteless grit of a deep frozen chocolate bar I admired the view in the bright light which shone through the cloudless sky. Each step took us further out of the valley and up into a new, hitherto unseen world. It is strange to say, but surrounded by such giant mountains it is only once you are high on the Lhotse Face that your position starts to actually *look* high. For the first time I could see past the summit of Pumori to the peaks beyond. In the distance I could make out Cho Oyu, its great summit plateau unmistakable at 8,188m / 26,860ft, and I smiled to myself. It was the first time I'd ever seen it.

The section above Lower Camp III was the hardest and steepest part of the face route so far. I was certainly feeling the effects of the altitude now and the energy we were expending was taking its toll. Still, the pace was broadly sustainable, at least for a few more hours, and we were still making progress. The blue ice was now as hard as iron and only the tiniest of white nicks in the surface gave any indication that a few Sherpa had passed this way to fix the ropes above. Kicking scarcely made any indent and each step was a precarious balancing act on a single crampon point as the wishy washy fixed line conspired to throw me off balance. It all felt horribly unstable. The hundred or so vertical meters between Lower and Upper Camp III took me over an hour, but we eventually crested a slight bump in the slope and arrived at a junction in the scarlet fixed line. A short tributary rope traversed up and to the right for about 50ft to its final terminus at an aluminum stake driven deeply into the snow. Just in front I could see the beginnings of a nascent terrace in the ice which would become our future home on the face. Right now, though, all that existed at IMG's Camp III were a few red marker flags and a small orderly stack of oxygen bottles which had been tied to the anchor.

Five to six hours is considered a solid time for this climb and we had made it in exactly four, a good performance for my first attempt I thought. At the anchor we took off our packs and after making sure they wouldn't slip and plummet a thousand feet down the face we sat in a mound of crunchy snow next to the metal cylinders. As I unwrapped another inedible frozen snack Thunang detached the radio from his backpack strap and called down to Base Camp to give them news of our arrival. Greg was immediately on the line and sounded pleased with our progress.

"Great work James, that's a good performance," remarked Greg. "How do you feel?"

"I feel good!" I replied. "A bit tired, and getting the points into the ice is a bit tricky, but otherwise I feel solid. We didn't go too hard and I think I've got plenty left in the tank."

"Great, great," said Greg. "You and Thunang are climbing well so keep it up. Take a bit of a rest and be careful on the way down."

"Yep will do," I replied. "Over and out from me!"

After the call we just laid back and relaxed, looking out across the Western Cwm and admiring the view in that warm sun and calm air. We were totally alone now; alone on Mount Everest and not in a bad way either. Far from it. The brightness of the untouched snow, the deepest dark blue of a high altitude sky, the endless panorama of the world's greatest peaks and that magical feeling of being high in the mountains and above all the world. Here we were as far removed from the stresses of life as one can be and I felt a glow of happiness as I sat there, alone and in true peace on this, the highest mountain on Earth. It was a dream. I wish you could have been there and shared in the reward that the universe had granted us.

After 15 or 20 minutes I began to feel a chill through my clothes as my body cooled after our climbing exertions. Thunang and I looked at each other and there was no need to discuss the plan. We both knew it was time to holster our backpacks and head back down. I was sad to leave, and yet I knew - or rather hoped - that I would be back.

Down was vastly easier and quicker than up. After less than an hour we were already at the bergschrund, and as a treat (for me, anyway) we rappelled down a rope hung across the lip a few yards away. Ostensibly the reason was to split the traffic directions to prevent a bottleneck at the ladder, but I just considered the rappel a fun prize for a good day's work. Just ninety minutes after leaving Camp III we were having tea with Mingma in the kitchen; a final reward for our efforts on the mountain that day. It couldn't have gone any better.

59
The Greatest is Gone

Our return to Base Camp the next day was blessedly uneventful. While the dangers of the icefall remained the same and we pushed hard to minimize how long we were exposed, as expected it was less physically punishing than the climb up and gave us a little more opportunity to appreciate the surroundings. It was a strange feeling to return through that icy maze, akin to descending slowly back to earth from the heavens; a sense that you are leaving a forbidden world and now emerging back into the "real" world. We were leaving the land of the gods.

Base Camp had not been idle during our absence. There were markedly more tents now, occupying every possible flat spot on the glacier, and each team's camp seemed to have expanded. The barely discernible path through base camp was now well worn, often with low stone walls separating each team's boundary and to shepherd the yaks in the right direction. There were so many more people there than before and it was evident that the season on Everest was now in full swing.

Things had also been progressing at IMG. A whole new section of camp had been constructed, this time for the Hybrid team which had now arrived. Similar to the Classic groups, the hybrid team had a little more support in terms of guide ratio; not a bad choice for those on their first expedition to the mountain. In fact, I had been part of this group on my first attempt in 2014. They had their own eating tent and cook, more a factor of the total number of people in camp than anything else, but with my team-of-one situation allowing me to flitter between groups I got to know them fairly well.

It was another strong team. Ryan was a US Special Forces soldier, one of two on our expedition, and was physically a beast of a man. He seemed a wonderful human, impressive but with humility and generosity. I liked him a lot. The other person on that team I found particularly interesting was Sharon, a teacher from Australia who was one of two women on our expedition. She was very Australian, if that is something I can say, but I like the Aussies a lot and enjoyed her company. Good people to be up on the mountain with, and another win for IMG's client screening process.

Life quickly settled back into base camp rhythm, at least until day two. We were mildly surprised to see Greg stick his head into our eating tent at lunchtime; we usually only saw him in the evening and sometimes at breakfast. You could tell from his demeanor that something was wrong. Gone was the congenial optimism, replaced by a frown and serious disposition. I immediately had a sense of foreboding; on Everest, bad news is generally terrible news, and only something important would warrant this special visit.

Once everyone had arrived and seated Greg told us what had happened.

"As some of you might have heard already, there was an accident on Nuptse this morning. A team found the body of a climber at the bottom of the face by Camp I and they've confirmed the identity. It is Ueli Steck."

"He is dead."

No one spoke as a shocked silence covered the room. Ueli Steck, probably the best mountaineer in the world, was dead? Not possible.

Ueli was a pioneer who had redefined our view of what was possible in the mountains. Building on the accomplishments of those before him, he had taken climbing to new heights. His speed record ascent of the Eiger North Face, one of the most feared climbs in the world, had made him a legend. This incredible, imposing face takes most expert climbers several days to climb. Ueli reached the summit in 2 hours and 48 minutes. No rope, no protection, just focus, skill and athleticism. It is a mind blowing thing to see and it became a huge motivation for me as I trained. I must have watched the video of his climb at least 100 times. I played the soundtrack as I hiked. I remembered his inspirational quotes at the end when my training got tough. It helped me understand that what I was trying to do was actually possible. I certainly wasn't Ueli, not by any stretch of the imagination, but he had reinforced my belief that amazing things could be done, and maybe even by me.

I had the privilege to watch him climb just a few days before. A small figure on the south face of Everest high above us, we watched as this person, alone and free, moved up the mountain on the difficult and rarely climbed Hornbein couloir. I didn't know it at the time, but I was one of the last people to ever see him climb. And now he was gone.

Ueli had been a personal friend of Greg and had visited him just a couple of days before the accident. For the rest of us, we had lost someone we respected and revered, someone who we had been brought closer to than ever, now we had briefly shared the same mountain as he had. It brought the tragedy that bit closer to us. I'm sad that I never had the opportunity to thank Ueli personally, as I feel somehow I owe him a small debt of gratitude for the inspiration and confidence he gave me to tackle this great challenge. It is a debt I shall not soon forget.

60
Raiders of the Lost Pantry

The winds on the upper mountain had been at hurricane force for several days and everyone was delayed in Base Camp, climbers and Sherpa both, waiting for them to abate. That morning Greg came into the tent as usual with the forecast and told us that we were heading up to Camp II the next day. I'd been down for a week now and was raring to go.

It was now time to make my first visit to the special "secret" tent in Base Camp. Discovering this on the first expedition had been one of the joys and I had been waiting for my first invite to this wonderland. For it was here where the snacks were kept.

Each year IMG ships a vast quantity of food from the US to Base Camp to help keep the climbers happy and well fed. As well as the general food bought in Nepal - the rice, vegetables etc…, there is a supply of western food both to cater to most people's tastes and to provide easy food options higher on the mountain. From noodles and oatmeal to Canadian bacon and skittles, the quantity required has to be seen to be believed as feeding 30 or more hungry climbers for nearly three months takes a lot. Greg and the team uploaded a photo to the expedition blog of all this stuff outside of Costco after they'd bought it all. Apparently this year it collectively weighed over 2,200lb. I can only imagine what the bill at the checkout register came to!

Everything inside the special tent was arranged in cardboard boxes and for each rotation you are allowed to take as much as you want. The proviso is that you, rather than your Sherpa, have to carry it up the mountain, which tends to keep people's enthusiasm somewhat in check. It's a surprisingly difficult decision to know whether you should take a Mars Bar or Snickers to 8,000m, and a surprisingly specific experience to know that a Clif Bar, while generally an excellent snack, becomes an inedible brick at -20°C / -4°F. Refining your snack strategy is determined by trial and error, and with my eyes bigger than my appetite I made my first big mistake of the expedition.

61
IcyHot

It was the usual start time from Base Camp, and I was content to trundle along towards the rear of the group. Thunang was not, but it would be too difficult to overtake the other Classic group climbers at least until we rested at the football field. The pace was still decent and I wasn't worried.

It was a surprise to see so many people at the football field when we arrived; not only was the rest of our team there but a number of Sherpa from at least two other expeditions. The guides were all in discussion, and we were soon told it might be a while. A Sherpa team from Himex, a well-regarded and strong company with a good relationship with IMG, were one of the groups already waiting, which suggested that the reasons for our delay were unlikely to be trivial.

Scouts eventually returned from higher on the icefall. There had been a collapse and a small segment of the route had been destroyed. However, although the area of damage was small, it was up a vertical section, which is not the sort of thing you can easily sidestep around.

"We'll go and take a better look," Dallas told us, "We will be as quick as we can, try to keep warm." And with that, he and a couple of our Sherpa headed into the maze. There was nothing to do but wait.

It was still before dawn and bitterly cold. A stiff breeze compounded the discomfort. I had left my thick down jacket in camp to save weight and space for the 20 pounds of snacks I had brought in anticipation of many days up on the mountain. I could feel the impact of each pound, and I found the climbing much more difficult than last time. I was soon wondering if I'd brought too much.

Time dragged on. I was becoming colder with each minute, and while my fingers and toes were OK my core temperature was not. I was shivering uncontrollably, and I knew I would soon have to climb in one direction or the other or I was going to get hypothermia. I wasn't the only one. By now our team were all huddled together like penguins, taking it in turns to shield the others from the wind as the countdown clock towards the abort of our rotation kept ticking down.

Dallas eventually reappeared and not a minute too soon.

"We've found a new route!" he told us, "We still need to put in the ladder, but we can get going now." I was unbelievably happy to hear this news, not only so we could now move but also that our rotation was still on. Stiffly we shouldered our packs and resumed our climb.

Perhaps 30 minutes ahead we stopped in a deep ravine of ice and stared up as PK ice climbed the last 2 meters to the top of a serac. The only ladder they had wasn't quite long enough to reach the top so all of us would soon be doing this, although we'd have the benefit of the fixed line which PK was now installing for us. Soon it was my turn, and with a 50lb pack it was more of a struggle that it should have been. Finally, though, I managed to muscle over with a spurt of adrenaline. Standing on top I felt we were doing OK once more, and as long as there wasn't another delay the few hours we had already lost wouldn't be the worst. Famous last words. Barely a hundred yards further on I crested a small ridge and ran into all of the climbers ahead now re-clustered together in another small gully ahead. There had been a second collapse on the route.

Fortunately, this one proved to be easier to navigate around, but we must have spent at least another hour waiting, standing beneath the overhanging glacier on the West Shoulder of Everest like pins in a bowling alley. It appeared that a number of the team were not concerned about this, but I was and so were the Sherpa, so we all hung back at the top of the ridge to at least give ourselves half a chance if the worst happened. As the sun began to rise above Nuptse and the snow began to ominously soften the signal came to advance, so we quickly negotiated through the repaired section before crossing the last crevasse to arrive at Camp I.

I was exhausted. The combination of cold and a heavy pack had taken an unexpected toll on my body and I needed a break. I sat down in the snow for a drink and snack, but Thunang barely took off his backpack. He was desperate to keep going and I couldn't understand the rush. I'd done the climb to Camp II already and although long it hadn't been particularly difficult. Still, he was insistent that we press on, so I rushed my snack and reluctantly re-shouldered my equipment for the second leg of this climb.

As we progressed into the Western Cwm I began to discover why Thunang was keen to leave. At such high altitude the light is brutally harsh with far more ultraviolet radiation than any desert. It has a power which is surprising. In the villages far below I'd seen people use a small arrangement of mirrors, called a solar concentrator, to boil kettles of water. Now deep into the Western Cwm we were surrounded by thousands of vertical feet of steep white walls while below us was a floor of blinding snow. We walked in a solar concentrator which was measured in miles rather than inches, and now endured perhaps the harshest solar radiation on Earth.

The temperature climbed rapidly. At 9.00am, as the sun and ourselves arrived in the valley it had been -15°C / 0°F. By 11.00am it was 30°C / 90°F, I kid you not. Within the space of an hour you go from freezing in the thickest down jacket you carry, to walking in a single thin thermal top and overheating like crazy. It is surreal, and even though it sounds quite nice it is anything but. I'd previously heard of the Western Cwm's reputation, but I had dismissed these stories as moaning. Now I understood the difficulties. I've run a double marathon in 35°C / 100°F heat and yet taking single slow steps in the Western Cwm that day was a greater struggle. My expected 30 minutes of casual sauntering became a two-hour festival of suffering and as I tiredly shuffled while reflecting on my hubris. This gentle climb was ten times more draining than the hottest day you can imagine, in an environment so different to our normal world that it has to be experienced to be understood.

By the time we finally, *finally*, reached the rocks at the lower limit of Camp II I was a broken man. There was a narrow gravel path past the tents, and although it is only a short distance it still took me another 30 minutes to reach IMG's area at the top. I cursed the team's choice to be so high in this camp. I just wanted this abysmal walk to end. Eventually, we could see Mingma, our Camp II chef, standing outside the cook tent and beckoning us inside. Dropping my pack and stumbling through the fabric flap I sat in silence on a stone bench which had been built along the side wall and sipped some sugary tea. Rarely has a welcoming drink tasted so good. I'd made it, but only by the narrowest of margins.

At least my struggles were over, I thought, but I couldn't have been more wrong. I didn't know it at the time, but the seeds of my destruction had already been sown...

62
Sickness and Suffering

The next milestone in my rotation plan was clear. Climb to Camp III, stay a night and then onward to Camp IV at the South Col. Sleep there for the night, and then return all the way back to Camp II. If I could do this I had a shot at the summit. We had a day of rest at Camp II after the trial to get here, and now it was time to see what I was made of.

The moment we left camp that morning I knew something wasn't quite right. I felt flat, drained of energy and strength. It was apparent that in the thin air I had not yet recovered from my prior exertion, but there was nothing I could do about that now. My only hope was to conserve energy with a slow pace and hope that another night's rest at Camp III would fix whatever was bothering me.

My dithering meant we left camp at the tail end of the team, and Thunang was in a frantic drive to make it to the front of the line before the Lhotse face. He hated being stuck behind slower climbers even more than I did, which was saying something. This time, though, I was either unwilling or just plain unable to muster enough effort to pass most of the climbers on the way to the bergschrund. We arrived in the middle of a fragmenting group.

Progress up the face was laborious, a real grind. However, if my pride had to take a hit to ensure tomorrow's success, so be it. Our climb took over an hour longer than on my first attempt, and when I arrived the camp was already busy. One of our guides shepherded me towards the middle tent on the upper of the two terraces as my home for the night. It was currently empty, but it wasn't before long I was joined by another climber by the name of Jim.

That tent was uncomfortable from the start. My spot, jammed against the back wall, was impinged on all sides. The vestibule had filled with snow and pushed in against the inner tent fabric to create a hard cold surface against which I was compressed. With no other place for them, my heavy boots lay at my feet and prevented me from fully extending my legs. My thick sleeping bag enveloped me like padding inside an amazon package and I was now trapped with zero free space and no way of expanding it. I remember thinking that it had all the mobility of a coffin, which was not an encouraging analogy given where I was.

We still expected a third tent buddy and had saved some space for him, yet as the afternoon wore on towards evening we wondered if anyone would arrive. Darkness was already beginning to fall when then there was a slight commotion outside and the zip to the tent was drawn back as a climber struggled his way inside. It was another Jim, Jim 3 if you also consider me a "Jim". Ten hours or more hours after leaving Camp II he had finally arrived and it was immediately clear that all was not well.

Most of us had noticed that Jim 3 had a bit of a cough for the last week or two. It sounded innocuous enough, and I had attributed it to what is known as the Khumbu Cough, a very common ailment at altitude caused by a throat irritation from the extremely dry air. While the Khumbu Cough can badly affect your sleep and make you susceptible to more serious infections like bronchitis, on its own it is merely a colossal pain in the neck. Wearing a thin buff, a balaclava-like garment, over your face virtually constantly for months was an effective preventative measure and many of us kept them on permanently. I personally found it very effective, even pulling it over my whole face when sleeping. Yeah, you wake up covered in drool, but it's better than hacking up your lungs like a maniac all day long. The only time you can't really wear the buff is when you are climbing due to the air restriction and icing, and that is often when the damage is done.

Jim 3's pervasive cough had now morphed into something more sinister, a violent and wheezing gasp.

"Maybe he's just irritated his throat during the climb," I hoped. We asked him how he was, but there was barely a one word reply. Not a good sign, but we put it down to exhaustion after his long hours on the face. Dallas checked him over and a short while later the Sherpa came to our tent bringing us all hot Rahman noodles. Jim 3 had no appetite and vomited up the small amount he had eaten. Definitely not good. Darkness descended quickly afterwards and with it came the frigid temperatures of night at 7,320m / 24,000ft. I lay in my sleeping bag, crushed, cold and unable to sleep as I listened to the coughing. Eventually, these noises were supplemented by delirious muttering and around 3am Jim 3's condition seemed to be worsening. The other Jim was also awake and we finally decided to call out to Dallas for some assistance.

Dallas is a fabulous climber and an even better guide. He is magic. It didn't take long before we heard the zipper on our tent fly and the beam of a head torch rustle into our tent. Help was at hand. He began talking with Jim 3, assessing his condition and what was to be done. He was soon on the radio with Greg at Base Camp, who was awake as always, giving him the update and discussing solutions. They determined that for now Jim should be given some bottled oxygen, after which they could assess what the next steps might be. With Jim's mask attached, the flow of oxygen seemed to help, and although the coughing continued he became far more lucid which was certainly a step in the right direction. The Sherpa made him some more noodles as Dallas was keen to get some calories and warmth into his body. He again threw some of it up, but a little seemed to stay down this time. And a little was better than none.

By 6am it is safe to say that everyone in our tent was broken in some fashion or another. Jim 3 was still on oxygen and had recovered enough to move but little else. The other Jim didn't seem too functional either and I had hardly slept for a moment that entire night. I felt like death; I'd say death warmed up except I was freezing cold, so it was really just like death.

The Sherpa brought us some hot water, part of which I added to my cup of instant oatmeal for breakfast, and as the light brightened with the dawn it was time to get ready. I changed my socks and pushed my feet into my stupidly frozen boots before following the two other Jims' out of the tent. It was a nice morning with good yet cold conditions. I snapped my crampons to my boots and watched some Sherpa already carrying loads past our camp. Standing there, as I looked at such unique beauty I felt just one emotion. Apathy. Total, abject apathy. The absolute last thing on God's green earth that I wanted to do right then was climb to the South Col.

I showed none of the careful preparation which had so far exemplified my approach on the mountain. I walked around outside wearing just my liner gloves, allowing my fingers to chill before I had even started the climb. Even with my thick mittens on I was soon banging them together in a futile attempt to return some warmth. It was the same situation with my feet, as I'd put on frozen boots without warming the liners in my sleeping bag. Through my apathy I'd sabotaged my own climb and Thunang could tell from my performance. We slowly ascended the first steep section above camp and at the top Thunang made a radio call to Base Camp. He was turning me around.

I half-heartedly protested the decision, but at that moment, deep down inside, I was happy that he was doing it. I just did not want to be there. With the decision made we were soon descending with the rest of the climbers, including an improving Jim 3, back to down Camp II.

63
Focus or Fail

Each step towards camp brought me closer to rest, and as the air grew thicker and warmed in the sun, so my physical discomfort receded. Yet each step also brought with it a growing realization of what I had just done. I had been weak when it mattered most, had given up when I most needed to commit. My inexperience had prevented me from recognizing what was happening and in those moments I had let my transient discomfort sabotage my goal. Had I just thrown away my no Os attempt as well?

I arrived at camp in a state of near despair, knowing that my fate was now out of my hands. I needed to talk to Greg and see where I now stood, but my fear of what he might say held me back. It took the entire day to pluck up the courage to call him, so scared I was to hear the bad news, and it was only in the late afternoon when I borrowed the satellite phone and called down to Mount Olympus.

"Do you remember slurring your words when Thunang turned you around?" he asked me.

I did not. I felt like I was in control at the time and it was unexpected to hear. I was mentally drained but I didn't think I was too badly affected by the altitude. My first climb above Camp III had basically been a disaster and here I was, making excuses. I was just desperate to be given a second chance, this time to show I could reach the South Col and reach it in a strong physical and mental condition. Maybe my pride had been hurt by the revelation that I had been less lucid than I remembered and I was now trying to restore my reputation.

"I wasn't, was I?" I protested, not remembering it happening. "I mean, if you say so I believe you," I continued, "but look, that whole day and night was just a mess. No sleep, too much exertion up the icefall, that went as badly as it could go. I can do it, I know I can."

"I really mean that," I continued. "There's a lot left in the tank, I just need another chance. Please."

I fully expected Greg to say no.

"Hey, so if you genuinely think you can do it then we should get you back up there for another try," he replied. And then a warning.

"That said, if this second attempt doesn't work out then we'll put on the Os. This is your last chance to prove you can make this step. Does that sound fair?" he asked.

Oh, that sounded more than fair!

For the rest of my life I will be eternally grateful to Greg for his faith in me that day. It would have been so, so easy for him to take the "safer" route and put me on oxygen right away. He could have taken exception to my initial unfounded criticism. He could have used my failure as evidence that a no Os climb was beyond my reach. Putting me back with the other classic group climbers would have simplified his life and saved him some sleep on those nights when I was the only climber going up the hill. And yet he chose to support me and my dream. As I look back on that moment I recognize the magnitude of his decision and what it really meant to me for the rest of my life. It meant the world.

That moment was the critical juncture of my expedition, and looking back perhaps this setback had been exactly what I needed. At some level I had forgotten what I was there to do. Obviously, at the intellectual level I still knew why I was on

Everest, but at a deeper level I had lost the drive and focus which had carried me all the way here in the first place. In the rarified bubble of Base Camp and ostensibly alone I'd become complacent. I'd spent so long on the ice that at a subconscious level my focus had drifted towards improving my comfort rather than summiting the mountain. I thought more about what was for dinner than about the climb. I'd been seduced and distracted, and in the process lost my ability to dig deep when it mattered. I'd gone soft.

Yet if circumstances on that rotation had been easier I would never have stopped to consider my mental state. Would my focus and drive have then let me down at a critical moment, a moment from which there could be no recovery? Like halfway through my summit bid? It's impossible to answer. All I do know is that from the second I hung up on the satellite phone I resolved that I had already made my last mistake. From now on neither discomfort nor difficulty would deter me from my prize. It was time to win.

It was also time to tell Thunang we would be heading back up the mountain. To say he was less than impressed would be an understatement. He implored me to give up on my no Os ascent, an option he had offered several times already. It was clear that we had different objectives for this expedition, and for me his perspective was scary. But not for the reasons you might think.

What scared me was me. I was terrified I would develop the habit of refusing his suggestion to put on oxygen, because what if one day he was 100% right? If I was delirious from a cerebral edema I might not be thinking correctly. I mean, I hadn't noticed that my words were slurring during that ill-fated Camp IV attempt so this possibility was more than just a hypothetical. Would I end up refusing the oxygen that could save me, all because of a conditioned response? It was frightening because I know myself and that's exactly the sort of thing I might do. I had to avoid this scenario at all costs, so I suggested to Thunang that we have a good chat about our new plan. The client eating tent was empty so I invited him in to have some tea. I poured us a couple of cups and we sat across from one another on the long picnic table covered with the red checkered plastic tablecloth.

It was a fascinating conversation; a rare insight into how the Sherpa think about guiding and their clients on Everest.

Every guided climb which Thunang had led in his career the overwhelming aim of each client was to stand on the summit. Not rocket science to grasp that, obviously. What *was* surprising was the totality with which this aim had been ingrained into his approach to the mountain and his job as a guide. It was a pure, singular focus on the result. Climbers on Everest just want to stand on the top and the methods to achieve that goal are irrelevant, period. Extra oxygen bottles at US$5,000 a time to make it easier? Why not! With 12 bottles of oxygen on summit day you can lower the effective height of the mountain down to nearly sea level - although in fairness you'll probably die from oxygen toxicity if you tried that. Hire some extra Sherpa to drag you up the last bit, a technique called short roping? Why not! At least one well-known professional climber used that form of assistance to reach the summit on a no Os attempt. Ultimately you can make the whole endeavor quite a bit easier and no-one will be any the wiser. And more to the point, they don't care even if they do. All they care about is that you SUMMITED!

It was Thunang's unshakable belief that the best outcome for both of us was to put me on the summit as easily and with as much certainty as possible. Climbing without Os was, in his mind, an unnecessary impediment which made us both worse off.

"Thunang, you might not believe me," I told him at one point, "but I would rather attempt the climb without oxygen and not reach the summit, than put on the oxygen and make it to the top."

His reaction was just so strange to see. Maybe it was the cultural differences but it was almost like he just didn't comprehend what I had just said; as though such a possibility just didn't compute. It was as though I had told him that my goal was to stop 50ft below the summit and then come back down. To him, the idea that a client would come here and purposefully jeopardize his or her summit chance was an anathema. I did my best to explain my motivations; that knowing what I could achieve was more important than "conquering" the mountain, that experiencing the death zone and the pure climb was the goal rather than summit photos, that doing this without Os would help me avoid the "what if" thoughts on my return to the real world. None of it seemed to make an impact. He nodded and agreed but I could tell nothing had changed in his approach or perspective.

In the end I gave up on trying to convince him and moved to Plan B. My sole aim in this discussion was to forestall a mistake on the upper mountain and Plan B was to align our goals by contract rather than shared philosophy. To do that I suggested a deal.

"OK so let's make a deal," I proposed. He nodded warily. "I will attempt the climb without supplemental oxygen. Please understand I'm going to try that, no matter what. However, I know it is hard and I might get in trouble. So here is the deal. If I *am* sick I will tell you. If you suggest using it at that moment I promise to put on the oxygen. That's my part of the bargain." Thunang nodded in agreement. Now for the tricky part.

"In return, you stop suggesting I use oxygen. The *only* time is if you think I have altitude sickness or the situation is getting dangerous. Other than that we just keep moving forward without it." This, I hoped, would keep us communicating. Otherwise I was incentivized to lie about my condition and pretend everything was fine.

Thunang thought this a reasonable compromise; he could just keep pushing me at the pace we needed to go and if I was jeopardizing our success he figured he could put me on the Os. From my perspective it reduced the number of "cry wolf" moments so I'd take his bottled oxygen suggestions seriously. Everyone's problem would be solved, or at least I hoped. Thunang agreed.

It was a timely discussion and a much needed one; our differing objectives were in danger of becoming a source of friction. Knowing I could count on my climbing partner was critical if I wanted to survive in this most deadly of games and Thunang saw the value of this also. I crossed my fingers, on both hands, and probably my toes as well, that this was going to work.

64
To the South Col

We took a rest day at Camp II before repeating the rotation for the South Col. With my new-found drive I was actually ready to leave camp on time for a change, proof that miracles are in fact possible.

A bitter wind was blowing down the Lhotse face that morning and with it came a torrent of sharp spindrift. We climbed into a glistening crystal stream which flowed as a stinging waterfall over the bergschrund and through the climbers below. It was awful, a most unpleasant period of climbing. Squinting at the ropes as my face was sandblasted by the ice I struggled to pull myself around the overhanging lip above the ladder as snow worked its way past my jacket collar. It was a taste of what bad conditions on the summit might bring and I was not keen to go through this endeavor more often than was unavoidable .

Oddly, conditions higher up on the face itself were a little more manageable. Like sand blowing over desert dunes, the flow of spindrift seemed constrained to a narrow layer just a foot or two above the surface and only our legs bore the worst of it. Beginning up the face I felt infinitely better than on the prior rotation and my resolve was absolute. It was time to push the pace and prove to the team and myself that I was stronger than we all perhaps imagined.

The additional traffic in the last couple of days had chipped some slightly better footholds into the ice, making the climbing a fraction easier, and combined with our pace we were soon at lower Camp III. It was still cold and windy so we dived inside the vestibule of some random unoccupied tent for some temporary protection. Looking past the nylon I could see the dark blue sky above the clear valley, interrupted only by the ice crystals which flashed in the sun as they zipped past. Brilliant rainbows of color darted in and out of existence as the air sparkled, and despite the harshness of where we were it was a tremendously pretty thing to watch.

There were barely any people on the face that morning and the climbing was uninterrupted. Even including our brief rest we reached Camp III in scarcely three hours and forty minutes. It had been a good performance and I still had plenty left in the tank for tomorrow. We called down as usual and the entire team seemed pleased. It gave me hope that our push to the South Col tomorrow might actually work.

Being the only people in Camp III we took a tent each, which compared to the last time was five star luxury! With little to do we lay back in our sleeping bags and rested.

Sunset that evening was stunning. Fluffy clouds peppered the horizon, their dark shadows obscuring small areas of bright pink and red which glowed behind. Later, as darkness fell, we could see the faint lights of Camp II glowing far below us in the valley. I was a demigod, looking down from the heavens at the mortals below. A demigod with a cup of hot spicy noodles, courtesy of Thunang. As we hunkered down and the temperature fell still further I reflected that this represented something of a pinnacle in my existence, especially as I was to now face another test set by this harshest of mountains. It was time to sleep without oxygen and this time I had nothing else to distract me from my rest. I was interested to see how I adapted to the effects of altitude. Could I sleep? It was time to find out.

Thunang actually had quite a job to get me awake the next morning. For 9 hours I slept like a baby. Emerging into consciousness I was greeted by a cup of hot water for my oatmeal, and as I slowly munched through it I thought about the climb ahead. This was it. Every step was now done carefully and meticulously, the polar opposite of my prior attempt. Fingers were kept warm, toes were kept warm, everything packed with precision. All systems were GO. Clambering out of my tent I stood on the face and looked up towards Camp IV with a face of iron determination. Today the mountain was mine and nothing was going to stop me.

With the better conditions there was already traffic already on the face moving past our camp. Teams were seeking to make up for time lost to yesterday's poor weather and there was a long line of Sherpa carrying loads up to the South Col. We had no choice but to join the procession and boy, was it a pain.

Proper fixed line climbing technique proscribes that you stay clipped to the rope at all times. To do this you have two points of contact; one is your ascender and the other is your so-called safety carabiner, which clips on the line ahead of the ascender and allows you to remain attached when you remove the ascender to pass an anchor. This technique also enables you to maintain contact with the rope as you move past another climber, by first moving the safety carabiner ahead of them and then the ascender. With only one climber to pass this is fairly efficient, but it becomes frustrating if there are several to pass in one go. Invariably one of them will start moving, stranding you in the middle of their little group. The Sherpa in particular aren't very tolerant of this, more in the sense that they just don't expect you to be clipping across everyone individually. They expect you to pass everyone at once. And that means completely detaching from the rope.

I always told myself I would avoid doing that exact thing, but faced with reality I found it to be impossible. You are tired, hypoxic, and the Sherpa "help" by moving your safety line for you, merely handing it person to person without clipping. Virtually all of the Sherpas take this laissez faire approach so you have to as well whether you want to or not. You can see the two thousand feet below you will fall if you - or they - screw up, and you know that many people have actually died making this exact mistake in this exact place. These moments were not fun. At one stage I remember passing five or six Sherpa who were irritatingly and unnecessarily *sitting* on the fixed line, forcing me to completely detach and traverse in front of them. Below was death. I don't mind taking risks, but unnecessary ones make me mad. Yet as I said, there is nothing I could do but tolerate yet another unnecessary human-induced risk factor to my climb.

Even with the traffic we made solid progress in good conditions. Soon we had passed over the first ice cliff where I had been turned around just a few days before, whereupon the route now turned to the left and began its long traverse up and across the Lhotse face to a feature called the Yellow Band. Named for the limestone layer which passes right through the entire mountain at this height, a very short, steep section of rock projects out of the ice and cannot be avoided. It was more awkward than I expected and took some time to climb because of the altitude. I was working hard and the knowledge that we would eventually reach the Geneva Spur, a larger and steeper rock band which separates the Lhotse Face from the South Col, drove me on. If I could conquer the Yellow Band and the Geneva Spur I would win. After discussions with Greg, Ang Jangbu and Funuru we had agreed that six or seven hours was the target for the day and I was desperate to make it. Breathing deeply I could feel my heart pounding as I moved, but at least I was moving. Unfortunately, so was the weather.

The upper level winds were starting to build as we approached the Geneva Spur and soon we faced rapidly deteriorating conditions. Cloud enveloped us, just wisps at first, but then thicker and more foreboding. It began to snow as the winds increased further and soon our climb had become a grind of epic proportions. Every single step was a cage fight against a ferocious headwind and even before we reached the base of the Spur it was evident that conditions at the South Col would be too dangerous. At the base of the Geneva Spur I knew we had reached the high point of today's effort. All the Sherpa were tying their loads to the fixed line to secure them and returning back down the mountain, and a general retreat was now in effect high on Everest. Thunang radioed camp to give them the news as I took a quick drink. It had taken me five and a quarter hours to reach an altitude of 7,850m, about 125m below the South Col. I felt I had done enough to prove my abilities even though I hadn't reached the col, and I hoped Greg would agree.

"James to Base Camp," I called on the radio, finger on the transmit button. It immediately sparked to life.

"Greg here. How's it going James?" he asked.

"Pretty good. We're right at the base of the Geneva Spur. The clouds are down on us and the weather is getting worse. All the Sherpa are turning back. This is as far as we can go, so we are planning on turning around," I responded.

"Understood. I completely agree, that's the right call," he replied. "You guys made good time up there, so I think you are back on track. Excellent work," he said. It was always nice to be congratulated by the boss for a job well done.

"Thanks Greg. I'll hand you over to Thunang, we'll start heading down in a minute," I said and gave the radio back.

Although disappointed we would not spend the night at 8,000m I had achieved what I set out to do, which was to restore the team's confidence in my abilities and get my attempt back on track. It was time to turn for home.

65
The Endless Wait

The worst of the weather fortunately remained above us and it was ultimately an uneventful descent. I had been on the upper mountain for 11 days now and I was looking forward to both some respite from the worst of the cold and a hot shower. Yes, a hot shower! Inside a special tent at Base Camp they had assembled a propane-fueled shower, routing the pipe to feed a normal shower head wired to the underside of the tent roof. A couple of flat stone slabs had been placed below the shower head for somewhere stable to stand and there was also a vestibule for undressing. Outside, at the top of the 30ft ice wall looming over the tent, was a large blue plastic barrel which provided the gravity-fed system with water. In the last few years all of the water for the shower was carried up to the barrel by hand, a back-breaking task for the Sherpa to make each 30 minute round trip to our camp's fresh water source. Such toil on my first expedition made taking a shower feel like I was a pharaoh of Egypt in a sort of slave-driving kind of way, so fortunately this season IMG had acquired a small solar powered water pump to relieve the Sherpa of this laborious task. We had to wait until 11am for the pipes to unfreeze and had to be careful not to inhale too many propane fumes, but otherwise the whole setup worked pretty well. With the air close to freezing there was always the awkward dash before and after showering to get undressed or dried, but standing under the hot water and soaping away 2 weeks of accumulated grime felt pretty magical.

The expedition had been going for almost 2 months now and nearly a third of our team had already returned home due to illness, injury or altitude-related issues. It is a slow attrition and devastating to say goodbye to people who were until recently an integral part of your life in the mountains. For some of them this was the end of the dream. Some might never again set foot on this mountain and I felt tremendous empathy and sadness for those forced to retreat. They'd pushed as hard as they could and their bodies finally said no. Still, as with my first expedition, I came to realize that we had all been on a journey that few people will ever embark on, and that gave me at least a little solace. I hoped in time they would recognize this too.

There seemed to be a level of relief for each of the team who were still in camp and still on target. It was well hidden, but I sensed we all knew we were the lucky ones. There was a sense that we should make this opportunity count. We each had our health, to a greater or lesser degree, and after the work of the prior few weeks there was a new optimism about things and a real drive to get this thing done. And yet there was also apprehension, a deep uncertainty which I believe we all felt at some level. How would we each feel and perform when we reached 8,000m, still an untested altitude for the majority of the climbers in our expedition. And what about the day itself? Would the weather hold? What would conditions be like? How many other teams would be on the mountain with us, and what about the idiot factor? How much would *that* dictate events? Of the thousand unanswerable questions there was one, however, which stood above all others.

When.

The Sherpa team had not yet fixed ropes all the way to the summit and until that happened we were certainly still stuck in base camp. However, once the Sherpa were successful another waiting period would begin, this one dependent on the weather. Or, more specifically, on the jet stream.

Responsible for the hurricane force winds at the summit, the jet stream is a nearly constant fixture on Everest's upper slopes for most of the climbing season. To even stand a chance those winds must drop, which means the jet stream needs to be redirected. Fortunately, this is exactly what happens when the monsoon pushes up through India. This creates a week or two of relative calm between the high winds of the jet stream and the snows of the monsoon. It is quite literally the calm before the storm. Every expedition must take that short window, which is why you may have seen pictures of Everest with climbers all waiting in a great long line near the summit. A whole year's worth of climbers have to summit in just a few mornings.

As I mentioned, our expedition employed two separate forecasters to help determine the best window, and it was a good job they did. That spring the jet stream had split, looping around and over the Himalayas to create a more complicated pattern than normal, which in turn impacted the climbing prognosis. Rather than the usual long window of lower winds, forecasters instead expected a series of shorter, less favorable opportunities, each lasting only a day and sometimes less. These could only be estimated perhaps five days ahead, which was a big problem as it takes five days to reach the summit from Base Camp. Once you start you are more or less committed, and you have just one summit bid, partly due to the finite supply of bottled oxygen and partly from the sheer physical toll of the attempt. In the thin air it is virtually impossible to recover in time for a second. This meant the timing of each attempt was absolutely critical, and it was now Greg's job to thread each of us through the eye of this moving and uncertain needle.

Each afternoon one of the guides would bring the printout of the latest forecast down from Mount Olympus to the eating tents so us climbers could take a look at our leisure. There were pages of wind diagrams, temperature forecasts, isobar maps and so on, but the estimated wind speed and temperature charts for the summit were the most scrutinized. Since arriving back in Base Camp both the wind and temperature had stayed frustratingly outside the safe zone for ascent. IMG has set a limit at 35 knots wind speed, about 40mph, as above this level the summit wind chill temperatures drop below -45°C / -50°F and climbing is especially dangerous. Brief windows would dip close to or even below that wind speed line before jumping back up, and paranoia grew as the day five summit wind forecast rose and fell with each new printout. Would today's forecast be *the* one, or had we already missed our best shot? Those monsoon storms would certainly arrive within the next three weeks and our expedition would then be over, summit attempt or not. There was no choice other than to put your faith in the guides, your belief in the forecasters, and to pray. I hoped the magic of Lama Geishi and the monks of the Puja had worked and the Buddhist prayer flags on my tent would do some good. At this stage I would take all the help I could get.

Tension in camp rose steadily with each passing day. Everyone had a return flight back home, and although it sounds ridiculous, this self-imposed cut-off became a greater source of anxiety than the dangers of the summit itself. You try not to think about it, but invariably you find your thoughts drifting towards the real world, just when your focus should be on the mountain. I had a feeling this might happen, and being fortunate with a flexible work schedule I had booked a return flight a week after the very last estimated summit window. That way, the worst outcome would be an early summit bid and a couple of extra weeks of vacation to unwind and recover. That didn't seem so bad. Others on the team had been less conservative, whether by choice, work constraints or mistake. Some had even booked a return flight barely halfway through the window period, which I thought was a risky move and one they were certainly now regretting. As you might expect, discussion of return dates and summit windows became the endless topic du jour.

"I think we should go, the forecast looks OK!" was heard at most mealtimes from at least one climber. Almost every day we'd also hear about another team who was attempting the summit although this was rarely accompanied by information regarding their success or failure. Successes are reported, failures are not, it seems, and most of the expeditions kept their cards close to their chests. Frankly, for the most part we would look at our weather forecasts and wonder whether these other expedition's forecasts were completely wrong, or ours were. There were some truly suicidal summit attempts according to our weather charts but still, "Team X are going up, why aren't we!" was a common mantra to be heard in camp at every breakfast, lunch and dinner.

I tried to keep my cool as in fairness I had been strangely fortunate with timing compared to some of the others. My initial failure to reach the South Col necessitated several additional days for the second attempt, delaying my return to Base Camp. By the time I returned everyone else had already been back for five or six days, and by now they had all been sitting and waiting for two weeks. That's a hell of a long time to live on a glacier with nothing to do but worry.

Around the 15th or 16th of May the forecast began to show some promise. A calmer window appeared to be opening up in the long-range estimates, and although much could change in the next few days the possibility was tantalizing. The winds were still blowing hard and it didn't look perfect, but for the first time there seemed to be an actual window below the magic 35 knot line. It was the first tangible glimmer of hope and chatter amongst the climbers grew to a fever pitch. Surely, *surely*, we would soon get a green light to make our bids.

On the evening of May 18, Greg appeared in the tent as he often did, armed as normal with the fresh printout and an update from the various goings on. Today, though, he seemed even more upbeat than normal. Today seemed different.

"Hey, so I'm sure some of you have seen the printout," he began, waving the papers. "I think it looks good for us, guys! It seems the better weather for the 22nd should hold. On the extended forecast there might also be another appearing on the 25th so we are in a good situation for all the groups." Smiles spread across faces. "Right, so folks in Classic Group 1 should get packed this evening, you are going up in the morning! 2am start."

This was it then, the starting gun for the main event. Not everyone was happy to be in the second, less certain wave, but at last we were going uphill. Greg came over after speaking and told me I would be climbing with this first wave. I was happy. I was going to grab my chances when and where they came.

66
A Rookie Move

I was already awake when the alarm on my phone went off at 2am, the nerves about the climb getting the best of my subconscious. I promptly turned on the little LED lamp I had wedged into the tent pocket above my head and began the slow process of dressing. I'd been careful to pack diligently the previous evening, not wanting to forget anything on this most important of mornings, so it wasn't long before I was eating a bit of toast with the others in the main tent. Still, my paranoia led me to recheck everything and I was yet again the last to leave camp. I preferred to bring up the rear, anyway.

With all the other climbers already gone I shook hands with Greg before walking with Thunang a short distance up the central hill in camp to pay our last respects at the shrine. Each time a team, client or Sherpa, headed up the mountain, juniper branches would be burnt on the shrine's stone plinth as an offering to Chomolungma, the Holy Mother, as Everest is called in Tibetan. In the darkness, with the smoke from the smoldering fronds dancing ephemerally through the light of my head torch I bent over the embers to inhale the fragrant incense. I tried in some way to connect with where I was, and to the place I was about to go. I felt this moment was somehow important and that I should acknowledge it. This marked the beginning of the end to my adventure, an adventure where the outcome was still so uncertain. In a few days' time I would be either an Everest summiteer or not, either healthy or injured. I might even be dead. I'm not one for superstition, but on this occasion I asked whoever might be listening for a little good fortune. As Thunang set off down the slope to the main path I took one last deep breath, closed my eyes for one final second and made one last silent wish. It was time to join him on a path towards destiny.

After 20 minutes walking through a dark and silent base camp we crossed the small meltwater river at the edge of the icefall. Well, at least it *used* to be small. Hopping across ice-covered boulders placed as makeshift stepping stones across the torrent was not a fun task by torchlight, but we made it safely, before heading into the maze of ice blades standing between us and crampon point. Each blade required a few steps of climbing, a straddle, and a hop down, and although we'd done them many times before they could occasionally be a little tricky without spikes. Still, we tackled each one without much drama or thought.

Near the end of this section I reached the top of one particularly nondescript blade and straddled across as I had so done many times before, placing a foot on what I thought was some gravel on the other side. Happy with that, I swung the other leg across in the darkness and stepped down. In the darkness I hadn't seen the danger and by then it was too late.

The gravel beneath that front boot was glazed with pure transparent ice and the slip was so sudden, so unexpected and so dramatic that I instinctively thrust out my arm down to brace myself. Another rookie mistake. Instantly I found myself sitting on the ice, holding my right wrist in my left hand.

You've been there, I'm sure. You know that feeling. That moment of dread. You don't want to move because you know, just *know*, that you've done something and you aren't ready to deal with the bad news quite yet. You are in shock and just stay motionless as your mind processes what has happened. I sat there on the ice in the dark, looking at my hand in the light of my head torch and tried to figure out what the pain really meant. I didn't know what I'd just done but it most definitely was not nothing.

Thunang turned around.

"James, are you OK?" he asked me as I sat there on the ground, wrist in hand.

"Yep, I'm fine," I replied as I deflected, stalling for time to overcome the shock and figure out what my response was going to be. "I slipped a little on the ice and banged my wrist."

"Ah you will be OK!" he replied. "Here," he said, turning back to me with his hands reaching out to take hold of my injured arm. With his fingers gripping the left and right of my palm he began vigorously wiggling and twisting my injured wrist, side to side, clockwise and counterclockwise. Now, I'm not a medical expert or anything, but grinding and shaking the joint is probably not the correct protocol in this situation. Protocol or not, it was absolute agony and a couple of seconds of this torture was plenty.

"No, no! OK, I'm better, you've made it better," I barked with a grimace through the pain, extracting my fingers from my hand as fast as I thought polite. "It just needs a bit of time."

"OK good. Let's go, we must be quick," Thunang replied and continued ahead.

Crampon point was only a few yards further ahead so I struggled to my feet. I needed a few moments to collect my thoughts. I didn't want to make a rash decision, such as returning to Base Camp, and I certainly didn't want anyone else turning me around either until I had made a proper self-assessment. I mean, perhaps the pain would start wearing off in a few minutes. I hoped I'd merely hyper-flexed the joint, and there was no need to have caused alarm and sow doubt if that was actually the case. I patiently waited for the pain to subside. It didn't.

Crampons on, I was soon heading into the icefall. Both my body and mind were now a mess.

What if I had just fractured my wrist, I thought? Surely my expedition would be over. It was my summit rotation and I hadn't even made it out of Base Camp! I just couldn't believe I'd come so far and worked so hard only for the prize to be ripped from my hands over something so unfathomably dumb. I'd hurt myself on the smallest, most innocuous, least dangerous piece of ice on the *entire* mountain. I was incredulous, just livid at myself for such a stupid mistake. It was a flood of emotion, all despair, anger and pain. As we walked through the start of the ice maze I found it impossible to focus until we reached the first rope.

The slope of this shallow section wasn't long or steep enough to need an ascender; just some balance, a bit of upper body strength and a working wrist. It was the first test. My expedition, perhaps the future direction of my life, hinged on this moment. The stakes could not have been higher.

I picked up the rope. It hurt. I pulled.

Hmmm. Actually my wrist didn't hurt as badly as I had expected from that pulling movement, just very painful rather than agonizing. Certainly not good, but not much worse than the pain of picking up the rope to begin with. I pulled a little harder. The pain grew linearly with the increasing tension but I could still apply a reasonable amount of force before it became bad. A glimmer of hope sparked through my mind.

"You know, James," I told myself, "If you swap your ascender to your left hand maybe you could do this...." It would be super awkward, it would be slower and it would hurt. But it might just be enough. And if it got better I could swap back.

Hell, there was only one way to find out.

67

Can The Crazy People Please Form A Line

Much deeper steps had now been kicked into the ice by the increased traffic, and while getting purchase on the ice was now easier the erosion had also stretched each step further apart. The physical exertion of heaving myself and heavy pack up each step negated any benefit from the traction. A small shuffle was always easier than a big lunge. Fortunately, though, it did mean I could rely more on my legs than my arms, which was exactly what I needed. It also slowed down the weakest climbers who struggled with each effort, and as you only climb as fast as the slowest person our entire team was soon reunited, compressed together behind a slower team ahead.

It is awful to be trapped in the icefall at night, held in place by the climber above and the climber below. In the cold and dark you feel your body temperature drop as your work rate falls. The extra time between each step gives you a chance to focus on the unpleasantness of the experience and the danger you are in, creating resentment towards the climber slowing everyone down. You feel as though their lack of speed and strength has ripped control of your climb away from your hands and placed it in theirs, and in this dangerous environment that was enough to make me quite angry. I reflected that this morning had not been one of my best.

In the pitch black we climbed at the end of a line of wavering flashlights until we crested a tricky step to stand on a small ledge at the edge of a crevasse. There must have been at least fifteen people waiting on the top of that ice vane, Sherpa and clients alike, pinned between the cliff we had just ascended and the deep crevasse on the other side. Three ladders had been lashed together as a bridge to cross it, followed immediately by four lashed vertically to ascend the next serac just a few yards beyond the bridge. It was intimidating, the bridge was wobbly and the drop was a big one, but this was the icefall and it certainly wasn't the worst bridge between here and the summit. Everyone on our team had been here at least twice before and we were prepared. Others, it seemed, were not.

At the front of the line of people was a woman trying to cross the bridge and it was clear to all that not only was this the first time she had been in the icefall, but that this was almost certainly the first ladder she had ever crossed. She seemed terrified. With a Sherpa in front and a Sherpa behind they coaxed her over, one agonizingly slow rung at a time.

Now, you might think I'm being unfair to judge her performance and her fear. It is not unfair. In case you think me harsh, I'm generally a very supportive, patient person when it comes to people learning new things. We are all beginners at the start. And just in case you think I was prejudiced, her struggles were nothing to do with her being female; I've seen extremely strong women climbers on Everest just crushing it. They are amazing. My judgment has everything to do with her lack of preparation. If you are too scared to cross a ladder you need to find that out before the middle of the icefall at 3am with a line of climbers behind you. It's like setting off in a racecar, hurling down the straight surrounded by other drivers, and then discovering at the first corner that you didn't bother learning about brakes.

Yes, crossing these ladders is not easy and it is certainly scary, but there is a time and place to learn that skill. Our team learned on a ladder set up in base camp a foot off the ground. We'd all done a daylight dry run in the icefall early in the season to experience that first real crossing at our own pace. The time for your first ladder experience is not during everyone's summit rotation with a large group of people waiting behind you on a narrow and unstable ice vane. A safe summit ascent seemed beyond her current level of ability and preparation and yet here she was, risking her life and all of ours.

As luck would have it my head torch died just as I reached the group on the vane. It was lucky because it gave me something to do while we waited rather than get angry. Unlike this climber I *was* prepared and dug out my backup torch from my pack while she shuffled forward. Eventually, she reached the other side of the bridge, sparking a great scramble of climbers behind, each almost sprinting across the bridge in a dash to overtake her before she began the vertical ladder. Everyone was desperate to avoid being stuck behind her on this next obstacle, which was harder than the bridge and frankly a lot scarier as you were essentially unprotected while climbing it. I was still fiddling with my torch as the climbers in front crossed the crevasse and Thunang nearly burst.

"We must go, quickly, *quickly!*" he insisted.

And for once I agreed.

68
There Must be a Free Buffet

Without any more delay we continued up the icefall and emerged into the Western Cwm as dawn reached the valley floor. From our vantage point we could see a line of people already moving over the wide crevasses on their way towards Camp II. It was busy! By this time I'd spent more than 20 days above Base Camp and had never seen anywhere near this many climbers on the mountain, not by a long stretch. It was jarring. I'd come to equate the upper mountain with peace and solitude, an ambiance which had now been shattered in the general commotion. The sheer number of people filled me with foreboding. Where had they all been? As with the climber in the icefall, for many it must surely have been their first time up here and I wondered how so many people could prepare so little.

IMG's Camp II was already bustling and I was allocated a tent with Cezar, a lovely guy from New York City. He was an older fellow who had moved from Puerto Rico to Manhattan some 40 years ago and never left. Small and wiry, with thick white hairs sprouting from his sparse beard, he had trained as hard as anyone for this climb; four hours a day by his reckoning. I had huge respect for his commitment. He was easy to get along with and an asset to the team, no doubt about it. I hoped he would summit.

We spent the day doing the usual Camp II things, which meant doing very little. Watching the Lhotse Face was more interesting than on previous rotations as far more people were making the climb. It seemed to me that other teams had a vastly different idea about the weather window than we did. The forecast before the 22nd the window looked rotten, with 50+mph winds expected above 8,000m for at least three days. If our forecast was right then all those people we currently watched as they moved up the hill were going to struggle mightily. Or die.

In any case, I had my own problems. My wrist had gone from bad to worse over the last few hours and had now swelled up quite badly. My afternoon was thus spent surreptitiously cooling it with chips of glacier ice in a Ziplock bag. I now couldn't lift anything with my right hand, forcing me to do even basic tasks with my left. I was convinced everyone would notice that I'd become incapable of pouring juice from the heavy kettle without spilling it, but no-one seemed to notice or care. It's amazing what people can miss when they aren't looking for it.

Still, I craved reassurance that I could still make it to the top yet I decided I had to keep it low-key for now. Was that a mistake? I wasn't sure if Greg and Ang Jangbu would let me continue if I told them, even if my climbing remained perfectly functional. If there was even a 1% chance they would send me back down then I couldn't risk it. If I found my ability to climb starting to deteriorate in any tangible way I would let them know; I had even less desire to risk my life than they did. Until then, however, I was going to stay quiet. I realize that this decision opens me up to criticism and rightly so, but I knew exactly what I could and couldn't do from a climbing capacity and I had tested my capabilities in the icefall. I was still in good enough shape and certain, absolutely certain, that I wasn't a liability to myself or anyone else on the team. If that changed I would come back down, but until then I was going to soldier on.

69
The Biggest Of Decisions

At 3am I wandered through Camp dressed in my down suit. I just couldn't stomach the usual breakfast of toast and eggs, and settled for just coffee and gnawing on a Clif Bar like a puppy on a bone. It sounds silly, but I found it hard to force down the western food up here, as good as it was. Maybe the Sherpa ate dal bhat for a reason!

Once again I started at the back of the group, once again. Thunang was worried at my lack of pace, once again. Held up by traffic and trying to conserve energy it was five hours before we walked into Camp III. With so many IMG climbers and so few tents up at Camp III, several of the Sherpa had to return to Camp II and would re-ascend once more the following morning. Thunang was one of the Sherpa chosen to go back down.

As the last man to arrive this time I was positioned by the tent door, which I preferred. The weather was calm and I had the best view in the house. I was assigned a tent with the same non-ill Jim as last time, and Brad. Brad was a pilot for Delta Airlines and a thoroughly wonderful fellow. In his younger days he'd flown a U2 spy plane for the US Air Force, which I found fascinating. The U2 remains the highest flying plane in history, and given its role in espionage few people ever flew one. Hanging out with someone who had come as close to space as it is possible to get without being an astronaut was a wonderful gift. You really do meet the most interesting people on Mount Everest!

As this was the summit bid, all of the Sherpa and climbers (except me) slept with their oxygen masks on, providing a low flow of oxygen to help them recover and remain strong. A couple of the clients had also used oxygen on climb up from Camp II, of which Brad was one. He'd been a little slow on his prior rotation and the guides felt that putting him on Os a little further down the hill would put him in a better position for his summit bid. His first ascent of the Lhotse Face had taken him ten hours; this one took five. Witness the awesome power of supplemental oxygen. Brad described it as "rocket fuel." Those who say it doesn't make much of a difference couldn't be more wrong; at extreme altitudes it's the greatest performance enhancing drug in existence.

Even with the oxygen cylinders and all our gear taking up precious space inside the tent I managed to sleep well, certainly far better than my night of trauma all those days ago. Waking with the dawn I heard the rustle of the guides stirring in the other tents long before our vestibule flap was unzipped and Dallas appeared.

"How is everyone this morning?" he chirped as we each shuffled stiffly into sitting positions. "Everyone feeling good?" he continued hopefully, eyeing the group. Then he turned to me.

"Hey so you might want to give Greg a call," he said and pulled the radio from his backpack. That was not a good sign. Turning on the power button he issued the "Camp III to Base Camp, over," call and waited for a response before passing me the handset.

"Hi Greg, how are things in Base Camp?" I asked.

"Good! Busy! I haven't slept as you guys are all up there, but we are in a decent position I think. Hey so I wanted to talk with you. We got the new weather forecast at 5am and we've been looking it over. The latest one shows a smaller window than we expected and the wind is going to pick up strength by late morning rather than late afternoon. With your later leaving time that's not good for you without the Os."

Disaster.

Climbers using bottled oxygen leave the South Col for the summit anywhere from between 8pm and midnight in a bid to beat the rush of people and the next afternoon's weather. Although very cold, the winds are generally lighter at night than during the day and at the summit these small differences can have a big impact on your chances. Bottled oxygen helps your metabolism keep you warm in those temperatures and you can more easily climb through the whole night if need be.

Without supplemental oxygen, though, such a long exposure to the deep cold is a much bigger risk. To mitigate it you must leave later in the night, usually between midnight and 2am, which means the climbing window must extend far later into the next day as your climbing time is also exacerbated by your slower climbing pace. I had estimated perhaps 14 hours from the South Col to the summit, putting me on the top by the middle of the afternoon. That's pretty late. To do this safely a big enough weather window was an absolute imperative, and without it I faced frostbite or death as likely outcomes rather than just possibilities. I now learned that this critical window was probably not going to be sufficient.

Plan B was to return down to Camp II and wait for the next potential window on May 25th. However, that forecast was still a long way out and the uncertainty was high. It could be better than the current opportunity but could also be worse, and worse meant no summit attempt at all.

"If you return to Camp II and go again that will be your last chance," warned Greg as we discussed the options. "There is no Plan C. If the 25th doesn't look good you will have to put on the Os."

I had an agonizing decision to make.

Should I continue up, having come so far, and hope that the window would in fact hold, or should I return to Camp II and wait. It was a high stakes decision made in minimal time with minimal information and in those seconds one main consequence stood out. Despite the risk, a small chance on the 25th still seemed preferable to zero chance on the 22nd. Some is better than none.

I asked Dallas what he thought.

"To be honest, I think you are right. If it was me I would head back down and go for the 25th."

I'd been fortunate enough to spend some time with Dallas during the expedition and knew he understood my perspective and goals about this expedition. I held him in extremely high regard and trusted his opinion. My mind was made up. I would descend to Camp II and risk the second window. I told Greg and gave the radio back to Dallas in a bit of shock.

At that very moment Thunang appeared in camp, having just reclimbed the Lhotse face. We told him I would shortly be heading back the way he had just come and to say he was unimpressed would be a monumental understatement. He suggested I could use oxygen and make *this* my window, which of course I wasn't having any of. He was breaking the deal! I felt terrible he'd climbed up just to escort me down but that was just the way it was. If I'd known a few hours before I would have halted his climb, but right now there was nothing I could do about it.

As the rest of the team adjusted their oxygen masks and joined the fixed lines towards the South Col, Thunang and I rappelled our way down the face. I desperately hoped I had made the right decision. My dream was coming right down to the wire and all I could do was cross my fingers. My destiny was once more in the hands of fate.

70
Up

There was a crowd of people making their way up from the lower camps that morning and as we descended past them I actually felt a little more confident in my decision. There was no way to know how many people would attempt the summit that night and I had no idea what a "normal" number looked like, but this seemed like an awful lot of climbers. I couldn't know what the next window would bring, but as with the weather, a small chance for a small crowd seemed better than the certainty of a big one. My thoughts wandered to our summit-bound team. I hoped things would go well.

The Sherpa in Camp II were surprised to see us, but we were soon treated to a hobbit style second breakfast in the Sherpa kitchen as there were no clients currently in camp. After a few hours the second wave of IMG clients began trickling in, fresh from Base Camp, and I began to repeat time, playing out an exact replica of the previous two days. The same rituals, same discussions, same nerves and anxieties, just different people. This time I shared a tent with Sharon, the gregarious Australian. Like Cezar she was another good tent buddy.

The next morning was the final recovery day, so we sat in the sunshine and watched the Lhotse Face while eagerly awaiting news from the summit. Luke, the main IMG guide for the second classic team, was with us at Camp II and was on the radio to Greg before breakfast. The report was excellent. The team had all left the South Col the previous evening as planned and everyone had already reached the summit! Everyone! Fantastic! I was ecstatic they had all made it. They were a really good group of humans who had worked hard and deserved their success.

Now came their real test; making it back to Camp II in one piece. More people die on the descent than on the climb up.

It was midday when the first summiteer stumbled into camp, and I mean stumbled. Knut was about as tired as I've ever seen a human being. We were all incredibly impressed and I'll admit I was shocked at his incredible performance. He had proven to be a fit and reliable climber during the previous rotations, but those solid efforts had given no indication that he would be the strongest climber on summit day. After all, one of the other clients was a professional mountain guide and there were two US special forces soldiers. Many of us were in our 30s and all had just been comprehensively bested by a 50 year old Norwegian. It was an awesome, awesome performance.

In between his sips of warm juice we gently asked him questions about the climb, and despite his fatigue Knut answered as best he could. He began to paint a vivid scene; a scene which would continue to develop over the next 8 hours as more members of the team returned from the summit. And it was not a pretty picture.

71
Down

From what he could tell, at least two other big teams had made their summit bid that night and at least one of those teams seemed woefully unprepared. On the way down Knut had seen several climbers who looked like they were starting to struggle. Still, as he had reached the summit so quickly he was already descending past these people before any major problems were evident. Others on our expedition were not so fortunate.

Several spoke of seeing a climber above them on the route literally dancing on the top of a cliff, over to the side of the route. This man had unclipped himself from the fixed line and his harness was down around his ankles, as though he had tried to take it off on purpose. They had called out to warn him, they had tried to reach him. But to no avail. He had stumbled, lost his footing and fell from the cliff to his death, right before their eyes. To see that tragedy from just yards away and be unable to stop it - well, that is something no one should have to experience. Just hearing about it left me numb.

Another spoke of a Sherpa falling ill from altitude sickness. The other Sherpa on his team came to his aid, with many helping him back to the South Col. While this act was honorable their departure stranded a group of clients high on the mountain. Abandoned, several soon got into trouble, with one in particular seemingly in real distress. He was passed by a member of our team who realized the situation and couldn't just leave him to his fate.

"He kept saying 'I just want to sleep'," Mo told us as he sat in the tent a short time after returning. "I kept trying to keep him awake, keep him moving down, but it was just so hard!" He was utterly distraught at the memory. "The guy just kept stopping and sitting down after every step. I had to keep lifting him to his feet."

Mo had given everything possible to get this man off the mountain, but at the South Col he'd been forced to leave him.

"I had to, it just wasn't possible to take him any further." Unable to physically move the stricken climber and himself now at the brink of utter exhaustion while still in the death zone, Mo had no choice but to continue his descent from the South Col. No-one could have done anything different, or done anything more.

"I have no idea what happened to him," he continued in a whisper, the emotions too strong and too raw to contain. "I couldn't do anything. Anything."

It was heartbreaking. This man, this hero, had given everything, risked everything, to bring an unknown climber down from the death zone and yet was finally forced to leave him or die himself. What became of this climber we never found out. What must that feel like? I cannot imagine. I have an immense amount of respect for Mo and for what he did. He should be immensely proud of himself as a human being.

These situations represent perhaps the most controversial aspects of commercial expeditions to Mount Everest. You stagger past an abandoned climber high on the mountain, alone and in distress. If you don't help they may die. Their life may rest on your action or inaction? Should you help? *Must* you help?

It is a complex question and so, so easy to say yes, of course you would. Yet most of those people who believe this is the only possible answer have probably not experienced a climb in those conditions. A rescue is hard and the consequences of helping can be severe. What if the delay uses up your remaining oxygen, or you choose to give them yours? What if their weight or lack of balance causes you both to slip or fall? What if you become so exhausted that you also become trapped on the mountain? What if you are already so hypoxic you can barely think, let alone make life-critical decisions for the both of you? What if they are injured and difficult to move, or at the brink of death? Many rescuers have died in these situations, both on Everest and elsewhere in the Himalaya. How do you then weigh the risks to your life against potentially saving theirs? It is far from simple.

Beyond the risk assessment there is also an ethical component. What if the climber had been grossly negligent and caused their own situation? Does that matter? And if it does, could you even know that was the case? We've already met a few people who should never have been on the mountain in the first place. Should you risk death because someone else cut a corner, whether by mistake or even knowingly?

Ultimately I don't have an answer for any of these questions. I'm certainly not trying to make the case that you shouldn't help. I seek only to shed some light on why "everyone for themselves" becomes a common outcome high on Everest. Those who choose that path are not bad people and we shouldn't judge those who make that choice. Until a person has truly been faced with such a situation I don't think they can know what they would actually do. Talking to a man who *had* faced this choice, his decision was to help, and trying to understand why was a deeply emotional experience. It made me genuinely scared of myself. The stakes were real and in a day or two I might be presented with an identical dilemma. What would I do? I like to believe I would help, but would I? I've twice rescued people in the mountains yet never in such critical circumstances or at such serious risk to myself. But frankly, I was terrified at what I might actually do.

72
Bitten by the Frost

As the sun dipped behind the mountains we heard news that several of our team still on the mountain were struggling to make it down. All had reached the South Col but exhaustion was now extracting a heavy toll. Two climbers had collapsed on the snow and a Sherpa team was dispatched from Camp II to potentially execute a rescue. Having such resources available is yet another reason why you should climb with a good guide company like IMG. It was a tense few hours until we heard the news: both had regained some strength and were continuing down under their own steam. Thank goodness! As we prepared for bed, 24 hours since those climbers began their ascent from the South Col, neither had yet arrived back at Camp II. It was nerve-wracking and disconcerting not to know the final outcome but they were in the best hands possible.

At 2am our wake up ritual was repeated. This time I forced down a bit of omelet along with the coffee and after double checking my gear I was heading to Camp III for the fifth and final time.

My focus was absolute. No mistakes, take it steady. The climb was unmemorable, exactly the way I wanted it to be. We arrived at Camp III in reasonable time, and with fewer climbers in this rotation I shared a tent with Thunang for the first time since Camp I.

Shortly before sunset we heard the loud whirr of helicopter blades rotating close by and felt the wind blast as it passed overhead. This was very unusual. The maximum working altitude of even these special helicopters was generally Camp II, and having seen a couple of frighteningly close misses on takeoff they were pushing the safety limits even there. I unzipped the tent fly and we looked up the face to see what was happening. A few hundred feet from our camp was a group of four or five climbers who were waving to the helicopter to send down the rescue line. The altitude was still a fraction too high, though, and after several attempts - including one which nearly blew our tents off the mountain - the helicopter was forced to retreat. With clouds drifting slowly up the valley and darkness rapidly approaching, the climbers now faced continuing their descent down the mountain on foot.

For the helicopter to even attempt such a dangerous rescue so late in the day indicated a serious situation, and it was. A group of Korean climbers had hugely overstretched themselves on their summit bid and one had become badly frostbitten, and I mean badly. I learned later from a Himalayan Rescue Association doctor that he subsequently lost both hands and both feet.

I look back on that moment as I write and I wonder about it. At the time it didn't even occur to me that I should climb over to see if I could help. Part of me wonders why not. Maybe it was my lack of medical training, that I would have been of little help even if I went. Maybe it was selfishness, with my thoughts immovably aimed towards my own summit attempt. Maybe because the Koreans themselves didn't ask us for help and continued down past our camp as though nothing was wrong. Or maybe it was our growing numbness to all the suffering in this place. Is that human nature? We've all walked past a homeless person at some point or another and not given them money. As on the mountain, after a while most of us just stop empathizing with the plight of others when we see hardship so often. In the rarified environment of Mount Everest those most basic behaviors are exposed; it is a place where you can glimpse the bare core of people. On display is the very best and the very worst that homo sapiens has to offer.

73
Earning My Geneva Spurs

Early the next morning I was back on the face and swiftly overtaken by the rest of our team. We hadn't even reached the Yellow Band and it was genuinely demoralizing to be passed by absolutely everyone. Still, I consoled myself that their oxygen masks were helping them. I hoped. This time the Yellow Band was much easier than before, but whether it was my improving acclimatization or an improving route which made the difference was hard to tell. I still had no real way to gauge my preparedness for what was about to come.

We traversed up and across the face to the base of the Geneva Spur much as we had done almost two weeks prior, before tackling the ascent of this section for the first time. The sense of achievement was quickly swallowed by the focus of exertion as I discovered the spur to be steeper and more challenging than it looked. The last part was a 70 degree cliff of soft snow, and climbing it was like trying to run up a sand dune with a heavy backpack. Lots of effort, little progress. At 7,900m / 26,000ft it was tough. Thunang had told me that once we topped this lip though, the last section was almost flat between there and the South Col, and after almost 6 hours of climbing without a break I was ready for a gentle walk and a chance to admire the scenery. At the top of the snow cliff I pulled myself over the edge, ready for some relief, but instead experienced something quite different.

It is a curious feeling to have your head nearly snapped off by the wind. Gale force winds tore across the South Col and out over the top of the Geneva spur, and as I crested the lip I was almost ripped off the mountain. We had been climbing up the protected leeward face in comparative calm and suddenly now faced the full brutality of the conditions. And brutal they were. At 7,950m / 26,100ft each step into the wind was a titanic effort, even as the rushing air sapped all warmth from my body. Goodness knows what the windchill was. Minus a lot. Step by tortuous step I literally dragged myself towards the flayed tents of Camp IV.

There were only a couple of tents still standing on the Col. With poles bent over and fabric violently snapping they threatened at any moment to lose their moorings and be cast into oblivion. Having that happen while I was in one was not a pleasant vision. One of the Sherpa emerged onto the Col, enduring the conditions as he beckoned us both into one of the standing tents. We opened the flap and clambered inside. The relief to be out of the wind was palpable, like coming home to a warm fire after a walk in cold dark rain. We had finally reached the South Col of Everest.

74
The Most Godforsaken Place on Earth

To see the South Col of Mount Everest with my own eyes had been a goal since I was young. In many ways the uniqueness of this place was more intriguing than the summit itself. This intrigue came from a single line of text in "Into thin air", a line which had stuck in my head through all the intervening years.

"If there is a more godforsaken place on Earth," Jon Krakauer wrote, "I hope never to see it."

The South Col is certainly unpleasant. Empty primus gas bottles and shredded strands of tent nylon are strewn across the rocky ground, glued down by a veneer of ice which coats the small black rocks scattered over this part of the plateau. It is barren, desolate and unloved. Unlovable. The environment is brutally harsh, a place of vicious winds and bitter cold. Human survival for extended periods of time is biologically impossible.

Yet in the moments when the wind dies down and the sun comes out, if wearing a down suit and not moving too much the conditions and altitude are tolerable. At those times it doesn't seem all that different from any other high mountain and the view does give some recompense for your pain. It looks bad, but not exactly god forsaken. So why his comment?

The reason is from something you can't see, hear or touch. You can't see it in pictures or videos. It is something which must be experienced. The South Col is a place of ultimate, unrelenting despair.

On your way up the mountain it is a place which harbors your worst doubts and greatest fears. Your insecurities bubble to the front of your mind. In a few short hours you will attempt to reach the summit itself. Are you ready? Will you make it? You know you are about to suffer some of the most difficult and exhausting moments of your life, and like the last few moments before plunging into icy water there is a sense and expectation of the pain to come. There is nothing to enjoy because enjoyment is the furthest thing from your mind.

On your way down it is no better. If you failed in your summit attempt you cross the Col feeling deep emotions of failure and disappointment. If you were successful you have been climbing for many hours and now the exhaustion really begins to bite. There is little time, no energy and little cause to feel the joy of triumph. As I mentioned, more people die on the way down and it is front of mind as you cross the ice. On the South Col you are acutely aware that help is impossibly far away; that if things go wrong no-one is realistically coming to save you. I imagine that descending to the bottom of the ocean in a submarine must feel somewhat similar. Sure, things are OK *for now*, but it is the anticipation of doom which must weigh on you. You can minimize the risks but not avoid them entirely. Even a minor problem can escalate towards death, and you know it. There is a visceral, continuous sense that on the South Col you balance at the absolute edge of existence, hoping not to fall.

Is it "godforsaken"? I'm not quite sure. Although even if it isn't, God certainly doesn't check in here all that often.

75
Killing Time and Brain Cells

With the wind absolutely howling outside I seriously doubted this summit attempt was going to happen. It had been hard enough to cross that flat traverse to reach the tent and I couldn't imagine trying to climb the Triangular Face in these conditions. With such wind the summit wind chill temperatures would be -60°C / -75°F and I would be frostbitten in minutes even if I avoided being blown off the mountain. The forecast said the wind would die away in the next few hours, but at this moment it was impossible to believe. It was time to cross my gloved fingers and hope.

Despite the precariousness of our situation there were some surreal moments to distract us as we waited in our sleeping bags. After an hour or two at the Col we heard the zip of our tent vestibule and the sound of the outer fly being drawn back with a deft heave. Moments later the inner zip was jerked upwards, deluging us with an icy blast from outside, before a climber came diving into our tent through the hole.

"Damian!" exclaimed Luke as the man wriggled towards us before wrestling the zip back closed. It was none other than Damian Benagas, one half of the most famous high altitude climbing brothers in the world. The Benagas Brothers were legendary.

"Hi Luke! How are you? How is everyone?" he replied, crawling a little further into the tent to shield us from the remnants of the incoming wind. "Hey, so I'm looking for a tent with four dead bodies in it. You don't happen to know where it is, do you?" he asked.

Never have I ever heard such a question and never will I again. Welcome to the South Col. Apparently several climbers had recently died on the upper mountain and had been placed in a tent somewhere nearby. Damian had the unenviable job of locating and identifying them.

"Urr, nope, don't know I'm afraid," replied Luke. "I guess they have to be here somewhere though, right?"

Indeed. There were only five or six tents still standing so I guessed it wouldn't take Damian long. A few more pleasantries were exchanged and Damian took his leave, unceremoniously worming his way back out the tent the way he had come in before disappearing into the maelstrom. We didn't see him again and I don't know if he found the bodies or not.

The second surreal moment on the South Col was more uplifting. With nothing else to do, Luke dug around in his pack and retrieved a small black case which contained a diminutive electronic device. A pulse oximeter! Looking like a big clothes peg, it is gently clipped onto your finger to measure the saturation level of oxygen in your blood. Guides often carry them on high altitude expeditions as they can be a useful tool when diagnosing a potential altitude-related health issue. While not an exact science, an excessively low number, say below 50%, was usually an indication that a climber was in serious danger. For context, at sea level anything below 92% means a trip to the emergency room.

Climbers occasionally tested their blood saturation levels out of curiosity, as the amount of oxygen you can absorb into your blood is an indicator of your acclimatization. Here on the South Col, Luke was also curious, not so much for his acclimatization but about how much difference his oxygen mask was making. It was fascinating to watch.

The impact was rapid and dramatic. Starting with a blood oxygen saturation in the 80% range he'd take off his mask and you could literally watch the number on the small screen fall in real time as his body struggled to absorb as much oxygen from the thin natural air. Replace the mask and it would rise back up.

"Ooo Ooo, can I try?" I asked. I was deeply curious about my level without supplemental oxygen at this altitude.

"Nope!"

I think he was genuinely worried about what my number was going to show. A figure below 50% was realistic and for a responsible guide what would that mean? That would be in the danger zone and put him in a difficult position. As I said I felt fine, from his perspective no news was good news.

"Oh go on!" I pleaded. "We both know it's going to be super low. We can just ignore the answer, I promise. I feel fine, I'm sure it will be OK." This was a discussion I really wanted to win and with no way of avoiding my pestering as we were literally trapped next to each other in a tent he eventually relented.

"OK. Just once though," he told me before clipping the little device onto my finger. I turned it on and relaxed, breathing normally. The device flashed for a bit until a number appeared onto the screen.

"What?" I yelped, looking up at Luke before looking back down at the bright blue number on the tiny screen. "70%? How is that even possible?" Luke had the same surprised look on his face. Here I was, at the South Col without breathing supplemental oxygen, showing a blood saturation level that was reasonable for a climber at Base Camp. Neither of us could really believe it. A few deep breaths and the number climbed a couple of points higher.

It was a revelation which made me smile. Was I really one of the lucky few who could tolerate these altitudes at some level? Could I actually do this? What I was attempting no longer seemed impossible, just very, very hard, and that was something I could deal with.

With the evening looming near it was time for some food. I had a bar of brittle chocolate followed blessedly by some hot Rahman noodles which the Sherpa had braved the elements to make for me. Along with the soup they brought warm water to fill our water bottles, ready for the climb to come. I carefully added some energy powder into the two one-liter insulated metal vacuum flasks which I would take with me to the summit. Plastic Nalgene bottles, even in an insulated sleeve, would quickly freeze in the conditions above us; a sage piece of advice I'd received from my friend Thom who'd discovered this the hard way during his ascent one year before.

Even with bottled oxygen, sleeping at the South Col is difficult. Without it, doubly so. I suppose I was in the mood to be unconventional as I slept so soundly that I didn't even hear Luke get up to organize his group for their departure. It was midnight when Thunang shook me awake.

"It is time."

76
The Face of Darkness

I immediately noticed two things. First, it was pitch black outside, which of course was expected. Second, it was now eerily quiet, which was not. The worst of the wind had died away and only an occasional gust now tugged at the tent fabric. Otherwise there was absolute silence. The forecast had been correct.

It was showtime.

Back in my BASE jumping days, the thrill of leaving the cliff edge was surpassed only by the moment you felt the parachute open above you. It was the moment you knew that you weren't going to die, at least not yet. The only equivalent emotional intensity was the anxiety I felt when packing the parachute before the jump. With no backup chute, even a small mistake meant certain death, so my paranoia during the process was twelve out of ten.

At the South Col I now felt a similar level of anxiety and pressure to get things right. It was critical, *absolutely critical,* that I kept my hands and feet warm at all times. In those deep temperatures even a few seconds of exposure will cause the blood vessels in your extremities to close, and once they do they won't reopen until the tissue warms. Unfortunately, the tissue can't rewarm itself because the blood flow is off, trapping you in a catch-22 situation that ends with frostbite. If you get cold hands or feet before leaving the tent they will never rewarm and the thickness of your boots and gloves won't matter. They can't save you. Sadly, keeping your hands and feet warm when it is -30°C / -20°F is not so simple when you have lots of things to do.

Eat a snack. Prepare my goggles and sunglasses. Put on fluffy fresh socks. Place everything into its predetermined pocket of my down suit. Reassemble the liners inside my climbing boots. Put my boots on while still inside my sleeping bag. Put on my harness. Tighten the buckles correctly. Take a drink of water to hydrate. Put on my balaclava. And so on. To perform each task I'd take my hands from within my sleeping bag and get to work. After a few seconds of activity they were thrust back under my armpits to rewarm. With so much stopping and starting my preparations took a while, but I knew from my aborted climb above Camp II that sacrificing warm fingers was a price not worth paying.

I was now almost ready. "Let's go!" implored Thunang once more, but I had one last task to complete. The physical side was in order but my mind was not. Like a sprinter in the blocks I needed a moment to calm myself and focus on the mission ahead. My determination needed to be primed, the fuse had to be lit. Fishing out my phone I navigated the menu with nose touches and found the playlist made for just such a moment. It was a strangely personal moment and I won't share the song here. Just know that as it played in the silence and I listened to the words, my mind focused and my determination stirred.

Now I was ready.

Phone pocketed, I sat up and crawled unceremoniously through the tent flap and out onto the South Col. It was like diving into cool water, a psychological shock as much as physical as I left our artificial cocoon to face Mount Everest at night.

It seemed incredibly dark on the col. I don't remember seeing any stars; perhaps there were high level clouds, perhaps the glare of my torch beam made them invisible. Perhaps I was just too focused to really take a good look around. The breeze quickly greeted me, and although not too strong I could feel it deepen the frigid temperatures still further. Pleasant it was not. There were no other people on the South Col at all now, just myself, Thunang and Philen, a Sherpa on our team who was carrying an emergency oxygen bottle for me should the worst come to pass. The isolation felt absolute, and after the constant crowds of the last few days it was briefly unnerving for our little team to be alone on the mountain. It was a sense of foreboding; that moment in a horror movie when all the other people suddenly disappear.

With crampons firmly attached we set off, crossing the shallow slope of an ice sheet in the center of the Col until we reached the base of the Triangular Face. I could now see the start of the fixed rope; a thin red line as the only splash of color amongst the white snow and gray rock. To the right and left, dark and impenetrable voids of purest black.

To my surprise I was now overheating. I'd put on an extra down layer and it was proving somewhat too effective. Much to Thunang's consternation I had to stop and take off this layer, which he tied to the rope for us to collect on the way back down. I remember being worried that someone might steal it! Not knowing the conditions on the upper mountain, surrendering a layer was a big risk, but I also knew that climbing while overheating could be equally risky. You sweat, you die, as my old friend Simon used to tell me. His advice was coming in very handy as I tried to avoid a mistake.

So then, of course, I made a big one. My goggles had begun to fog a little so I lifted them from my head in a foolish attempt to clear the haze. As I did so I carelessly breathed out right inside them, instantly creating a layer of hard frost on the inner lens which was impossible to remove without making things worse. I had no alternative but to put them back on as they were. Visibility, which had been low in the weak torch light, fell to near zero. I could now only see the snow directly under my feet and a few yards of the rope ascending steeply above. It was diabolical.

We were now climbing above 8,000m / 26,250ft and each step was a devastating struggle of will. It is hard to put into words just how difficult it was to keep moving. Imagine sprinting up several flights of stairs. You know that moment at the top, when you are bent over and gasping for air, your body and mind temporarily overcome with the effort? Near the summit of Everest, every single step feels like that. Unlike sprinting up stairs, though, there is hardly a rest before doing it again. Three, four, maybe five breaths and then step. Imagine doing this all night, in the coldest depths of winter with wolves snapping at your heels. If you slow down, you fail. If you stop, you die. If you continue, you suffer.

And people say summiting Everest is easy.

Still, despite the challenge I knew that every step was one closer to the summit. As my favorite Lake Tahoe T-shirt reads, "Pain is temporary, glory is forever." I wasn't going to let something as temporary as pain stop me now.

77
Death At Dawn

After an eternity I became dimly aware that a world existed beyond the darkness. Almost imperceptible at first, merely shades of black on black, I began to make out the serrated silhouette of the horizon. It was the coming of the dawn. My hands and feet were cold, but not dangerously so, and the rays of sun would soon bring some relief from my torment. I had triumphed against the night. The ambient light eventually became bright enough to momentarily stop and swap my goggles for sunglasses, and suddenly I could see! A deep crimson glow reflected from the slope of Lhotse rising steeply behind me on the other side of the South Col and for the first time I could see Makalu, the world's fifth highest mountain, which had previously been obscured behind the Lhotse face. I found a new strength in those moments and a new motivation. I finally felt like I was getting somewhere.

We soon approached the top of a thin gully where the route then passed over a small ledge of snow. I climbed onto this tiny plateau and saw, to my great surprise, what I initially thought was a shop mannequin, lying on its back beside the anchor point. Its rigid form had been dressed in a yellow down suit and a pair of Millet high altitude boots, while the elbows had been positioned by its sides. Both hands were raised to head level, palms outwards, as if a shield against some oncoming horror. There were no gloves on the fingers; contorted, twisted fingers covered with a thin white layer of translucent frost. The head was bare, with no head torch or balaclava, and the short, jet black hair was ruffled. Beneath, a face stared wide eyed and unmoving into the distance.

Even in my hypoxic state it didn't take long to realize this wasn't a shop mannequin. It was a man, frozen to death on the snow.

That poor soul must have died mere hours before we reached him. I only glanced upon his face for just the briefest of instants but the image I saw will be etched in my mind for the rest of my days. It was the look of fear in his face and the terror in his eyes as he stared into the abyss, knowing he would soon die, and die alone. I can scarcely imagine the emotions that he must have felt in his final moments. It is a crass and insufficient comparison, but the impression was as though he had stood before a zombie hoard, hands up to protect himself as they overwhelmed him. Fear was quite literally frozen onto his face.

It is difficult to write about this experience, not just because of the gravity of what I experienced but also of my reaction. It was strange. On the one hand it was profoundly disturbing to see someone who had just died with such desperation and anguish. I could barely look at him. There was no sense of morbid fascination but rather only sadness. Yet on the other hand I felt somehow disassociated from the whole event. You know you might see a body on the climb but I expected a more visceral reaction, perhaps. It was almost as though my brain subconsciously decided that, for the moment at least, it wasn't real and in some way turned him back into the mannequin I first thought him to be. In those moments my empathy dial had been turned right the way down, that I had become more psychopath than human being. Perhaps it was the hypoxia, or exhaustion, or perhaps it was from being so utterly focused on my objective, but there was no introspection, no reevaluation of what this meant.

In any case there was nothing I could do for him. Later I would grieve, but for now my thoughts must return to the task ahead.

The climber was still attached to the fixed line, so I clipped my ascender past his body, and with a deep breath I continued to climb.

78
All or Nothing

Beyond the gully, the snow slope widened a little as the route continued for another 100m / 300ft or so until it finally intersected with the corner of the ridge above. At this junction sits a tiny, exposed plateau known as the Balcony; an apt name given its spectacular views and precarious location. Reaching the Balcony is the first milestone of every summit bid on the main Nepalese route up Mount Everest, and it's the first place with enough flat-ish space to have a somewhat safe rest. I sat down beside a couple of colorfully decorated oxygen cylinders, their bright images no doubt serving to identify them for a specific guide company. For climbers on oxygen it is common to switch your current bottle for a fresh full cylinder at the Balcony, giving you plenty of oxygen for the summit climb and your return to this point, upon which you switch back to the first cylinder for the remainder of your descent. This strategy reduces the chance of running out of oxygen near the summit, which is obviously the most important situation to avoid.

Sitting on the snow at the edge of the Balcony I looked across a cloudless dawn sky all the way to the Nepalese lowlands and India beyond. Waves upon waves of mountains, each tinted a progressively darker shade of blue by the distance, extended across the Himalaya as far as the eye could see. It is strange to say, but the Balcony was the first moment on Everest that I could truly appreciate just how high up we were. We were now at 8,400m / 27,600ft and only one other mountain peak in the world was higher than where we now sat. Thousands of feet below I could see the glaciers which carved away both sides of the Everest massif, and I looked down on peaks which had previously towered high above. No doubt about it, the Balcony was a special place indeed.

I was pretty tired, and grateful for a few minutes rest. We both fished our water bottles from our pockets to have a quick drink, and once done Thunang radioed down to Base Camp.

"Hey guys, how are you doing?" came Greg's voice, clear despite the swirling breeze.

"Yeah, pretty good," I replied, leaning towards Thunang to speak into the handset which was still attached to his backpack strap. "It's tough going and I'm pretty tired, but otherwise I'm feeling OK. Hands and feet are warm so that's good!"

"Great, great, that's good to hear," Greg responded, but the expected satisfaction in his voice was absent. I was expecting a more optimistic reply. "Hey, so you guys took 5 hours 15 to make it up there," he continued, "That's not so good."

Ahh.

"Also, we got the latest weather forecast, and it looks like the window is going to be smaller than we thought," he said with a more serious and somber tone. "You guys aren't going fast enough to make it."

Double-ahh.

In Base Camp we had a discussion about my targets for summit day. The team was more aggressive than my 14 hour estimate, more related to the size of the available window rather than my abilities, I thought. In short, I was always going to be against the clock, hemmed in between the risks of a too-early start and the afternoon weather. I could see why Thunang wanted to get started early and in hindsight I should have taken his advice. My target for the Triangular Face had been four hours. Slower than that I would struggle to beat the weather. I knew four hours was ambitious, but I thought I could outperform expectations. Apparently I could not. I was a good distance behind schedule and if I couldn't speed up I would certainly be turned around before reaching the summit or be forced to use oxygen. Both were unpalatable choices.

"So maybe you want to put the oxygen on?" Greg suggested.

As usual that question made me mad. I was so close, *too* close, to give up without giving it everything I had. I took a mental inventory. Had I already given it everything? I didn't think so. Part of me knew that I was still pacing myself, knowing I wasn't yet half way up and still needing to come back down. Part of me knew that despite the pain I had some untapped capacity for suffering. If I turned around now or put on Os I would always wonder; did I *really* need to? It was a question that would consume my soul.

I knew what I had to do. When the going gets tough, the tough get going. For me it was time to get tough *and* get going.

"Greg, I can make it," I told him. "I really can. I was probably pacing myself up the triangular face a bit too much. I feel OK so I want to keep pushing on without the Os and see if I can climb faster."

"OK, well if you think you can do it. But you have to get a move on. If you can't, we'll have to put on the Os or turn you around."

"Yep, understood," I replied, "I'll keep pushing and we'll see where we get to. Thanks!"

And with that I stood up and looked at the first section of the Southeast Ridge. It didn't seem so bad.

79
The Color Of Emotion

The Southeast Ridge leads up from the Balcony to the South Summit, a small false summit some 300-400 vertical feet below the true summit of Everest. The ridge begins with a somewhat moderate incline before steepening for the remainder of the ascent. A third of the way up, rocky outcrops begin to interrupt the snow and must be scrambled over. Ordinarily not so tough, but at this altitude it is a different ball game. Once at the South Summit there are still two significant obstacles to tackle, the Cornice Ridge and the Hillary Step, but to reach the South Summit is to break the back of the climb. If I could make it there and the conditions were still fair, I knew I should, *should*, reach the top.

It was head down, pedal to the metal time. The only way to speed up was to take less rest between steps, so instead of four or five recovery breaths I forced myself down to a consistent three. The strain was diabolical. It was the absolute limit of what my body could tolerate, and my mind reacted in some truly strange ways.

I began to hallucinate.

When I say hallucinate, it was different from what you might think. I wasn't physically seeing solid objects which weren't there or frolicking with unicorns. Instead, it was more like a form of augmented reality. My mind's eye overlaid an image on what I was seeing as a visual representation of what I was thinking, almost like a head's up display of my inner workings. And it was quite amazingly weird.

A set of blue horizontal bars, stacked on top of each other like the equalizer on an old Hi-Fi display, somehow hovered in front of me, slightly above and to the left. Nothing *physical* to see when I looked directly in that direction but it was there in my peripheral vision nonetheless. Each time I took a step these bars would light up, indicating how close I was to my hypoxia limit perhaps. The more hypoxic I was the higher they would go, just like on that hi-fi display. Each recovery breath allowed the lights to recede back down. It was strange.

However, what was even stranger was that each breath now created a distinct emotion of the color "blue" and a sensation of "left".

It is difficult to describe how you can *feel* "left", but it was nevertheless unmistakable. It was almost as though I was using only my left lung to breathe even though I was certainly using both. The closest analogy to normal life I can think of is laying on my bed after too many drinks and staring up at the ceiling as it slowly spins. You have the sensation of "spinning" yet nothing is moving. "Left" was a similar extrapolation and fortunately far less nauseating. Feeling the color blue was equally weird and equally difficult to describe. It was like the color blue really was an emotion and I could feel "blue" in the same way we can feel "happy" or "sad". It was a sensation of being bathed in blue light, both inside and out. I know this makes little sense, but it is the best explanation I can come up with.

Taken together, these hallucinations were singularly bizarre.

Even weirder still, becoming more hypoxic without actively stepping, such as bending down to re-clip past an anchor, resulted in a similar but different vision. These actions slightly constricted how much air I could get in my lungs and that small change was enough to push me beyond the limit. Violent and involuntary hyperventilation often followed; a terrible, desperate need for air as I suffocated. Similar to the blue bars, another set of Hi-Fi bars then appeared in my field of vision, except this time they were yellow and hovered to the right. I now felt a strong sense of "right" rather than "left", and the emotion "yellow" rather than "blue".

I reached the stage where I couldn't unclip and then re-clip the rope in one go without the bars maxing out and the edges of my sight starting to gray from tunnel vision as I began to pass out. To avoid this, I had to clip in two stages; unclip, stand up and hyperventilate, then bend down to re-clip. On each part the yellow bars would still shoot up and I would need a second or two for them to come back down. I was operating at the very edge of consciousness.

As I climbed in these conditions I had one final hallucination. Higher and further to the left than the blue bars hovered the head of a man. I don't remember much about the face, only that this man had a medium length white beard. Think "ye olde fisherman" type beard rather than Santa Claus. A weaker presence than the bars, this head was silent and vanished if I tried to focus on it. It was like an ephemeral guardian, some kind of grizzled angel watching over me as I climbed, able to see but unable to make contact from the other side. Interestingly, when I told Thom about it he exclaimed "I've got a white beard! Dude, that was me!" And you know what? He might well have been right.

Despite the pain, worry, fear and hallucinations, I admit I thought this whole experience was kind of awesome. It was epic-level suffering yet at the same time I was totally captivated by the strangeness of it all. I wanted to climb without supplemental oxygen in part to experience the death zone for what it actually was, and boy oh boy, was it giving me the works. Even the hallucinations were all part of it; a unique experience in a unique place. Despite the pain and the pressure that strangely made me very happy indeed.

80
The Best of Times, The Worst of Times

Hallucinating wasn't my only unique and special experience on Everest that day. A short distance up the Southeast Ridge I remember one of the rare occasions when I briefly stopped to look around. Beyond the precipitous drop just a few feet to my left I looked westwards across the Himalaya and saw a sight I shall not soon forget. Across the indigo sky, blues blended into pastel yellows and deep reds as bright orange hues foretold the coming rays of sun. It was glorious. And then there, in the center, pushing through all these colors, appeared a vast black triangle. As though standing at its base I looked out as the apex extended beyond infinity at the farthest horizon. It was the shadow of Mount Everest itself.

I remember seeing a similar photo in a book when I was just a young boy, and remember the wonder I felt as I looked at this spectacle of nature. Such power, such isolation, such beauty! It captured my imagination more than any other picture of Mount Everest, before or since. Still, I never expected I would have the opportunity to see it for myself. As that boy, Mount Everest was an impossible place, and even when in Base Camp all these years later I thought the chance would pass me by. I figured I would be too low on the mountain to see it or be foiled by the weather, such is my usual luck with mountain summits. It was truly a shock to turn around and see this dream realized before my eyes. With the time pressure of my climb I stopped only for a few seconds to admire the sight and I didn't even take a photo. Yet those seconds and that view are seared into my memory now, so vivid and joyous was the experience. Even now I can feel my eyes moisten up a little when I think about it. It was a moment which will last a lifetime; a single moment worth the cost, suffering and risk of both my Everest expeditions in their entirety.

Nothing good lasts, though, and I had barely recovered my breath before resuming the task at hand. We were approaching the first of the rocky outcrops along the ridge. It took a bit of adjustment to use my crampons on rock, given we'd barely stood on anything other than ice for a long time, but even this climbing was more pleasant than the dark torment of the triangular face. At least I could see where I was going!

The terrain of each outcrop proved to be a harsh master, though, and my pace slowed. A little below the base of the final outcrop we met Luke and a small group of the IMG climbers on their way down. They were the first and only climbers we had encountered since leaving camp over seven hours ago.

"James! How are you?" Luke asked as we met.

"Doing OK," was about all I could muster as a response between heavy breaths. It took a few more seconds to get enough air in my lungs to be able to talk. "How did everyone do?"

"Everyone made it, the whole team! They are all heading down, so far no problems."

"Fantastic!" I replied. That was music to my ears and I was genuinely happy for everyone. So far so good.

"Hey, let's radio Base Camp," advised Luke. "We can let them know where you are and give them an update."

Luke began transmitting on the radio, but I was a little far away and the wind was swirling too much to hear the conversation. After a minute or two Luke put down the radio and turned back to me, standing slightly above him on the slope.

"Hey, so you're not going to like this," Luke began as he relayed the message from Greg. "Greg says that the weather forecast just worsened again and you don't have much time. You'll have to turn around in the next two hours or so."

I nearly lost my cool. Well, in fact I did lose it. The happiness I'd felt a few moments before was quenched in a torrent of visceral, primordial anger. I can't remember ever being so angry in my whole life. Not at the team, even though they might have thought otherwise at the time. I knew the weather wasn't their fault and they did the best possible job with the forecast at hand. I was angry at fate. For nearly eight hours I had figuratively and literally destroyed my body, quite possibly permanently, to reach this point only to hear that it would likely all be for zero. To get so close after such a gargantuan effort, only for the summit to be snatched away; well I couldn't comprehend it. As with a rollercoaster, the higher you go the further and faster you fall. And this was vertical with my feet trapped in concrete.

Thunang suggested I put on the oxygen. A reasonable suggestion, of course, but in my emotional state that was the wrong thing to say. I don't remember my exact words, but Luke later told me that it was a lengthy reply that mostly consisted of swear words. I ashamedly don't doubt it. In my mind there was only one solution at this point, at least that I was willing to consider: go for broke. I felt knackered but otherwise physically OK; there might be a tiny bit extra if I held nothing back and just sprinted for the top. I knew the unacceptable risks of climbing into bad conditions and knew they were not worth taking, but I also knew that I might just be able to make this even narrower window without using the oxygen. If it still wasn't enough then I would put on the Os and make a supercharged dash for the top.

Damn it, I was going to try.

"Fine, *fine!*" I eventually declared in resigned defiance. "Right, well then let's get going. Let's go, *let's go!* We can make a turnaround decision on the South Summit."

Without waiting for a reply, confirmation or even to say goodbye to Luke I turned up the mountain and pushed on. It might have been a little rude, but with time pressure at 8,700m / 28,500ft civility kind of goes out the window. From now on, rest breaths were for wimps. After about five steps I started to pass out from hypoxia; I guess at least a few rest breaths were still needed, wimp or not. Yet there did seem to be one final extra half-gear available. Until I had pushed at my absolute limit or the weather intervened I wasn't going to quit.

81
For There Were No More Worlds To Conquer

I attacked the last awkward band of rock below the South Summit, stumbling a little as my coordination suffered from the pace and self-induced hypoxia. But I kept pushing on. Every single breath became scientific, systematic and consciously exact. Breathe in as deeply I could, first pushing down the diaphragm, then expanding the lower lungs, then the upper chest, and finally expanding my back at the shoulder blades to fill the absolute last bit of available lung volume. Each exhale reversed the process, with abs contracted, diaphragm compressed and throat tightened to squeeze out every last cubic inch of air. I followed this breathing pattern with perhaps more attention that I was applying to anything else as the fight became internal rather than external.

Beyond the rock outcrop we ascended a short, steep ice cliff which gave way to a snow-covered flat area on the top of a small mound. Looking at the drop on all sides I felt a wave of joy. I had reached the South Summit at last. In front I could see the path down towards Hillary step and the beginning of the final cornice still high above, which continued to obscure the top of the mountain. I was suffering terribly but success was now within my grasp.

Then suddenly there were people! It was the remainder of the IMG team coming down from the summit. With their faces obscured by balaclavas and oxygen masks, the muffled congratulations of our mutual progress were hard to make out, especially in my hypoxic slow mental state. I recognized Phillipe, though, as he took an extra moment to stop and properly say hello. Very kind! I also recognized Sharon from her distinctive blue and yellow Marmot down suit which was a source of light-hearted amusement at Camp II as it made her look like a Minion. Dallas had the same suit, though, so it is certainly not a criticism. We gave each other a cursory wave as we passed. She doesn't remember it at all and I don't blame her. Things get fuzzy up there for all of us.

At the South Summit Thunang once more radioed Base Camp to give them an update on our progress. This time the conversation was different.

"That's awesome, James, fantastic work!" came Greg's reply when Thunang told him we were at the South Summit. "You are way ahead of our estimate. Great work!"

Boy, did he sound happy, a total U-turn from our last conversation. I guess our update with Luke hadn't given him a sense of exactly where we were on the Southeast Ridge and this was the first time since the Balcony that the team at Base Camp accurately knew where we were. Five hours had been the original target for this section and I'd smashed it, climbing from the Balcony in just three. After my slow progress on the triangular face I imagine they were surprised I had made it at all.

It was a small victory to treasure. The greater prize was the time I had managed to recover. I was now even ahead of the original schedule and we were just about back inside the weather window. With luck there should be enough time to summit and begin our descent before conditions deteriorated too much. We were finally winning.

From the South Summit the route descends 20 or 30 feet down to the penultimate obstacle on the climb, the so-called

Cornice Traverse. Here a sharp ridge, perhaps 30ft long, connects the South Summit with the final section up to the summit. On the left, a 3,300m / 11,500ft drop straight down to the Khumbu Glacier. On the right, a 4,000m / 13,000ft drop straight down into Tibet. Peter Habeler, the joint first no Os Everest summiteer along with Reinhold Messner, once called this ridge the most exposed place on earth. I thought it would be scarier. The wind had pushed the snow into a low cornice on the Tibetan side, allowing the path to traverse a few feet below the knife edge of the ridge itself. It was no longer the tightrope walk I expected but rather a narrow goat track. I also found the visuals less heart-stopping than I previously imagined. Each face was sloped at perhaps 60 degrees. They were as dangerous as vertical if you fall, but not quite as heart pounding as a sheer cliff. Plus hypoxia probably helped to dim the fear. Frankly it was actually enjoyable to momentarily stop in the middle and peer down into the abyss. I wanted to see what infinity looked like.

At the end of the traverse we reached the Hillary Step. Iconic, fabled and feared. I'll be honest, it didn't seem especially difficult and if it wasn't so famous I probably wouldn't have remembered it all that much. For sure it was a steep scramble and it was certainly awkward, with progress made over large steep boulders covered in ice and snow. Yet technically and physically it didn't seem much worse than the Geneva spur. I was almost disappointed that it wasn't more difficult. In fairness, there is some debate whether there has been a shift in the rock up there which has simplified the climb a little. I have no idea. In any case, I found the most strenuous section of the step to be the snow cliff up to the final ridge. From there it would be a relatively modest incline up to the summit.

As I hauled myself over the lip of that final snow section Thunang, who had climbed the step in front of me, turned back and gave me a big smile.

"I think you are going to make it!"

"Ha!" I blurted out. "I think you might be right."

I think that was the first time he truly believed I was going to reach the summit, with all of about 100ft remaining. I was actually quite surprised at his congratulation, because we hadn't reached the summit and you couldn't see the top from where we stood. I didn't actually know at that point how far it still was, so in my mind I was being congratulated far, *far* too soon. In fact, both the location of the congratulation and his newfound confidence in my prospects felt jarring. Were we counting our chickens before they hatched?

That said, I was also very grateful for the kind words and to have him there on the climb with me in the first place. He'd worked tirelessly to make this expedition a success for me, from helping me clip the rope past the anchor on the trickiest sections on the upper mountain to carrying my mittens near the summit when I removed them for better dexterity. He is an excellent guide and fabulous climber, and without him the climb would have undoubtedly been a more difficult or perhaps impossible endeavor. It was good to have him there, and I felt happy that we would, *should*, both soon summit.

From the Hillary Step the ridge curves gently around to the right, following a large cornice as it continues upwards. In some ways this segment of the climb is both the easiest and hardest part of the whole climb. It should be simple; a twenty to thirty degree slope of compact snow, and yet it is not. At an altitude of 8,840m / 29,000ft you now walk so slowly that the unseen end feels forever out of reach. You are at your goal, except that you aren't. Time drags to an unbearable extent. I would look down at my feet, take a small step, and look back up. Nothing had changed. Repeat.

Suddenly, look down. Step, Look up. Something!

The cornice blocks your view of the summit until the last thirty or forty feet, and now there it was. Exactly 10 hours after leaving my tent on the South Col a small triangular metal structure appeared from around the ice at the far end of the ridge. Covered with colorful prayer flags, they fluttered in front of nothing but indigo sky. There was no more mountain to climb. A few more steps, this time filled with joy and relief, and I was there.

I had reached the highest point on Earth.

82
The Summit of Mount Everest

We were alone at the top of the world. There was no crowd of climbers, no line of people waiting for a summit photo. There was no-one else at all, no-one to dilute the pure essence of the experience. I had barely dared to dream that my summit would be this way. I felt like one of the pioneers of old who had reached the top when few had ever been there, when the magic spell of this unique place remained unbroken.

It was the first time since the Balcony that I could rest and fully absorb the view. And what a view it was. To the North I could now see Tibet properly for the first time, as I placed one foot in China, one in Nepal. Across the horizon, the world's greatest mountains stretched from one end to the other, from Kanchenjunga and Shishapangma in the East to Cho Oyu, Annapurna and Dhaulagiri in the West. Along the other axis I could see the entire width of the Himalaya, from the plains of India to the edge of the Tibetan plateau, hundreds of miles in either direction. For the first time you have an unobstructed view of the terrain and all its myriad complexities. There is a most visceral sense of scale. It is the difference from looking up at a tall building from ground level and looking out across the surroundings from its top floor observation lounge. Sure, I'd felt this place was big, but only when looking down on everything did I get a real sense of just how big it actually was. Vast glaciers gouge their way through deep valleys so far below that it was difficult to comprehend them as real. Icy peaks reached up towards us, yet never came close. Mountains which were intimately familiar were hard to identify, so different was the perspective. I just couldn't believe that Pumori, which towers 6,000ft above the tents of Base Camp, could look so small and insignificant. I actually had trouble identifying the peak, so lost it was in this gargantuan landscape. It was truly awe inspiring.

To stand on the summit was a completely different sensation than traveling on an airplane. Maybe it is the connection you have with your environment rather than being cocooned in a bubble; the difference between watching a football game on TV and actually being in the stadium. Or perhaps it was the 360 degree view rather than looking out of a window. Or maybe it was the silence or the cold wind. It's hard to explain. It just felt infinitely more *real*.

I had imagined this moment for a large part of my life. I always expected my final steps to the summit would be a delirious crawl, literally dragged there on all fours by my guide in a half-conscious nightmare. In the book "Into Thin Air", Krakauer describes his feelings at the summit as a mix of nothing but cold and exhaustion. Peter Habeler described standing on the summit with only a vague understanding that he was on Mount Everest at all.

My experience was different. I stood on the summit and felt… fine.

I was extremely tired, of course, but once I had stopped climbing I felt, you know, OK. It's not the most descriptive word but it encapsulates exactly how I felt. My breathing was fast but there was no hyperventilation. There was discomfort and lethargy from the exhaustion, but no pain. The hallucinations were gone and I had no confusion. In fact, I had no acute mountain sickness symptoms at all, not even a headache. Just standing there it didn't feel all that different from Camp II or even to Base Camp. I knew exactly where I was, and I could speak and think clearly, although I was definitely mentally slower than normal. Dallas told me he once removed his oxygen mask at the summit and said it didn't feel all that much different either. At the time I was skeptical, but now I believed him. It's only when you start moving that the altitude hits like a sledgehammer.

All that said, I was mindful to enunciate my words properly when we called Greg on the radio, just to remove any doubt or worry about my condition. The only physical sign which felt obviously out of place was my heartbeat, which continued to hammer at a rapid pace.

Despite the accomplishment there was no euphoria in the moment. Instead, the overwhelming emotion was a deep and fundamental satisfaction. I'd done something "epic" that I had long dreamed about, and had - thus far - beaten the odds. I was in a magical place. Yet for all that, still in my mind was the knowledge that I had only reached the halfway point. You know you are in a place the human body is not supposed to be, and from somewhere deep inside a voice was screaming at me to keep my guard up, not do anything stupid, and to get the hell out of there while I still could.

Happiness and satisfaction my subconscious would allow. Euphoria would have to wait until I was safely back down.

We took some photos, including some of me holding pictures of my friends and family. In that way I felt they had been there with me. Then, at the very summit, beneath the tripod and prayer flags, I placed a fist-sized granite stone which I had carried from Camp II. On it I'd inscribed the initials of those dear to me; my family, friends, and my friend's dog Miss Kitty, who is the most awesome of doggies. It was my way of sharing this journey and to bring them all with me to this special place. With a bit of luck these names will remain frozen into the ice at the top of the world for a thousand years. In which case I guess I probably should have remembered to write my own name on that rock as well.

As I looked around I knew I had been fortunate, at least in Mount Everest terms. The winds at the summit were gusty but not overly strong, which was as lucky as you could reasonably hope for. The temperature was warm for the summit at only -23°C / -10°F, giving an apparent wind chill of perhaps -35°C / -30°F. Combined with my low body warmth from the hypoxia that was unpleasant but just about tolerable. Still, this was not a place to linger. We could see clouds forming below in the valleys below us and time was of the essence. I spent the last minutes trying to absorb as much of this place and this moment as possible, internalizing what I was feeling and hoping to remember those few seconds forever. Under such pressure to descend it was hard to take much thinking time at the summit, but a few moments made all the difference. I felt so grateful at this opportunity to be there, and for the help I had received to make it possible. I felt so proud that I had battled my limits and had overcome them. A few seconds, with my eyes closed and absorbing the experience, were moments of deep peace.

I opened my eyes, turned to Thunang and gave him a smile and a nod. It was time to begin our journey back down to Earth.

We had been on the summit for 15 minutes.

83
The Descent Back To Earth

My singular objective was now our safe descent back to the South Col. I thought about my parents, my sister, my little niece and nephew. I needed to make it back for them. "Climb for yourself, return for others," was my motto.

My descent down the Hillary step was messy. On one of the larger moves I managed to slash a crampon spike right through my down suit near the knee. I missed my actual leg so even with feathers flying everywhere I didn't panic. The hole wasn't all that big and there was nothing that a strip of duct tape couldn't temporarily fix at some point, plus I had two layers still intact under the suit so I figured I would keep warm enough. I quickly put the incident out of my mind and continued on. At the base of the step, as the route moved out onto the Cornice Traverse, I picked up a small stone as a souvenir. Carrying rocks both up and down Everest was probably not one of my best ideas, but hey, I figured it was too late now. We across walked the exposed traverse and I struggled mightily up the return snow path at the South Summit.

The clouds were rising quickly now and half way down the Southeast Ridge they caught us, enveloping us from our left as we continued to descend. Light snow began to swirl. Fortunately, the visibility was still reasonable and the winds remained moderate so there was no reason to panic. Frankly, at this stage we were committed and there was nothing else to do except descend as quickly and as carefully as possible. Speed was our only weapon in this lop-sided fight.

Although less painful than the ascent, our return wasn't nearly as fast as I had expected. Previous descents down the Lhotse face from Camp III had been very rapid, just 30 minutes to retrace a two-hour climb as we were helped rather than hindered by gravity. Yet near the summit the lack of oxygen was the limit on my speed rather than gravity and fatigue quickly began to weigh on my body. It was just above the Balcony when my body finally ran out of fuel.

Over the years I've done some pretty tough endurance events. I've cycled 200 miles over three mountain ranges in a day and run 301 miles in a week. I thought I knew what tired meant, but until my descent of Everest I did not. My exhaustion was ten times more severe than any of those other challenges. I could take only a few steps before having to rest, oftentimes needing to physically sit down in order to regain just a few more seconds of endurance. Standing was literally too difficult and in its own way this was as brutal as the ascent had been. It was as though someone had turned me off. Like a marathon runner at mile twenty I had hit the wall, and high on Everest this had a catastrophic impact. My body had burned every ounce of sugar it possessed and was now burning living muscle for fuel. I was eating myself alive.

Once more I began hallucinating. This time, however, rather than floating colored bars I envisioned the head and torso of a German banker, floating above me and to the left. Seriously, don't ask, I have no idea. He was a middle aged gentleman, in a dark suit, white shirt and rimless glasses. He wore a tie but the color I don't remember. This time, unlike the white bearded man on the ascent, the apparition could talk and soon began dictating when I was allowed to get up and how many steps I was allowed to take before resting.

"Four steps! Schnell!"

I would obey his command and collapse back into the snow until I received the next order to move. It was even weirder than the colored bars. Once again I think it was my body's way of trying to regulate this fantastical stress which it found itself under. Your heart and brain can only use sugar and its derivatives as fuel so they were both really struggling to get enough energy to continue working. As you can't turn either of them off without some fairly terminal consequences my body somehow had to walk the line between moving and sustaining these vital organs. Those subconscious commands to my conscious mind seemed to be its way to control the situation.

Good work, body!

The main goal was to get down as low as possible, as quickly as possible, while minimizing the damage I did to myself in the process. I was dying a little bit each minute, and even on oxygen so was Thunang. He knew it as well. He would descend a short way ahead for added motivation and although I tried my best to keep up I had reached my absolute limit. As we approached the South Col in fits and starts rather than in steady steps the weather conditions improved a little, and by the time we had reached the end of the fixed lines we had left the worst of the weather above us.

We retrieved my down vest from where Thunang had tied it all those hours before and started our short walk across the glacier to the tents. It was an appalling effort. I was so close I could almost touch our camp yet the effort to reach those tents seemed insurmountable. The slightest incline was akin to pulling a sled full of bricks up a cliff. It felt like an age and perhaps it was, but eventually I made it. I was too tired to do much cheering.

Snapping open the heel bails of my crampons I kicked them mercilessly onto the ground to the side of the tent vestibule and crawled half dead into my yellow crypt. It was about all I could do to remove my boots, slither into my sleeping bag and open a chocolate bar. I was utterly spent and maybe irrevocably broken. But I was still alive. And I was happy.

Happy for the summit, happy I was still alive, and happy that my wish for an even higher mountain had not been granted. It had taken 15 hours of continuous maximum effort to reach the summit and return, a total round trip distance of just 2.2 miles.

84
Almost Human

There was zero possibility I could safely descend beyond Camp IV that day and we now had to risk another night at the South Col as the lesser of two evils. People have died in their tents doing this, the cumulative stress causing a heart attack during the night. I wasn't kidding about the damage I was doing.

The Sherpa were total heroes and made me some spicy Rahman noodles to help get some internal warmth and calories back inside my body. I was exhausted, but once I was resting in my sleeping bag I otherwise felt reasonably good. Nothing actually hurt, per se, and I still didn't have any altitude sickness symptoms. There were only two slight irritations. The first was removing the chunks of ice which had accumulated on my ragged beard from the snow and my breath freezing in the cold air. It was more of a novelty than a problem and I found it quite amusing to see just how much had accumulated there. I looked like one of those proper adventurers you see in magazine pictures, with their icy beards and their tell-it-like-it-is, get-the-job-done, no-nonsense demeanors. That's not how I usually roll, but hey, it's good for Instagram.

The second was more of a genuine irritant. I had forgotten to apply any sunscreen before setting out. When it's dark and minus 30°C, sunscreen usually isn't top of mind. For the last 10 hours I had been destroyed by the sun's rays. My face was red and swollen, my lips cracked and dark purple. Already the skin on my cheeks was beginning to blister and peel. I remember thinking that this sunburn was going to be epic and I remember my bemusement at the thought of it. Here I was, with my life still in the balance, worrying that if I survived the night I would have to deal with cracked lips. As a Special Forces soldier once told me about the time his colleague jumped out of an exploding airplane without a parachute, "Deal with one ***** problem at a time." The guy apparently survived, by the way. I felt incredibly grateful to be alive and that I still had all my fingers and toes. My one problem right now was to remain that way for the next 12 hours. Cracked lips and looking terrible could be the next one.

Blessedly all went well and I slept like a baby once more. Such sleep wasn't a surprise after the efforts of the previous day, but given the risks it was nice just to wake up at all. It is an odd experience to wake up and have as your first thought: "Oh good! I'm still alive!"

Even in my sleeping bag I could feel my weakness yet I was infinitely better compared with the prior day. My stomach wasn't feeling great so it was a candy bar for breakfast, but I was soon getting ready for our descent to Camp II. Crawling out of the tent a little after sunrise, I was greeted by unusual calm on the South Col. A high cloud layer draped a thick overcast gloom across the landscape, and along with the general messiness of Camp IV the atmosphere was almost depressing. Thunang helped the other couple of Sherpa to pack up the last of the IMG equipment and we eventually resumed our journey down. Even Thunang now seemed to be affected with fatigue and we descended with a tacit, unspoken agreement that neither of us needed to do anything heroic. Arriving safely continued to be the real prize, and we had no desire to become a statistic. It was still critical to keep concentrating, but as we descended into more nourishing air the time pressure abated a little. I felt like we were going to make it.

Just before the Yellow Band we passed a number of climbers heading up the mountain, two of whom seemed to be climbing without Os. We passed without saying a word, everyone too tired to talk. I wished them luck in my mind. As far as I can tell from later reports, neither of them managed to summit. Soon we passed Camp III where I was back in now familiar territory. Taking care not to trip at the finishing line as we arm-wrapped down the lines on the Lhotse Face, I tried to absorb the experience. This was in all probably the last time I'd ever be here, and I was at peace with that fact. It had been a long, wild ride and I had drunk my fill from this particular cup.

The additional energy I had absorbed during my slumber was soon spent and our pace slowed. Even Thunang was occasionally sitting to rest now. We did a final rappel down the bergschrund and around midday I staggered into Camp II, exactly like the climbers I'd seen a few days before. I expected just a couple of the Sherpa to come out to greet us but to my surprise they were joined by Funuru! He'd finagled a ride on a helicopter for an unrelated errand and was there to congratulate us. Funuru was the world record holder for ascents of Cho Oyu, another 8000m peak, so if he's impressed I guess I must have done something pretty wild. It was a wonderful feeling to have this legendary climber celebrate with me.

Both Cezar and Sharon were still in Camp II. Sharon had also stayed that night at the South Col but had departed before I'd woken that morning. I wasn't even aware she had been there at all. We were now both on the same descent schedule and it was nice to have some additional company for the final day. Cezar had injured his leg on one of the aluminum anchors while descending the day before and was now waiting either for a helicopter to get him out or to recover enough to walk down. In the end he had to walk, which I'm not sure he was too happy about, but luckily he is a tough fellow and managed to muscle through.

I caught up on the gossip of what had happened to everyone on their climbs, but I don't remember talking much about my own experiences. We'd all shared something unique, and yet our individual experiences were quite personal to each of us. Everest is far more about conquering yourself than the mountain, and those parts of our psyche, the parts way deep down, are sometimes hard to articulate. And at that stage, I'm not sure any of us had yet figured out what our climbs even meant.

85
Fate and Fortune

It was whiteout conditions in the Western Cwm the next morning; the first time I had seen that on the mountain. Everything was just so quiet and incredibly still; a different feeling from the other occasions I had climbed through that part of the valley. It was as though the mountain, mystically revealed for the last few months, was vanishing back into the mists of legend. The only sounds were the crunch of crampons, the huff of breathing and the faint rumble of high winds at the summit. Maybe it was an indication that the weather window had now closed and I feared the worst for those climbers we had passed the previous day.

That final descent through the cwm and down into the icefall was eerie. Teetering seracs and sword-like icicles appeared through the dense white mist like phantoms. You'd look up and suddenly see a 30ft icicle, a sharp spear of ice, pointing right down at you. It is unnerving yet I was still happy; it felt as though the worst had passed and fate couldn't *possibly* be so cruel as to deny me now. I was content to be irrationally oblivious to reality, just this once.

Six hours after leaving Camp II we reached a familiar sight. Anchored into the ice was the final rope on the icefall. Transformed from a slippery slope into a broad staircase by all the footsteps of the last six weeks I barely used the rope for those last few meters, but for symbolism held it until there was no more to hold. And then that was it. I had reached the end of the icefall and the last obstacle on Mount Everest. All that remained was the simple route across the glacier and a short trip through base camp to our tents, at which point my summit rotation, my climb, my whole expedition would essentially be over. However, as my wrist still hurt quite badly I didn't feel I was safe quite yet. Euphoria would still have to wait.

At crampon point we met another climber taking off his spikes. He had an appropriately grizzled beard and his red jacket was covered in sponsor patches. Could it be? Of course it was! I hadn't seen the Hungarians since my first rotation up the Lhotse Face all those weeks beforehand and now one of them sat beneath a vast line of prayer flags which had recently been ambitiously strung high across this part of the glacier. Just one Hungarian sat there, though. He seemed tired and his mood was low. I didn't have the heart to ask him how things had gone.

As I look back at that moment I realized how focused I had been for those last few weeks. My only assumption at that time was that he was depressed because his summit attempt must have failed. The summit had dominated every single thought I'd had for weeks, when not a single decision was taken without one eye on how it would affect my prospects; not a sip of tea, bite of food or casual walk. As I looked at the Hungarian, a failed summit attempt was the only reason which occurred to me to explain his mood. At the time the absence of his partner barely even registered a "huh" in my tired mind. Had his partner been killed or injured, explaining both his mood and the other man's absence? Or had a disagreement splintered the partnership? Before or after the summit bid? Was there a summit bid? These questions didn't even occur to me. I later discovered that his teammate had suffered from altitude sickness a little below the South Col and had been forced to abandon the attempt. The climber I had just met had continued on, but was himself forced to abandon just above the col. Both were OK but the summit was not to be theirs this time around. For me, it was a final, sobering moment on the mountain, one last confirmation of the strange things this place does to our minds and our perspectives of what "normal" behavior and thought should be. In some ways I was glad to be leaving.

I took off my crampons and walked, *very* carefully this time, across the small ice vanes to the meltwater stream which marked the outer boundary of Base Camp itself. A quick hop across the stepping stones and I was back on the main path through the camp. In 20 minutes I would be back at my tent.

Nearly home.

86
Reality is No Fun at All

From such isolation I was suddenly surrounded by what was, in comparison, a mass of people going around their daily business. It was a genuine shock. Forty-eight hours ago I was battling some of the most extreme conditions on Earth. Now I was walking past people lounging in deck chairs as they soaked up the rays of early morning sun while sipping hot tea. It felt so incredibly disjointed. Maybe this is how astronauts feel on their return to Earth. In an instant you go from space, to hero, to standing in line at Starbucks where no-one knows who you are. I found it makes for an uneasy sense that you don't belong anymore. You have now experienced something fundamental about the world which others apparently have not.

Perhaps that explained my feelings as I walked through camp. I expected to be merrily skipping along, ecstatic from my achievement and my safe return. And some part of me was. Yet there was a melancholy undertone to that walk as well. Perhaps seeing these people was a reminder that all I'd done was stand at the top of a mountain. It had been my focus for more than a year, yet the importance of this quest was fundamentally relevant to me and to me alone. I hadn't discovered anything, or saved any lives. I certainly hope I can be an inspiration to others, yet seeing all these people who didn't know or care confirmed that at the end of the day, climbing Mount Everest is ultimately about exploring yourself. No more, no less. Reinhold Messner spoke of this when he made that first no Os summit 40 years before I did, and nothing about that realization has changed since.

At the end of those 20 minutes the shrine at our camp, with its tall pole and fluttering prayer flags, emerged into view from around the gravel-covered ice. At the outskirts, Thunang shook my hand, gave me a hug, and with minimal fanfare departed to the Sherpa section. It was a quick goodbye and as he walked up the path the moment hit me, as though my subconscious now knew I was finally back in the real world. My guide of the last two months had delivered me safe and sound back to Base Camp, and now our climb together was over.

Tears flowed without warning. They were tears of joy and of profound happiness. I think part of me actually wanted to cry a little, to release some of the emotion which had been constrained for so long. Finally, *this* was my moment of euphoria and through the tears I smiled the kind of smile that makes your face hurt. Those moments don't happen often, and they don't last long, but they are the moments which I believe makes life worth living. I shall remember those few seconds forever.

I scrambled the short distance up to the shrine and as I walked past I paused, running my hand against the stones much as I had done 12 long days beforehand. I said a silent "thank you" to the Goddess of the mountain. She had brought me a mixed bag of luck during my time on those icy slopes, yet in the end she had come good in fine style. She had allowed me to enter her domain and return more or less unharmed. Many others had not been so fortunate. I was profoundly grateful to have returned from this most dangerous of endeavors.

I wiped away the last of the tears and walked over to the cook tent where outside stood Kaji and Purna, both waiting to welcome me home. Kaji shook my hand and gave me a bottle of Coca-Cola as a reward. Apparently this was by far and away the most requested thing by returning climbers. It was a lovely gesture to welcome us back to camp. Once again, the IMG team was doing things right.

Greg soon came down from Mount Olympus and congratulated Sharon and I on our successful climbs. He was over the moon that we had both succeeded. It ended up being a fairly short conversation, and I had to remind myself that while this climb was a life changing experience for me, I was summit number 20 for Greg this season alone. The real world was beginning to appear, and after those moments of euphoria I was already going from astronaut to that line in Starbucks.

87
A Glorious Finale

It was nice to be in Base Camp without the pressures of the climb. Several other team members were still there, although the entire Classic phase 1 had already left, all by helicopter. For all its creature comforts and the jelly bean jar I was also ready to leave. The shock of my return to civilization was beginning to recede, and I was now looking forward to some warmth and a real bed after living for so long on the ice. The Sherpa were already dismantling the camp around us and it was time to go.

The next morning all the remaining climbers and guides took the helicopter straight back to Kathmandu, with the exception of Sharon and her guide Jonny. We'd decided to make the walk back to Lukla rather than fly. Greg had been organizing things on the second helipad near our camp and I had a chat with him while the others went ahead. I figured I'd catch them up soon enough. Wrong! I walked the entire day on my own.

It was actually a good outcome. It gave me some time and space to process the experience. You are never really alone on Mount Everest and this was the first time for a long time I had more than an hour or two without other people around. I stopped on the moraine ridge a few miles down the valley from Base Camp and turned for a last look at the summit of Mount Everest. Once again it seemed so high above, once again an impossible goal. I played the soundtrack song to that Ueli Steck climbing video I had seen so many times during my training; I had planned to do it at the summit but had forgotten. It was another emotional moment and I felt pretty good about the universe. This was the good bit of life, the bit which makes all the hassle, fuss and lies of the real world worth tolerating. In those moments I finally made my peace with the mountain and as the song ended I turned back to the path to continue my walk.

I never saw the summit again.

A few hours later I arrived at the teahouse in Lobuche where I had stayed for a few nights on the trek up and ordered a cup of milk tea for old time's sake. It was nice to sit indoors for the first time in two months. Then it was onwards down the valley, past the swollen river at Thokla and through the cemetery where I again paid my respects to Scott Fischer and the other fallen climbers. From there the path descends that long staircase down towards the valley floor and it was late afternoon when I arrived at the Himalayan Hotel in Pheriche. I had no idea where Johnny and Sharon had gone but I was done for the day and made the executive decision to stay there for the night regardless. My body was still weak and I was plenty tired. In any case, I liked the Himalayan Hotel and this was my last chance to hear that 80s CD.

Ah, better lucky than good. I entered the communal area to see Sharon and Jonny drinking tea from one of the large ubiquitous thermos flasks while generally enjoying the last of the afternoon sun shining through the tall windows. I joined them and we spent another pleasant evening at my favorite teahouse on the trek. At this time of year the rooms didn't even seem that cold. There were surprisingly few trekkers about, a symptom of the time in the season I supposed, and that was fine with me. A slower re-entry into civilization was exactly what the doctor ordered.

The next day we walked to Namche Bazaar, a 20 mile stretch which wasn't too bad in the increasingly thick air. It had been 62 days since I'd seen a tree, and when we reached the tree line a short distance from Pheriche I gave the first one I saw a big hug! Below the plateau we were now surrounded by thick rhododendron forests and with summer approaching the warm air was again sweet with flowers. It was wonderful, like natural aromatherapy. My spirits were lifted as I felt a reconnection with the natural world after so much time surrounded only by dead rock and cold ice.

As we walked we began to be passed by runners! It was the Everest Marathon! In the lead up to the trek I had considered running it; after all, I did happen to already be in Base Camp. However the entry fee alone was a staggering US$1,000 and I figured I'd already destroyed enough of my body and mind for one adventure. In my current state I don't think I could have physically completed it anyway. It was genuinely impressive to see the folks speeding by on the rough terrain and extreme altitude. As the sun was setting we descended the path into Namche Bazaar to the sound of techno music blaring from some speakers, evidently the finish line for the marathon. It was sponsored by a Russian vodka company I'd never heard of so I'm sure they all had fun, but for me it was all a bit much. All I wanted was a well-deserved beer at the Khumbu Lodge. I was quickly in the common area to order a can of Everest beer as I looked through the windows at the mountains beyond. Ah, my second favorite place on the trek!

It was a bit busier here than in the Himalayan hotel; evidently we'd caught up with the tail end of the trekker wave. I still felt a sense of isolation from the people around me though, and as I sat at a table with Sharon I could tell she shared some of that disconnect as well.

I'm sure it would have otherwise remained unknown but I looked like a man who had just climbed Mount Everest, i.e. utterly dreadful. With purple lips, swollen cheeks, peeling skin, straggling limbs, unkempt beard and no haircut for three months I looked like a shipwreck victim. I'm sure a few of the trekkers wondered just what the hell had happened to this vagabond and eventually I got talking to a couple of the people sitting on the next table over.

Instant celebrity! I guess some of them were interested after all. Actually pretty much everyone in the communal area came over and started to ask questions. It was nice to see that others valued what we had suffered so much for, even from curiosity. We talked for a while, but after a couple of beers and many miles of mountain trails I quickly reached my limit and retired for the night, safe in the knowledge that it had been a good day. I never understood how anyone could take the helicopter straight back to Kathmandu. I guess some have time pressure, but to forgo this decompression and the carefree experience of the trek back down was a golden opportunity they would miss. Namche had been overwhelming enough and I couldn't imagine the shock of flying straight from Base Camp to the bustling capital. The trek back had been my favorite time of the previous expedition and a great experience on this one.

88
To Infinity Pool and Beyond!

We were never going to make the day's early flight so I preferred to take it easy and absorb my last proper day in the Khumbu. By early afternoon we arrived in Lukla and checked into the Paradise lodge as though we'd never left. As luck would have it, Terez, my wonderful doctor friend from the Himalayan Rescue Center in Pheriche, was sitting in the common area of the teahouse! She had spent the last couple of weeks in Lukla, dealing with frostbite cases and other patients during their medical evacuations from Base Camp to Kathmandu. It was great to sit there, catch up over a pot of Sherpa tea, and hear what had been happening on her side of things. Naturally we also talked about my adventures since the last time I'd seen her, and as I reached the part about slipping on the ice it occurred to me that she'd know what I'd done. She *was* an ER doctor in real life, after all!

It took her about 5 seconds to confirm that I had indeed broken my wrist! I'd fractured one of the little ones at the base on the hand rather than the main forearm bones, which explained why some movements were agony but I could still climb. I had been a lucky chap, and that was all the more reason to celebrate. Terez knew a few of the local lads in the village so we all went out for a drink that evening. I'm pretty sure my rehabilitation back to civilization was complete after the first couple of shots and thank goodness I don't get bad hangovers. We were flying to Kathmandu the next day and now at least I was partially prepared to return to the modern world.

At breakfast we sat in the teahouse while Lakpa, IMG's man on the ground, figured out the hieroglyphic airline schedule and managed to get us on a flight. Terez had already been waiting two days for a seat so Lakpa made sure she was on the same flight as myself, Jonny and Sharon. There is mutual respect between the Sherpa, the teams and the HRA doctors so Lakpa was more than happy to pull a few strings on her behalf. At around about 9am he gave word for us to walk across to the airport, where once again the calm of the Khumbu transformed into airport chaos. I'm not sure the airline logo was even on our boarding passes this time, let alone a flight number.

We eventually found our way into the small orange-walled departure lounge. As we sat there and watched the planes arrive my eyes drifted to a small TV fixed to the wall between the large windows overlooking the runway. It was showing a movie. Now, remember that Lukla is one of the world's most dangerous airports, and indeed Terez had saved the lives of some people in a fatal plane crash at that very airport the week before, a terrible and traumatic event for everyone involved. The movie was "Alive", a film about a fatal plane crash. Eventually, one of the airport workers came and changed the channel, but not before everyone had a good chuckle at the irony, including Terez I might add. You couldn't make this stuff up.

The flight was scenic as always, although Mount Everest remained hidden. Forty-five minutes after takeoff we arrived in Kathmandu to be greeted by the usual wonderful chaos. Mohan met us at the airport and I was at the Hotel Tibet in no time. It was like I had never left.

The mirror in the bathroom was the first time I'd seen myself since, well, the last time I stood in front of this mirror in the

Hotel Tibet. I knew I'd lost weight, but the sight that greeted me was a shock. There was a bathroom scale in the corner so I hopped on. Crikey. 130lb (9 stone 3lb) for a guy who is 6'0ft tall and had been full-on binge eating for the last 4 days. I'd lost 40lb during my time in the Khumbu, nearly 25% of my body weight and the majority of it muscle. When I said my body was burning living muscle for fuel I wasn't kidding.

Terez sent me a note the next morning. Would I like to go to a rooftop spa that afternoon? It was at one of the nice hotels and you could get a guest pass for cheap. Sure! And so it was that I sat on a lounger on the 15th floor roof deck, sunning myself in the warm air - with lots of sunscreen on this time - as I gazed across an infinity pool towards the city outskirts and the green foothills beyond. In my hand I held a dramatic, vivid blue cocktail in a martini glass, a fitting symbol of my dramatic, vivid journey. I raised a toast to the last three months. To the people who had made it possible. To those who had been thwarted in their efforts, and to those who had been successful. To fate, to the experience, and to my ultimate good fortune.

What a journey it had been.

Epilogue
Stupid. Worth It.

I'm often asked "Was it worth it?" The answer is complicated.

I made a lot of sacrifices to turn this dream into a reality. A thousand hours of strenuous physical training. A hundred thousand dollars, all told, between the two expeditions. Months living in a tent away from my friends and family. Many days of pain and suffering. Damage to my body and brain, some of it perhaps permanently. The emotional stress put on my loved ones. And the risk to my life. Each one is in itself a big deal and combined make this undertaking the absolute opposite of trivial.

And for what? To have the opportunity to spend 15 minutes at the highest point on Earth? If standing on the summit had been my only definition of success then I would say it was not worth it.

But that was never my definition of success.

I'd seen the shadow of Everest silhouetted against a fiery sunrise. I'd experienced the death zone and discovered my unusual reactions to it. I crossed the cornice traverse and climbed the Hillary Step. I'd looked down into an abyss from a bridge made of ladders. I slept at the South Col of Everest and climbed the ice of the Lhotse Face. I pushed my body to a level beyond anything I have ever previously attempted. I'd spent quality time with the Sherpa and learned something of their culture. I'd been blessed by a Lama and made friends with some wonderful people. I learned to bounce back from failure and to channel my determination to succeed against difficult odds.

And for 15 minutes I was the highest person on the surface of the Earth.

With those definitions of success my adventure was absolutely worth it. There is no question in my mind. Reaching the summit was the icing on the cake, the final experience to savor amongst a myriad of unique experiences. When I told Thunang that reaching the summit wasn't the most important thing about my climb I was telling him the truth.

So if there are lessons to learn from these pages then perhaps they are these. To enjoy the journey of life and redefine what success really means to you personally. The idea that you can turn something painful into something wonderful just by reframing the experience, because everything is a matter of perspective. And if nothing else, that we can do something pretty amazing when we put our minds to it. I'm nothing special, and if I can do something like this then you can do what inspires you. And that is something I truly believe.

So find your own personal Mount Everest.

Look up.

And climb!

The End.

About the Author

James Brooman was born and raised in England. Professionally, his career has been in finance and technology, and has earned an MBA from Dartmouth College. In the gaps, however, he is a mountaineer, runner, cyclist and adventurer. He has climbed Mount Everest, run solo from Perth to Sydney, cycled from Alaska to Argentina and BASE jumped in Norway. He has also been kidnapped a couple of times.

James hopes this makes him interesting at dinner parties, but is still not quite sure.

Printed in Great Britain
by Amazon

15564386R00214